I0793153

IMAGES
of America

CALIFORNIA'S HIGHWAY 99

MODESTO TO BAKERSFIELD

On the Cover: This photograph shows a single vehicle traveling on State Route 4. In the 1920s, State Route 4 (Legislative Route Number 4) was redesignated as Highway 99 (US 99), and in the 1960s, it was redesignated again as State Route 99 (CA-99). (Copyright © California Department of Transportation.)

IMAGES
of America

California's Highway 99
Modesto to Bakersfield

Keith Warwick, PE

ARCADIA
PUBLISHING

ISBN 978-1-4671-3213-8

Published by Arcadia Publishing
Charleston, South Carolina

Printed in the United States of America

Library of Congress Control Number: 2014931005

For all general information, please contact Arcadia Publishing:
Telephone 843-853-2070
Fax 843-853-0044
E-mail sales@arcadiapublishing.com
For customer service and orders:
Toll-Free 1-888-313-2665

Visit us on the Internet at www.arcadiapublishing.com

To my lovely wife, Patty, who is about all that I am about.

Contents

ACKNOWLEDGMENTS

I wish to thank the following people and organizations for providing encouragement, photographs, ideas, and technical assistance:

Bob Schmidt
The California Department of Transportation
The California State Library
The City of Hughson, California
The City of Chowchilla, California
The City of Waterford, California
The Kern County Library, Bakersfield, California
The Library of Congress
The Manteca Historical Society, California
The McHenry Museum, Modesto, California
Patty Warwick

I am also thankful to the editorial staff at Arcadia Publishing for their guidance. Unless otherwise noted, all images appear courtesy of the author.

INTRODUCTION

This book captures the spirit of Highway 99 as found both on the highway and in the cities and towns along it. In the 1920s, State Route 4 (Legislative Route Number 4) was redesignated as Highway 99 (US 99). It was redesignated again as State Route 99 (CA-99) in the 1960s.

CA-99 is a major highway through the Central Valley of California. Its northern endpoint is at CA-36 near Red Bluff, and its southern endpoint is at the intersection with Highway 5 near Wheeler Ridge. This book, however, will primarily cover the stretch of Highway 99 between Modesto and Bakersfield as it traverses Kern, Tulare, Fresno, Madera, Merced, and Stanislaus Counties.

CA-99 started as a California state highway about 1910, just after cars became popular and commonplace. It was designated Legislative Route Number 4 and linked Sacramento and Los Angeles. Around 1915, the roadway was paved, and in the 1920s, the roadway was redesignated as US 99—sometimes referred to as the Golden State Highway. In the 1930s, sections of the road were widened to three lanes. Later, between the 1930s and the 1950s, the road was widened to a four-lane expressway and, in many cases, bypassed the downtown areas of the towns and cities that it connected.

The cities and towns that are along Highway 99, near Highway 99, or are considered to be part of the 99 corridor include Salida, Modesto, Shackelford, Ceres, Empire, Hughson, Denair, Turlock, Irwin, Delhi, Livingston, Atwater, Merced, Chowchilla, Fairmead, Madera, Fresno, Fowler, Selma, Monmouth, Sanger, Parlier, Reedley, Dinuba, Kingsburg, Visalia, Farmersville, Exeter, Tulare, Lindsay, Porterville, Pixley, Earlimart, Delano, McFarland, Bakerfield, Greenfield, Lamont, and Arvin. Many of these towns were already settled by the time that Highway 99 was established, but many began as simple intersections. Several of these cities, particularly Modesto, Fresno, and Bakersfield, are largely urbanized areas, while many of the smaller towns are barely discernible. These cities and towns were, and are, very different, but they have one thing in common: Highway 99.

Many say that Highway 99 is a fun highway to drive on and one on which you get to experience a slice of Americana. As a result, many businesses along Highway 99 have long aimed to be the most entertaining establishment along the way. When stopping at a diner along Highway 99, it was oftentimes the owner or his family that served you. You were in their home, in their neighborhood, and on their main street. You were in their town, and you were welcome. There were no rich or poor on the highway—just thirsty travelers stopping along the way at places like the Giant Orange.

The focus of this book is the segment of the 99 between Modesto and Bakersfield, which runs through or by numerous cities and towns. Some of the photographs in this book are not from within the boundary of Highway 99 but contribute to an understanding of the highway's charm. Highway 99 is an older highway, genuine and real, and from the 1910s to the 1970s, it was lined with numerous, unique, locally owned and operated motels, attractions, cafés, and juice stands.

There is also a socially significant aspect to the highway. Cesar Chavez and his aides traveled on it while helping California's farmworkers improve their lives. Those who moved to California to escape the Dust Bowl of the 1930s traveled on the highway, and many of those hardworking people settled in the Bakersfield area.

Traveling on the highway today evokes nostalgia for simpler times. The highway captures the mood of teen culture in the 1950s, and there is a unique charm and character to the highway that is significant to the residents and visitors to California's Central Valley over the past century. The roadway has never been upscale or presumptuous but is, rather, truly egalitarian. There were many filling stations along Highway 99 where customers could choose between ethyl and regular gasoline, and the attendant checked the oil and radiator and washed the windows without even being asked.

For this book, the author visited and photographed the foundation of the last Giant Orange juice stand on this stretch of 99, and the highway can be seen in the background of the images. Between 2000 and 2010, the site's orange structure was collected by the City of Chowchilla so that it could be established as an exhibit for the city's museum. The foundation, railroad tracks, and the town of Fairmead (near Chowchilla) are all visible in the images of the Giant Orange stand. They help to establish the unassuming location of this historic establishment.

When "our brother" Bob Dylan sang "The Times They Are a-Changin'," he was commenting on the social climate of the time. But his words could also apply to Highway 99, which was changing too. The author hopes that this book reminds you of the highway before its times changed.

One

Background

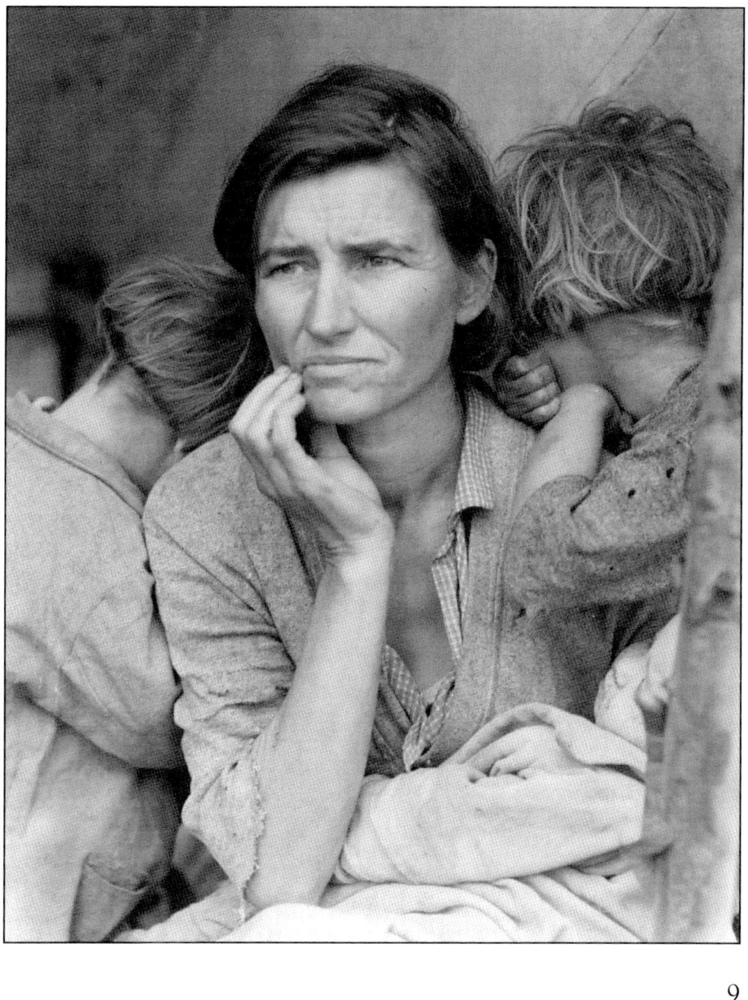

This famous Dorothea Lange photograph—showing a Depression-era woman and her hungry children—outlines the pain, suffering, hunger, and poverty of the era. This family was struggling because of a failed pea crop. At that time, there were more people needing employment than there were jobs available. (Courtesy of the Library of Congress.)

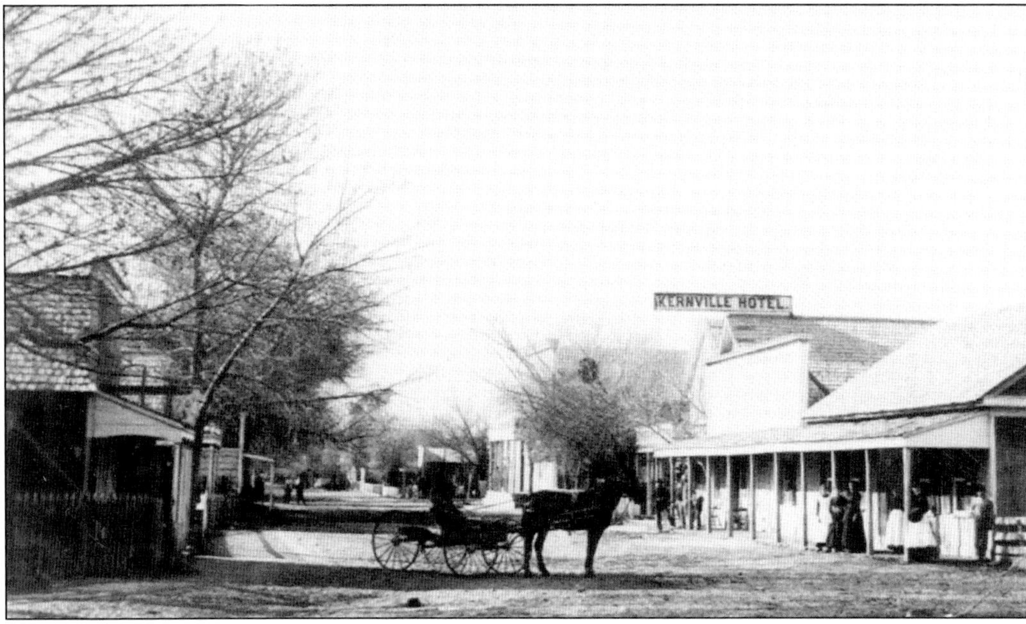

Horses and wagons are present on a Kernville street in this photograph. The Kernville Hotel can be seen on the right side of the street. Kernville is located northeast of Bakersfield, in Kern County, on the banks of the Kern River—which was named for topographer Edward Kern. The town was formed during a gold rush. (Courtesy of the Kern County Library.)

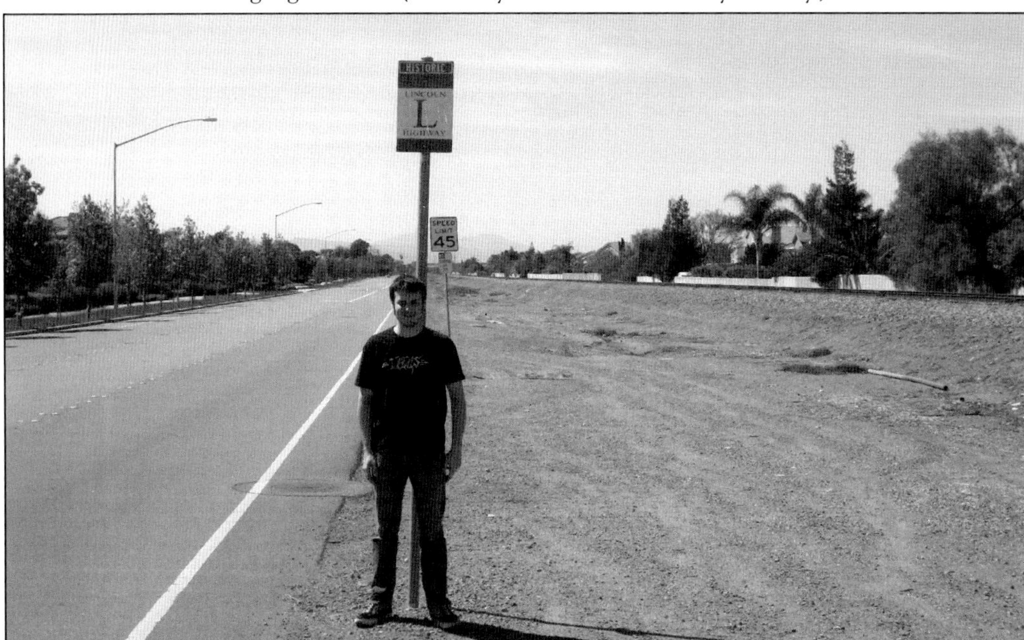

The Lincoln Highway in California combines pieces of Americana and bits of nostalgia. It is a simple, unpretentious road with an egalitarian theme. Highway 99 and the Lincoln Highway share the same road in places between Sacramento and Stockton. In 1912, an entrepreneur and visionary named Carl Fisher recognized the need for a coast-to-coast highway that was designed for automobile travel. This highway was completed quickly and was dedicated in October 1913.

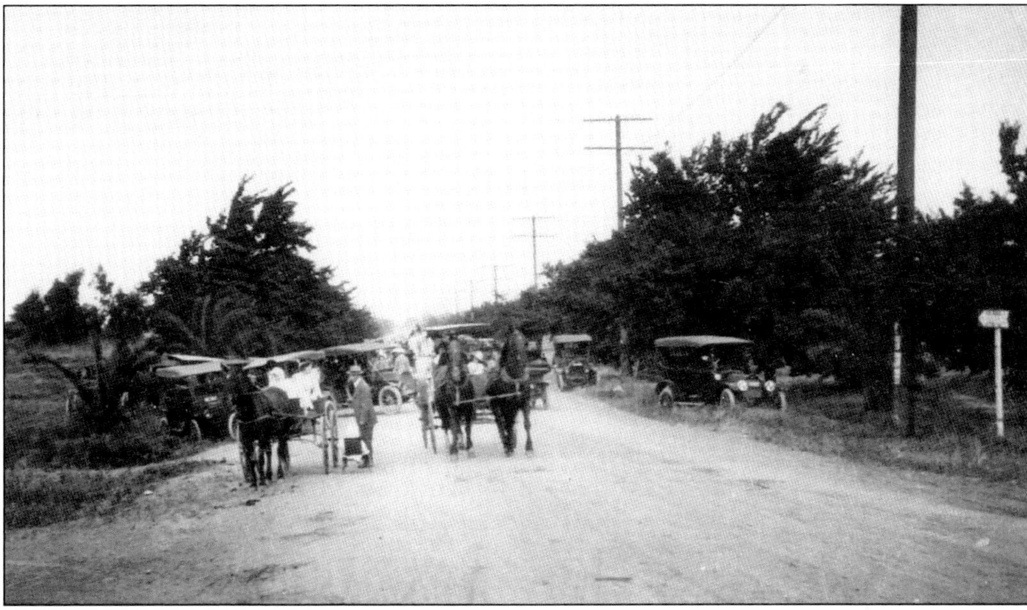

Accidents such as this one, involving both cars and horses, occurred during the period in which carriages, wagons, and cars shared the road. The pictured accident occurred in 1913 on the section of Highway 99 (then State Route 4) north of Fresno. At that time, the roadway was generally developed but unpaved. (Copyright © California Department of Transportation.)

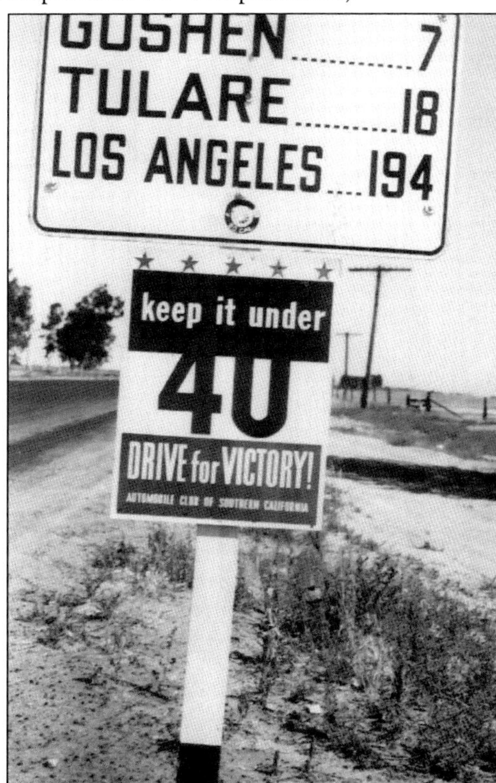

At different times in its history, Highway 99 extended as far south as the Los Angeles area. Highway 99 is sometimes referred to as an egalitarian area, because all travelers equally shared the roadway without regard to their financial status. Note the sign listing the mileage to the small farming communities of Goshen and Tulare and the major city of Los Angeles. Due to wartime gasoline rationing, drivers were encouraged to keep their speed to less than 40 miles per hour at the time that this photograph was taken. (Courtesy of the Turlock Historical Society.)

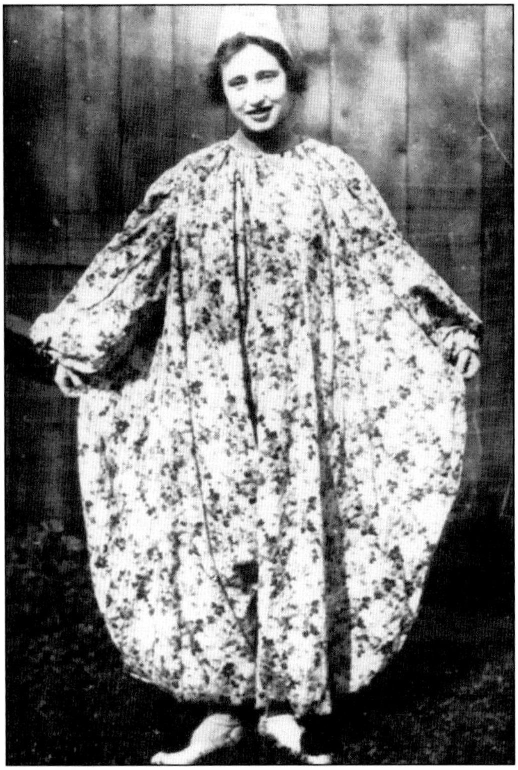

This is a photograph of a young Taft resident dressed in a masquerade suit. In the time before television and video games, live theater, music, and comedy played an important part in people's lives. The city of Taft was incorporated on November 6, 1910, and it is interesting to note that the first officers to patrol the streets of Taft were called city marshals. (Courtesy of the Kern County Library.)

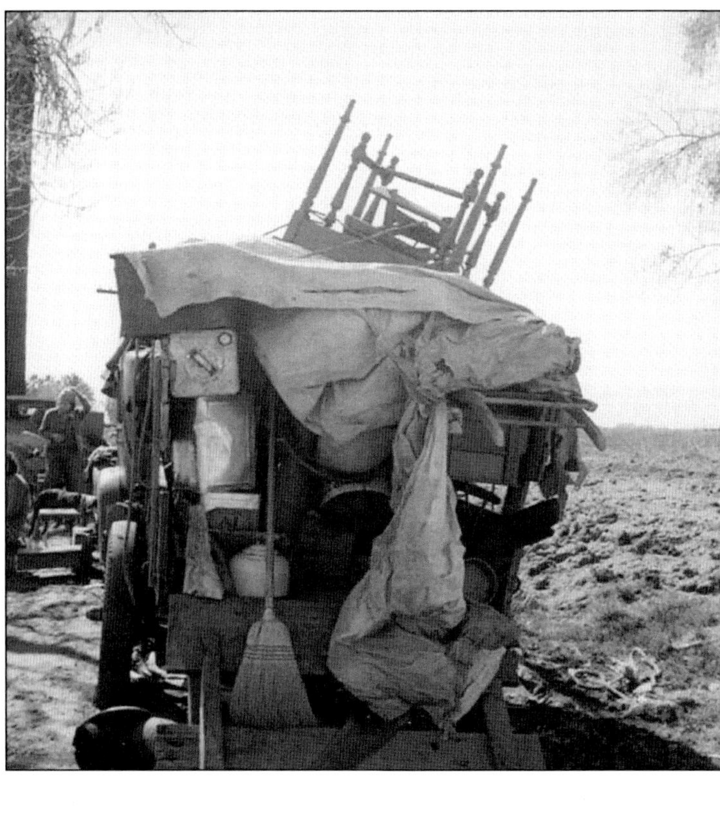

This photograph of Depression-era travelers was taken on Highway 99 south of Bakersfield. These travelers typify John Steinbeck's 1939 novel *The Grapes of Wrath* and its 1940 film adaptation. The migration of residents from Oklahoma and the surrounding states in the 1930s brought over a million people to California. Many were seeking farm labor jobs in California's Central Valley and settled in the Oildale region of Bakersfield and other towns along Highway 99. (Courtesy of the Library of Congress.)

This photograph is of a Mr. Chung, who worked as a cook, standing in front of an oil sump in McKittrick. Several "Chinatowns" were located throughout the Central Valley from the 1850s on, with prominent examples in Bakersfield, Fresno, and Holt. (Courtesy of the Kern County Library.)

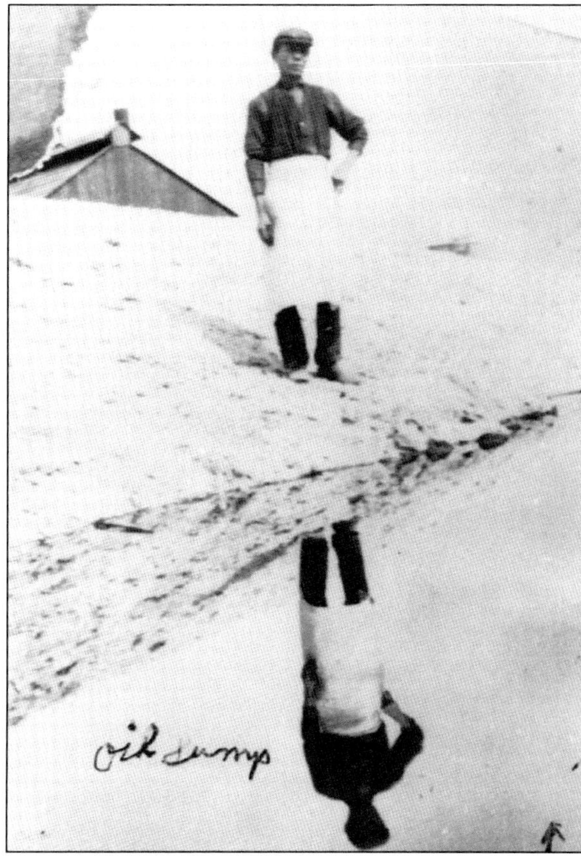

This is a view of the El Tejon Hotel at Seventeenth and K Streets, where Bakersfield's Bank of America building now stands. This photograph establishes Bakersfield's level of development prior to the establishment of Highway 99, which connected Bakersfield to the other cities in the Central Valley. (Courtesy of the Kern County Library.)

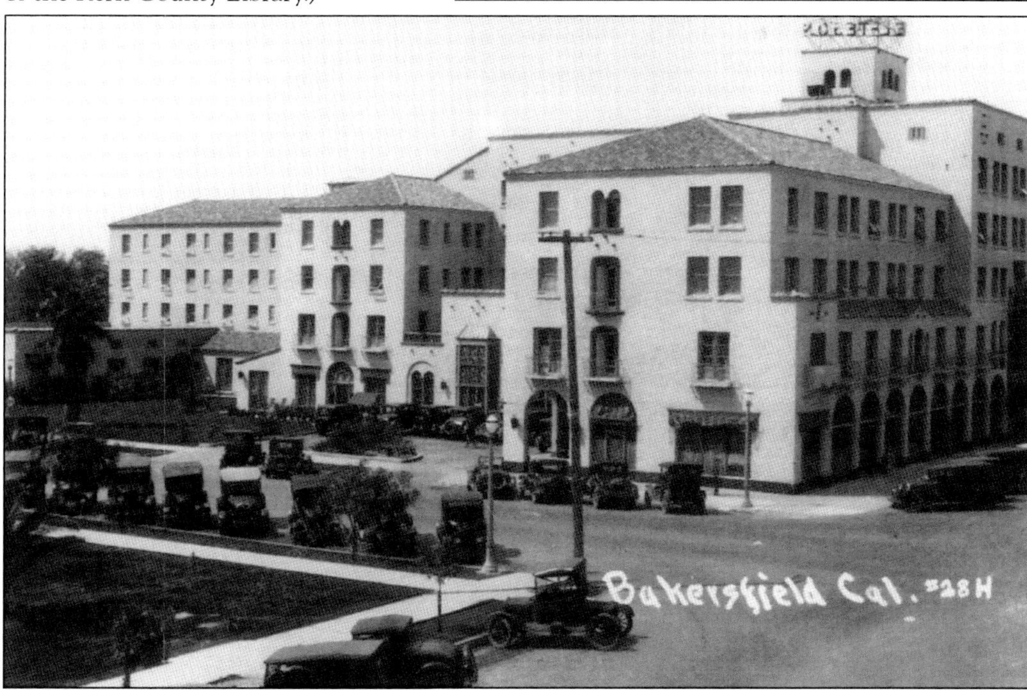

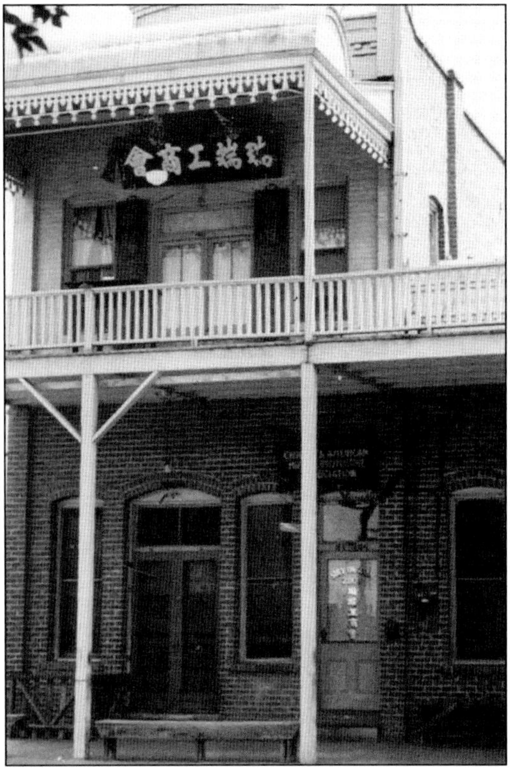

The Suey On Association, a fraternal organization of Chinese merchants, was located at 2110 L Street in Bakersfield. Bakersfield had a noted Chinatown, which was established prior to 1900 and was representative of similar neighborhoods in Fresno, Holt, and other cities and towns in the late 1800s and early 1900s. (Courtesy of the Kern County Library.)

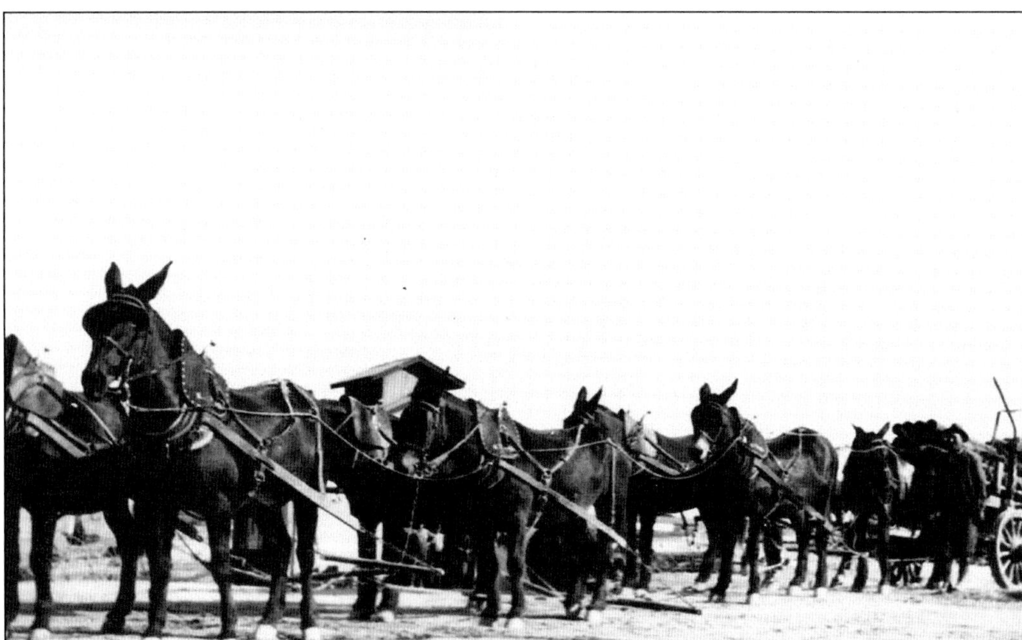

This image shows petroleum industry mules pulling a load of pipe. After oil was discovered near the Kern River—just north of Bakersfield—in 1899, the town grew rapidly. The installation, maintenance, and repair of the utilities and oil pipelines provided a lot of jobs at that time. Petroleum remains a major industry in the Bakersfield area. (Courtesy of the Kern County Library.)

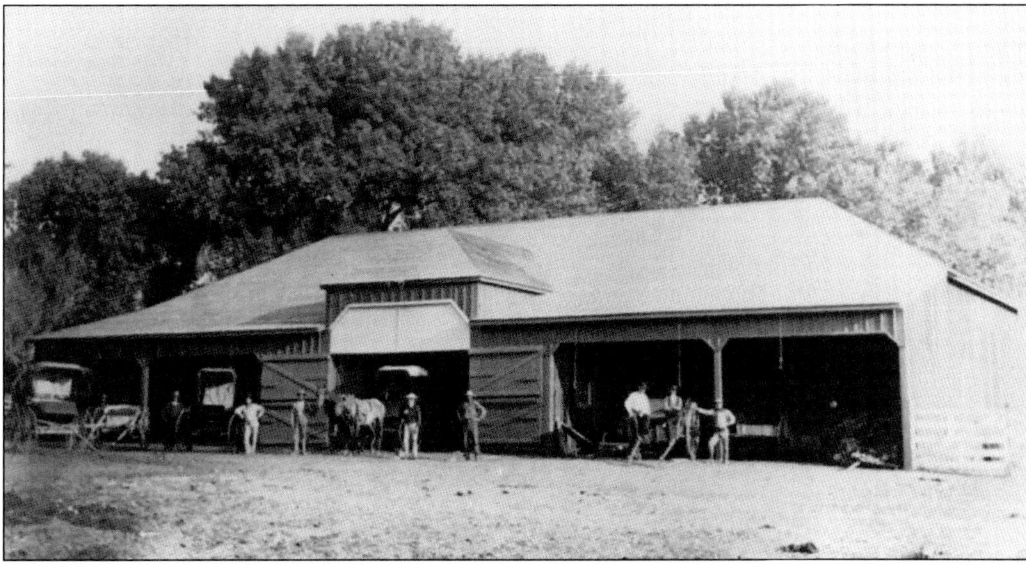

This image is of a carriage barn that was used to house and protect horse-drawn wagons and carriages. The individuals standing in front were caretakers or the owners of the wagons. This photograph dates to a time when horses and automobiles were used simultaneously. This often resulted in interference between these two modes of transportation, but horses were used for recreational purposes as well as for transportation. Kern County recreational activities include horseback riding, hunting, trout fly-fishing, white-water rafting, kayaking, shooting, hiking, and camping. (Courtesy of the Kern County Library.)

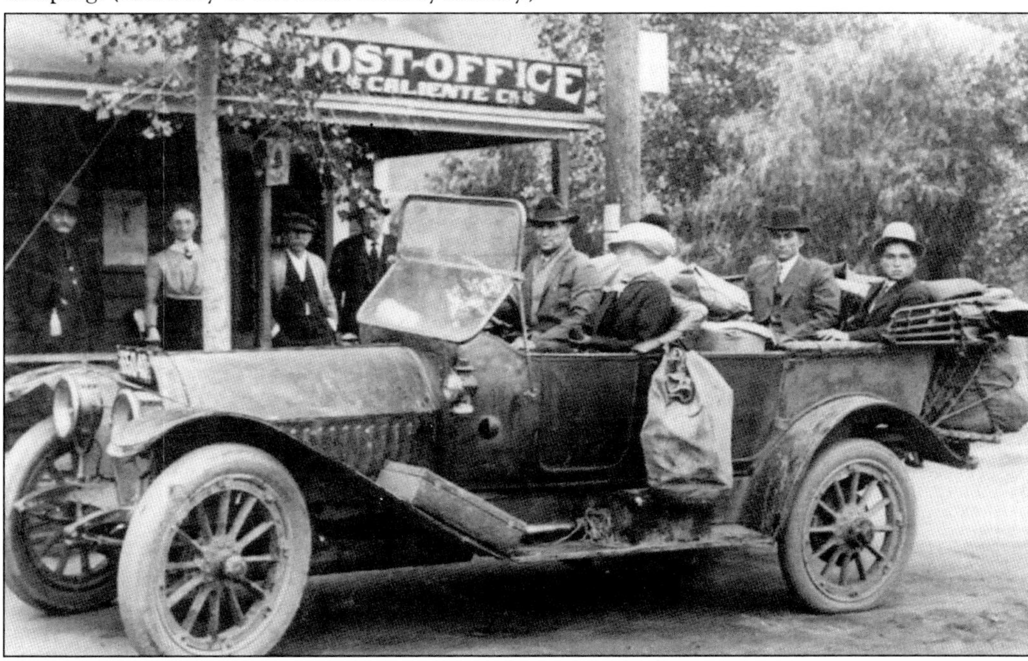

The Mitchell automobile served as an auto-stage, replacing the stagecoach through Caliente. It is seen here parked in front of the Caliente Post Office. Caliente (formerly named Allen's Camp and Agua Caliente) is an unincorporated community within Kern County. The population at the time this photograph was taken is estimated to be 500. (Courtesy of the Kern County Library.)

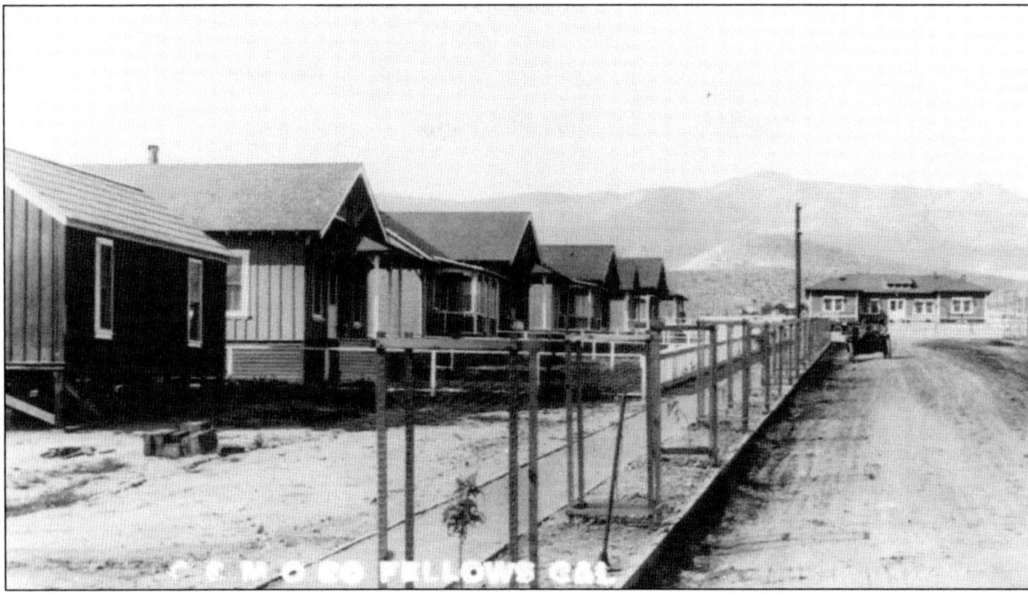

Worker housing is visible on the left side of this photograph of Vernette. Note how spartan the accommodations were at that time. The headquarters building can be seen at the end of the street. Vernette was a railroad siding three-quarters of a mile north of Fellows. (Courtesy of the Kern County Library.)

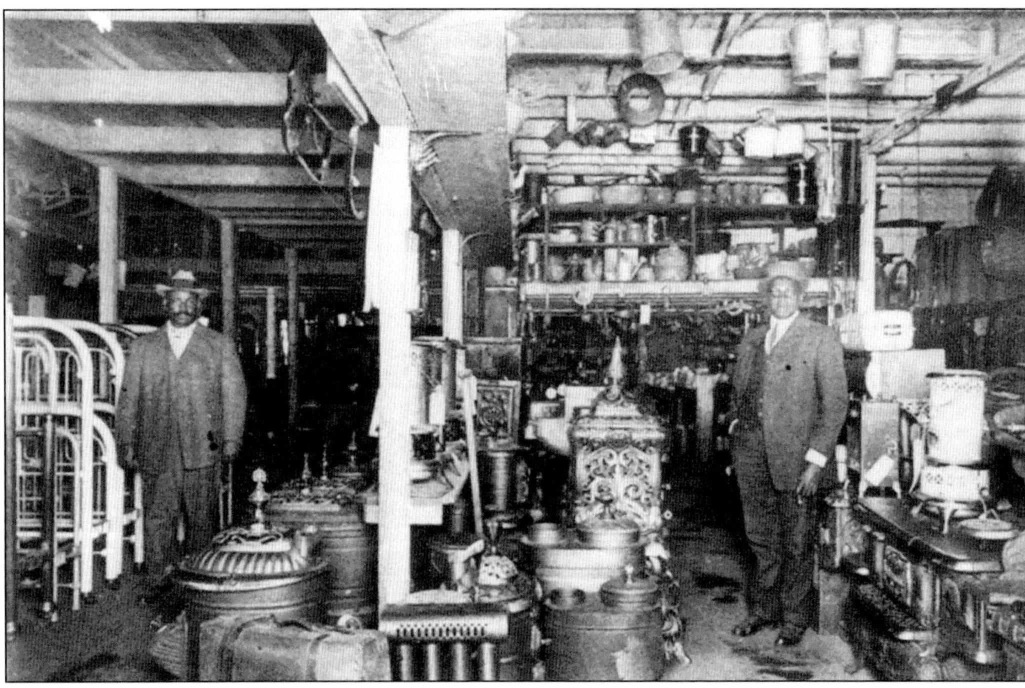

This photograph shows two gentlemen standing in a store that one of them owned. The store was located in Bakersfield and sold a variety of tools and household supplies. It was located on Nineteenth Street between K and L Streets. (Courtesy of the Kern County Library.)

Oregon Route 99 has much of the same nostalgic value that California's Highway 99 does. It extends north from the southern border of Oregon to Junction City. Oregon Route 99 includes portions of the former US Route 99 and runs along the same route as Interstate 5. (Courtesy of the Library of Congress.)

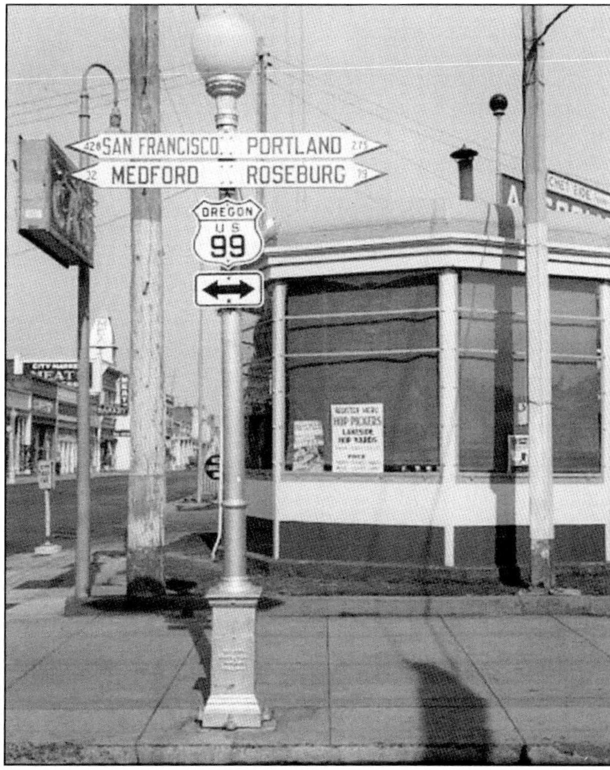

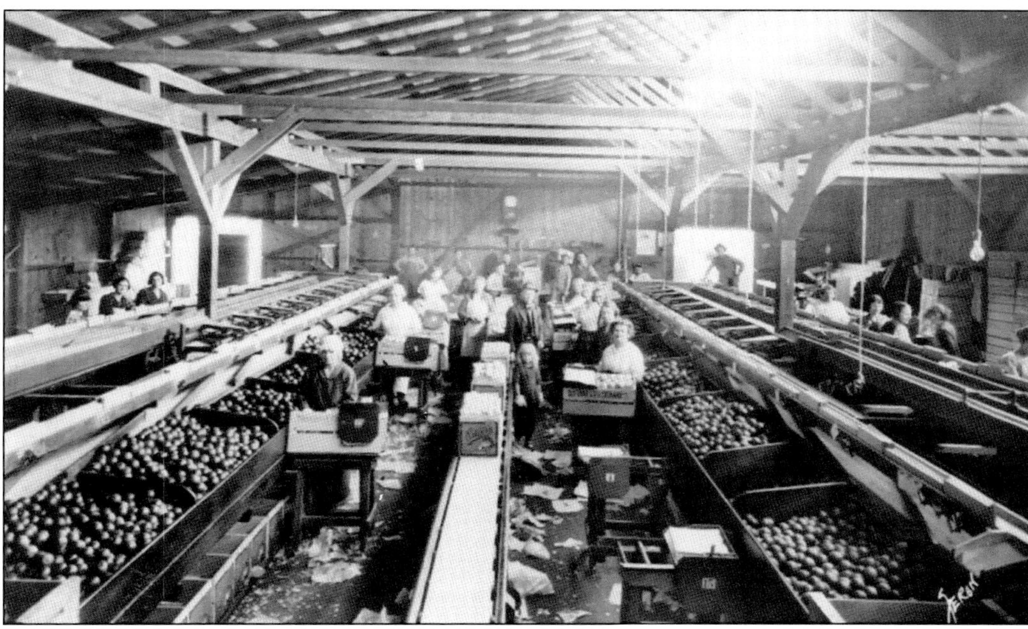

Orange production was a major industry in Kern County and along Highway 99. This image shows men and women working in Kern County packing oranges. The citrus crop remains a symbol of Highway 99's agricultural base. The Kern County Department of Agriculture and Measurement Standards in Bakersfield monitors the citrus industry in Kern County. (Courtesy of the Kern County Library.)

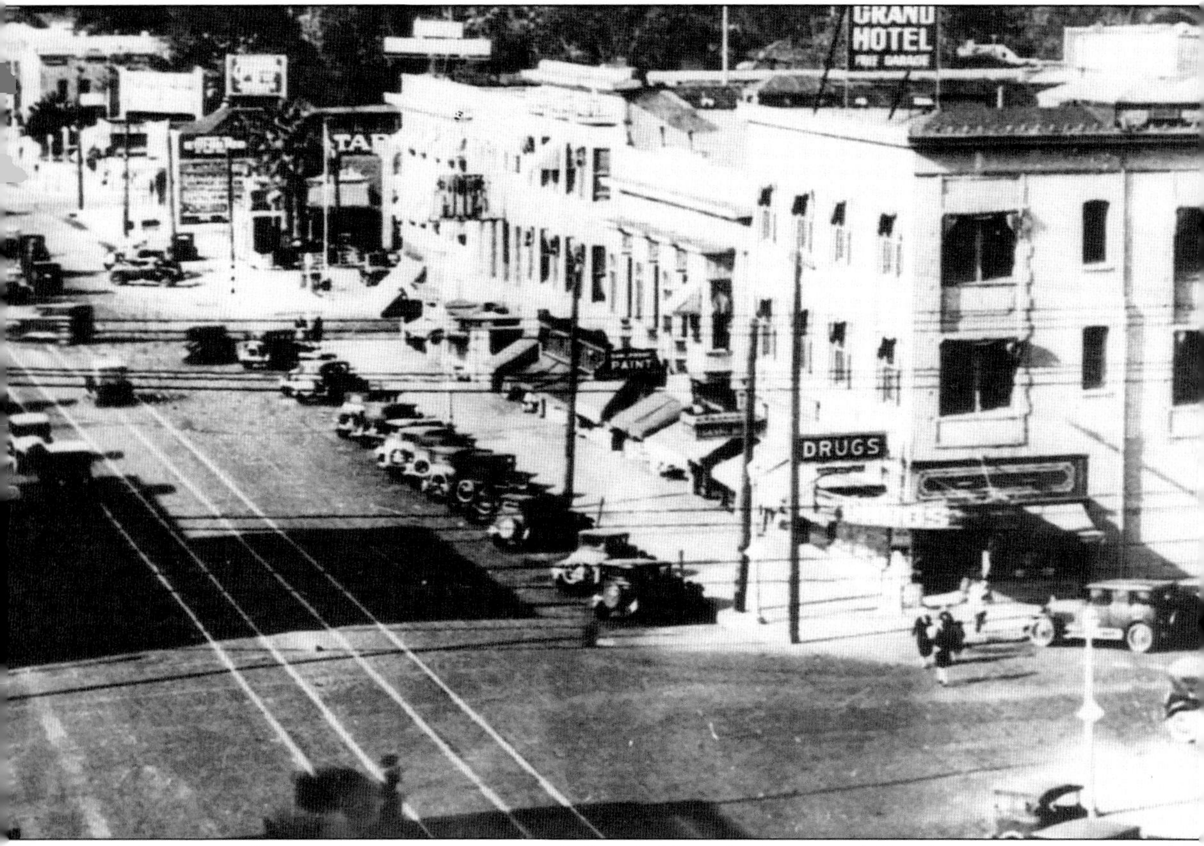

This image shows a busy street scene in Bakersfield, with the Grand Hotel and a drugstore in view. The Grand Hotel offered free, covered parking as well as other amenities. The area was well developed, with multistory office buildings. (Courtesy of the Kern County Library.)

Two

EARLIER DEVELOPMENTS

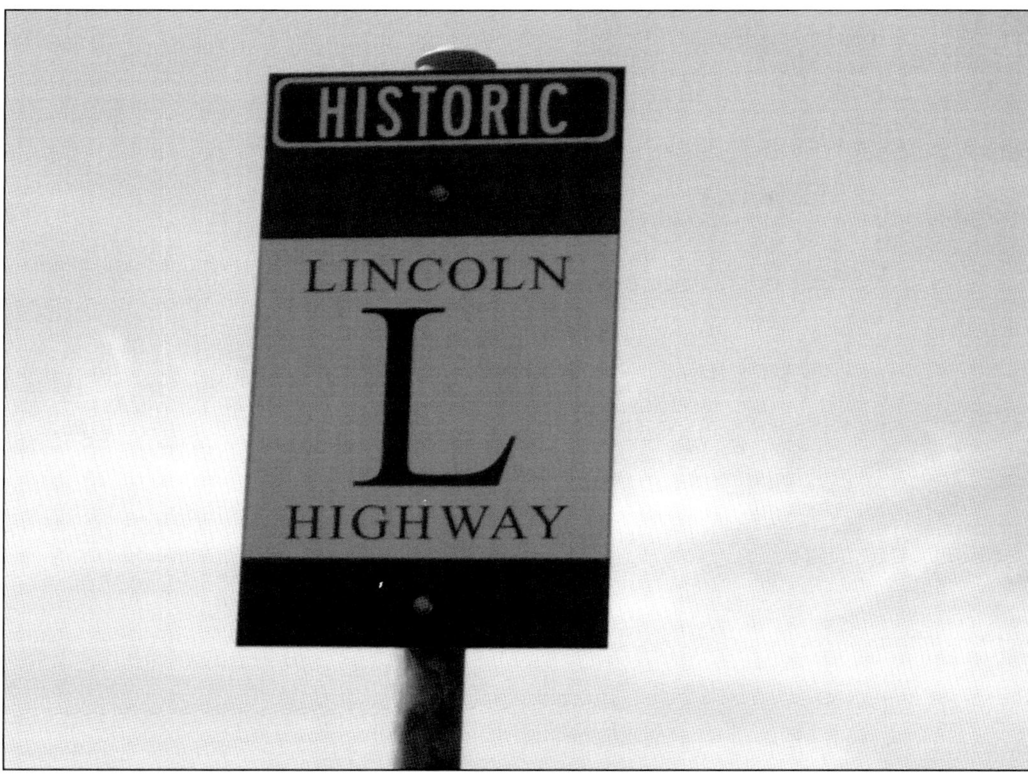

Many of the developers of the Lincoln Highway—which intersects Highway 99—were successful industrialists of the time. The Lincoln Highway originated in Manhattan's Times Square, which was already an American landmark, and ran to Lincoln Park in San Francisco.

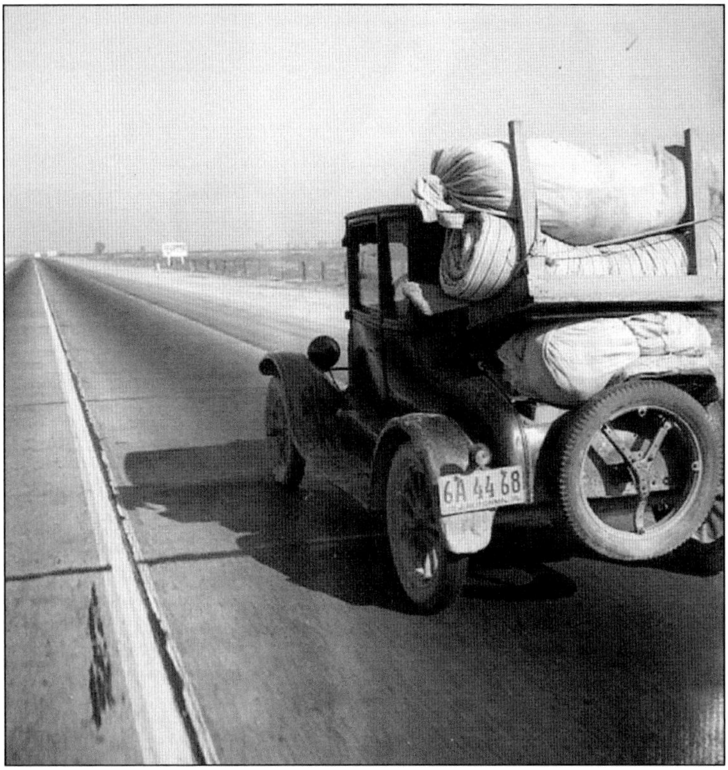

This late-1930s photograph of Highway 99 shows individuals that fled the Dust Bowl. By this time, the highway included a paved shoulder for convenience and safety. By 1950, millions of people born in Oklahoma, Texas, Arkansas, and Missouri had left that region in order to find employment. (Courtesy of the Library of Congress.)

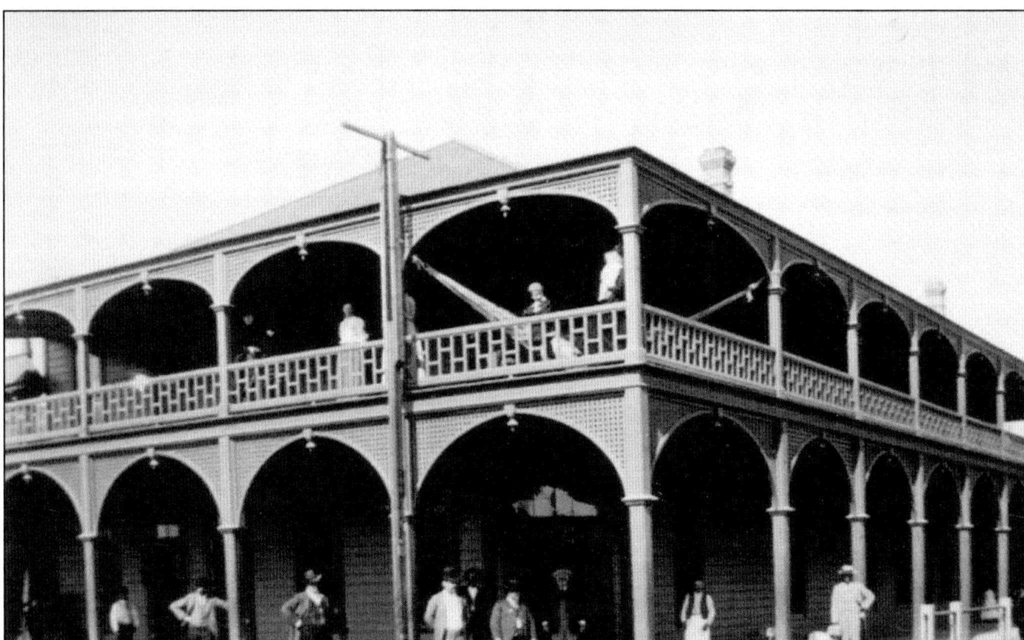

The Ingleside Hotel, seen here with people standing in front and on the balcony, replaced the Bakersfield Town Hall around January 1890 and then burned down that August. It was located at the northwest corner of Seventeenth Street and Chester Avenue. The original Beale Memorial Library opened on that site in 1900. (Courtesy of the Kern County Library.)

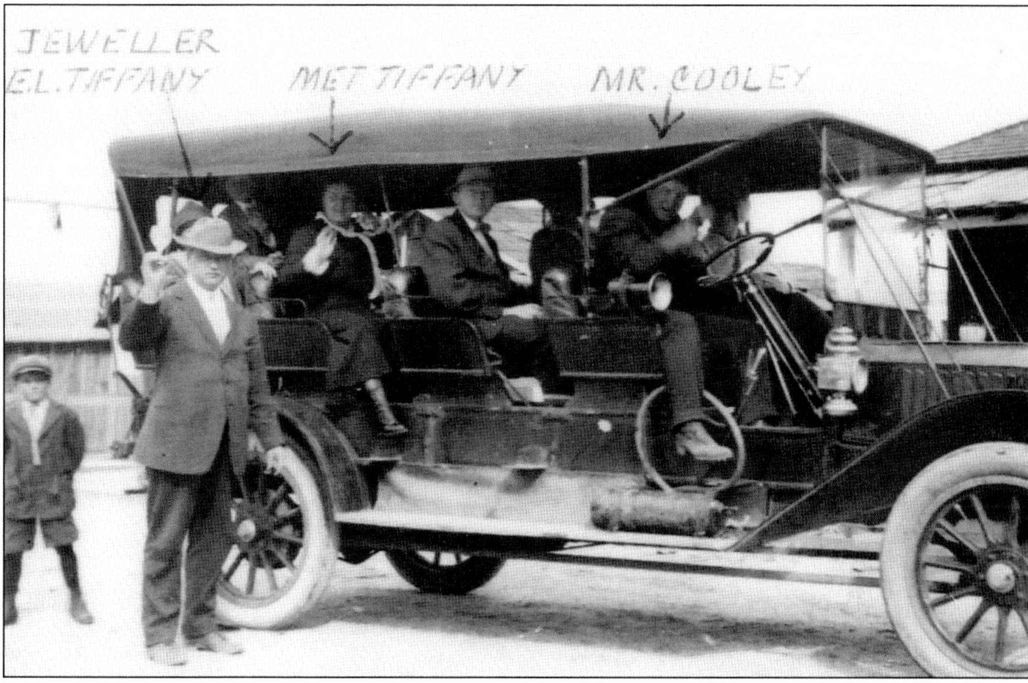

In this 1912 photograph, a Taft jeweler and his wife are leaving for their honeymoon to Richardson's Ranch in Cuiaba, California, aboard the Maricopa bus. Highway 99, and roads that connected to it, were used for personal and recreational use in addition to their agricultural and industrial purposes. (Courtesy of the Kern County Library.)

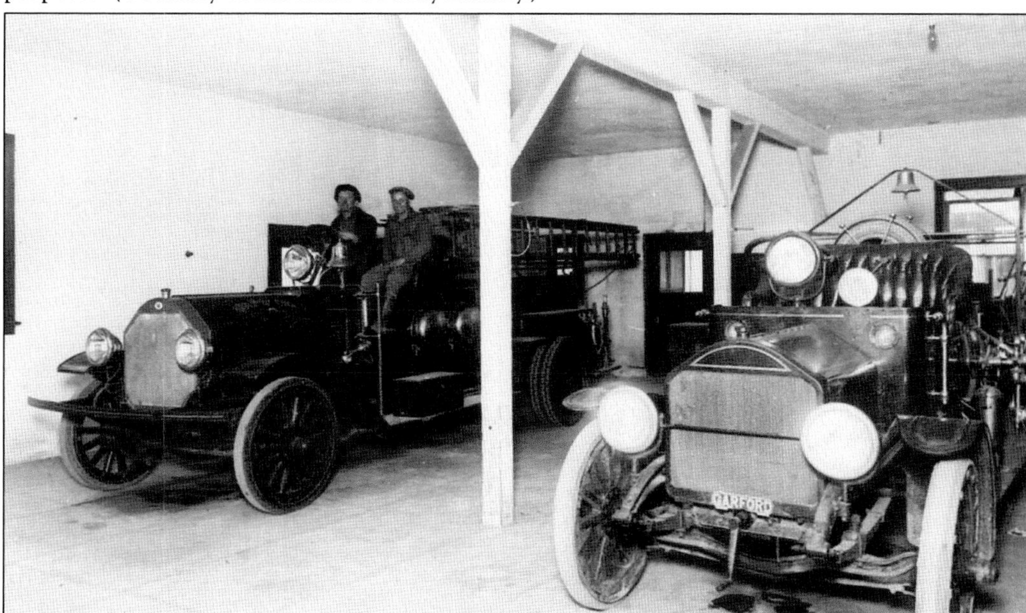

This 1921 photograph shows fire trucks in Taft, California. Note the pride that the firefighters took in their equipment. They took care of the equipment not only so it would be ready to fight fires but also because it was a reflection of their professionalism. The city of Taft was incorporated on November 7, 1910. (Courtesy of the Kern County Library.)

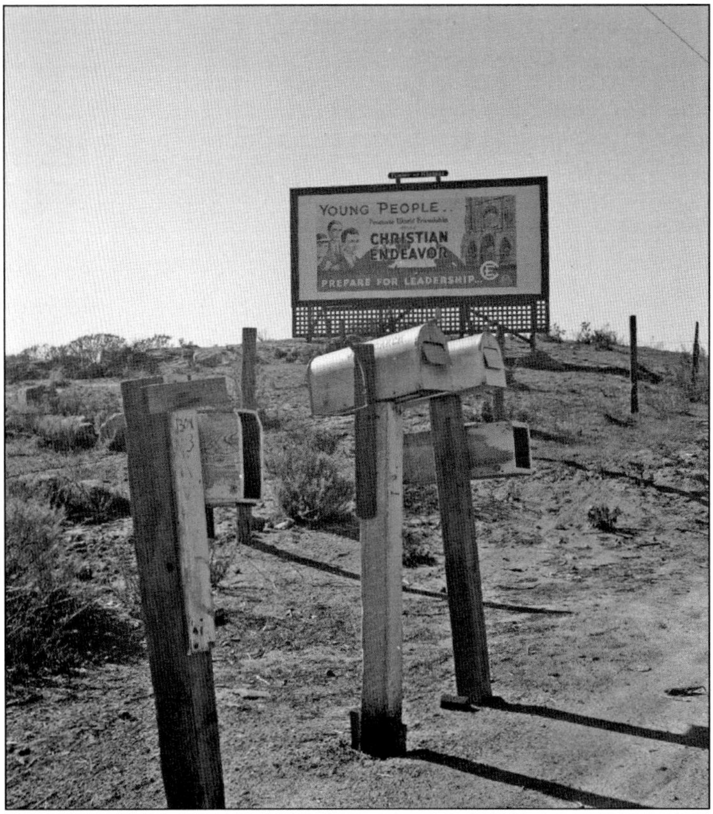

In the 1930s, a large billboard was erected along Highway 99 that described an organization called Christian Endeavor. This was a nondenominational evangelical organization founded in 1881 by Francis Edward Clark in Portland, Maine. The organization promoted leadership skills and a willingness to serve. (Courtesy of the Library of Congress)

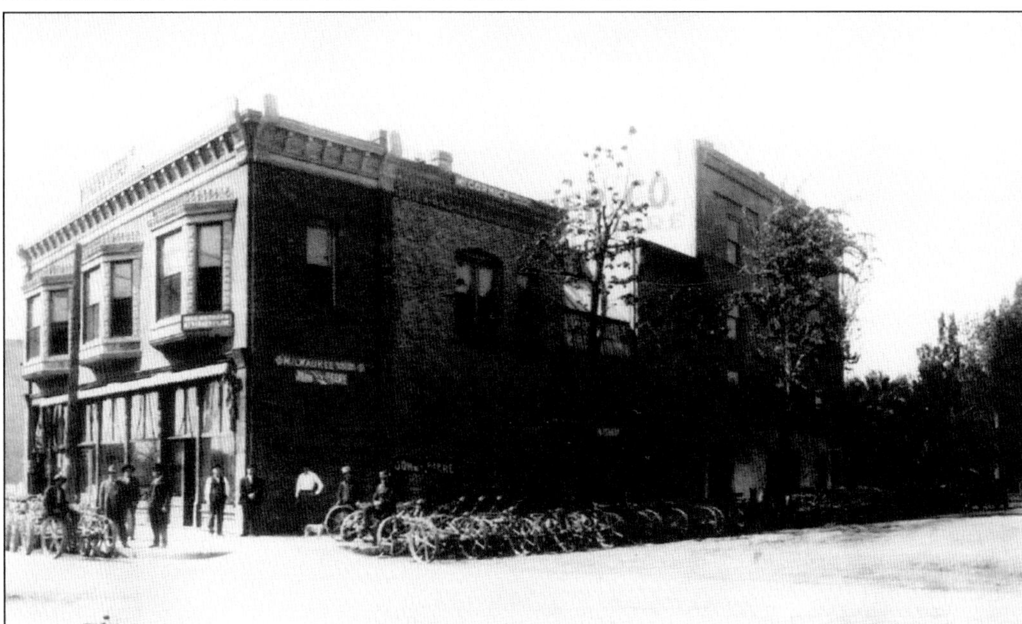

This street scene of downtown Bakersfield shows a bicycle business. Highway 99 and earlier routes were routed through this area. Although many streets in downtown Bakersfield had been paved by this time, some of rural Highway 99 had not been. (Courtesy of the Kern County Library.)

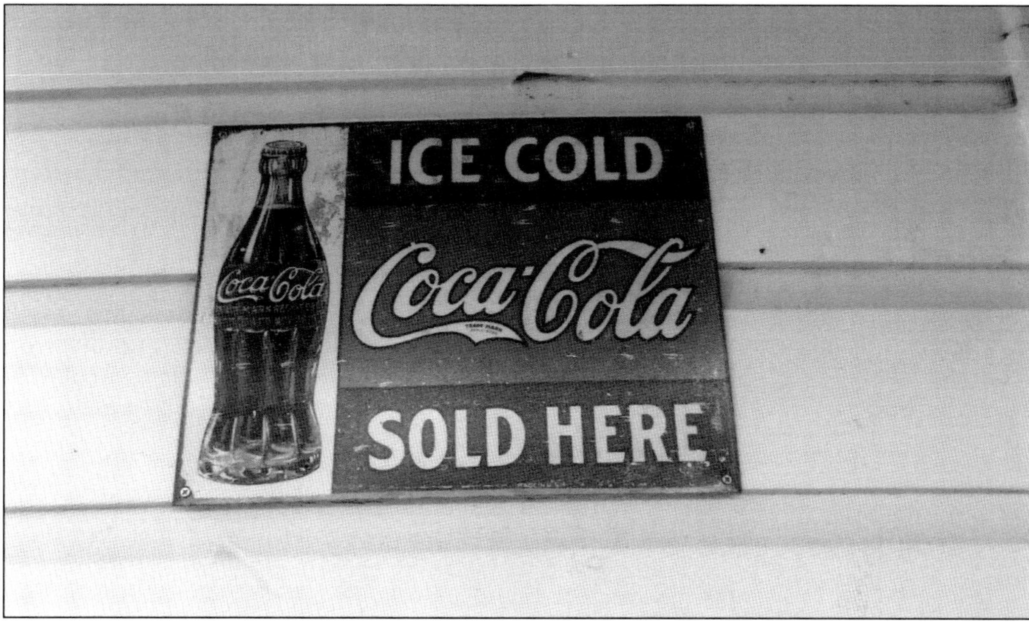

This photograph shows a Coca-Cola sign. Signs like this showing the logos of different brands of soft drinks were seen along the highway and included Bireley's Orange, Grape Nehi, Coca-Cola, and various root beers and sarsaparillas. The Coca-Cola Company began operations in the late 1880s, but Bireley's Orange soft drinks became an American staple by the 1930s, and Grape Nehi was first sold in the 1920s.

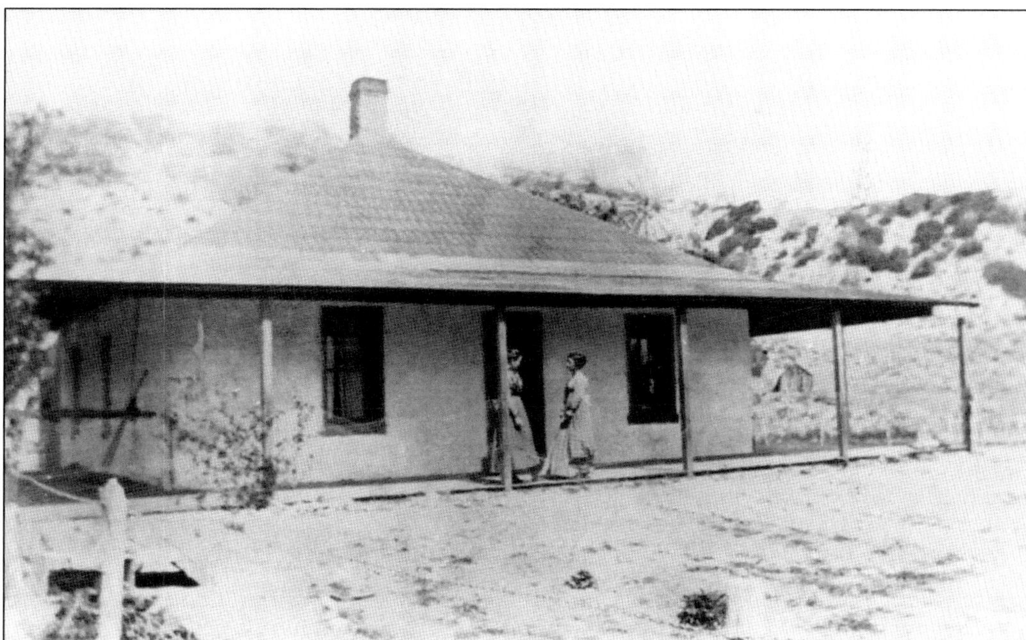

This photograph, taken in 1900, shows a ranch-style home in Kern County. A crudely constructed barbed wire fence surrounds the house, and a windmill for the well can be seen in the distance. This simple but functional home was situated across from the Lebec Post Office. (Courtesy of the Kern County Library.)

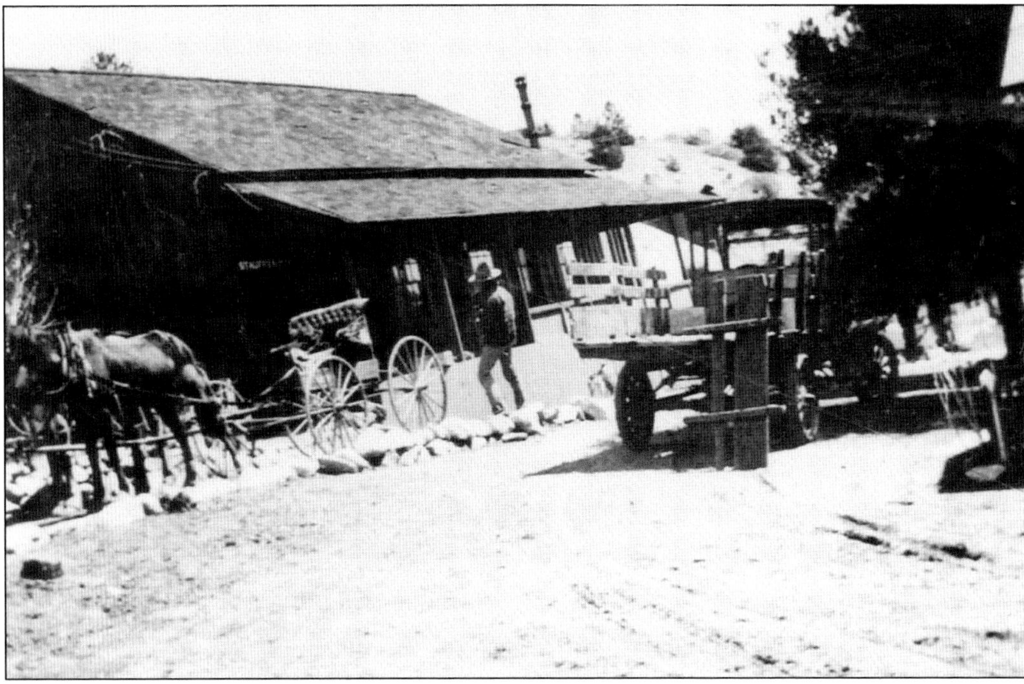

This is an image of the historic Stauffer Post Office, with a man in the foreground loading supplies. The post office was located southwest of Frazier Park. Stauffer was a mining town located along Seymour Creek. (Courtesy of the Kern County Library.)

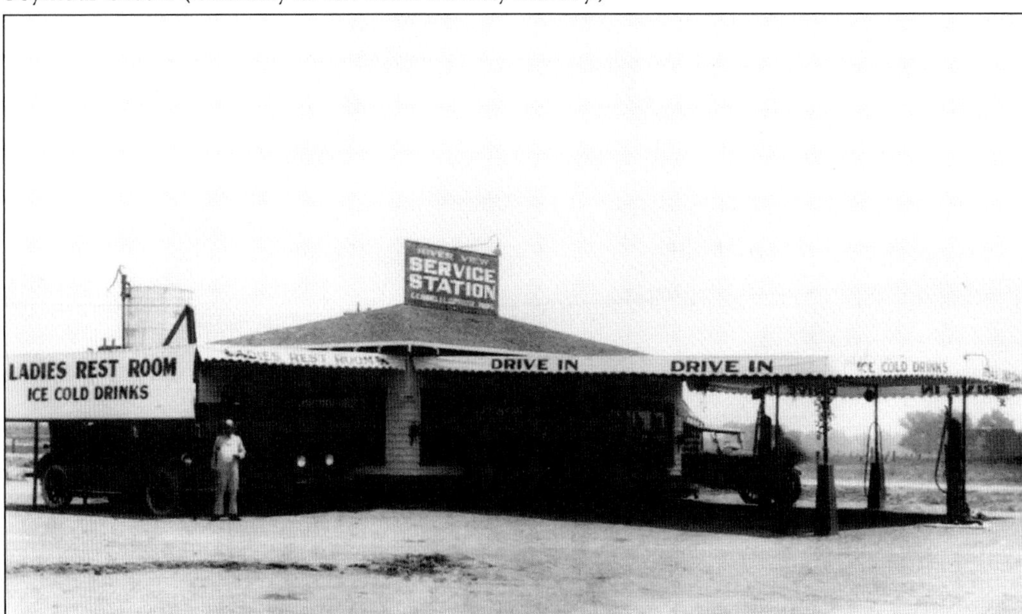

This 1920 photograph shows the River View Service Station, which was a multipurpose stop for weary travelers. It provided care for the vehicle, restrooms, food, and drinks. The cold drinks were a welcome treat in a time when vehicles did not have air conditioning and were often uncovered. The River View Service Station was located at Beardsley Avenue and North Chester Avenue in Oildale. (Courtesy of the Kern County Library.)

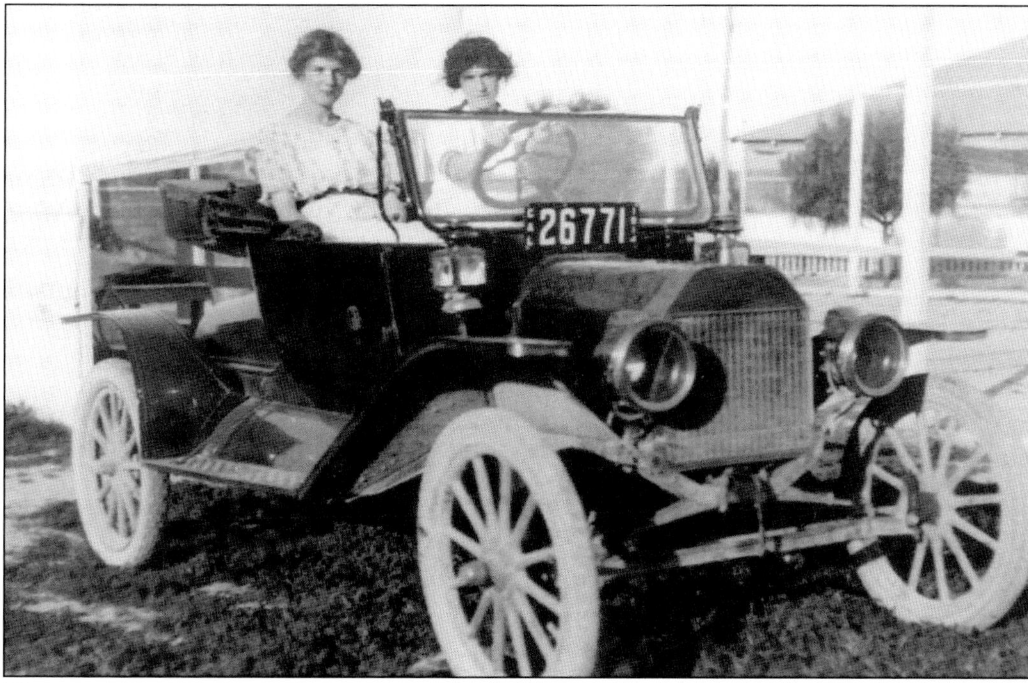

This image shows two young women in an early automobile. Top speeds were low at the time, but poor conditions often made roads the limiting factor, not the cars. The tires were not much different than the bicycle tires of that time. (Courtesy of the Kern County Library.)

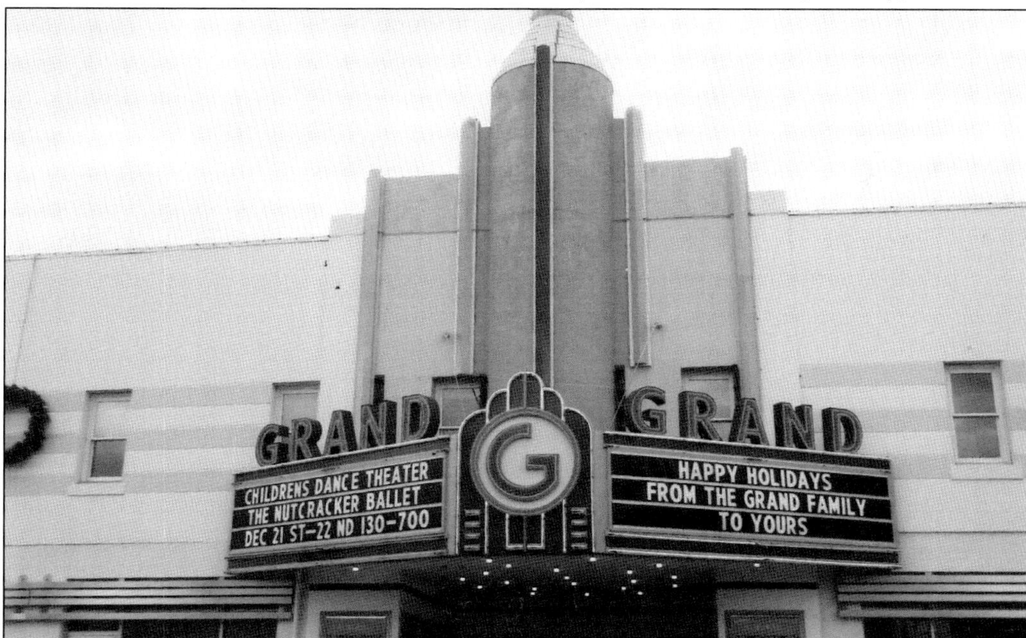

The Art Deco–styled Grand Theatre in Tracy opened on August 11, 1923. Most of the towns and cities along Highway 99 had a theater like this one—typically located downtown. These theaters were originally designed with only one screen, were often ornate, and their seats were often adorned with plush cushions upholstered with scarlet-colored velvet.

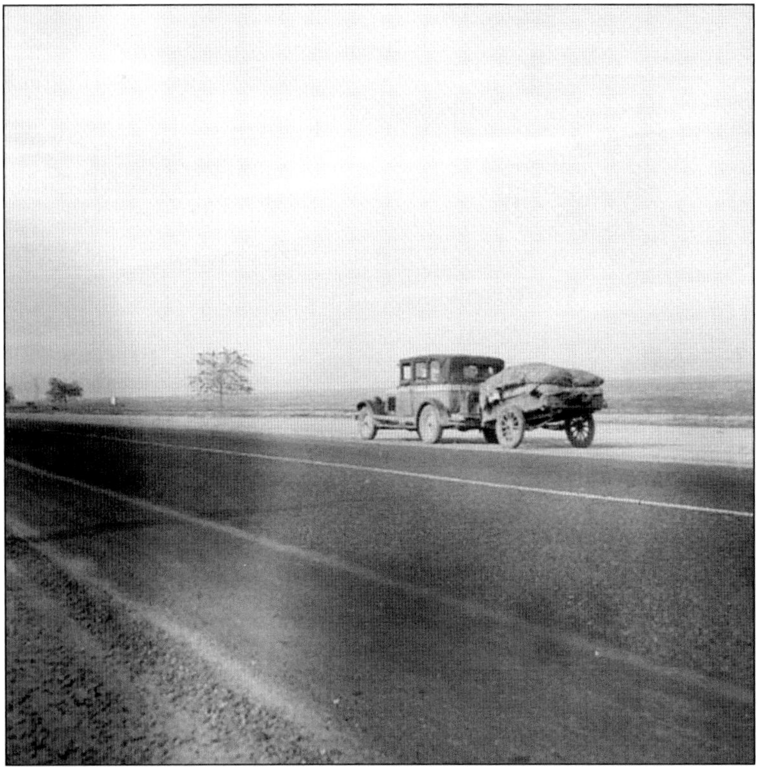

This photograph is of a car traveling down Highway 99, which had already been paved by the mid-1930s. The paved roads allowed for safer and more efficient travel and reduced wear and tear on travelling automobiles. Most of those who moved to California during the Dust Bowl were very poor and often needed financial and social assistance. As a result, the Resettlement Administration was established in 1935 to reduce American rural poverty. (Courtesy of the Library of Congress.)

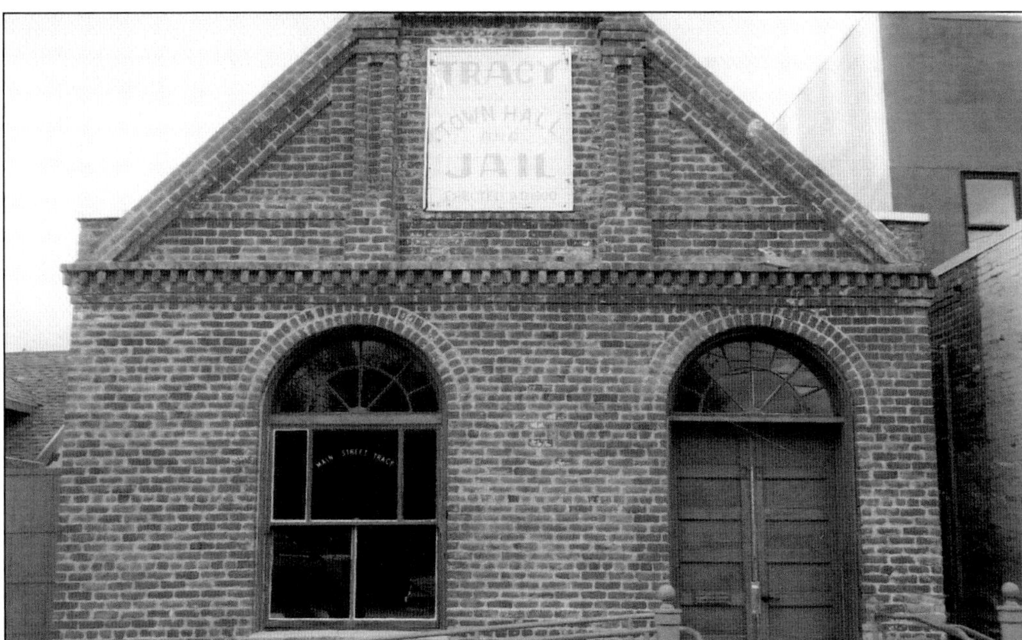

The Highway 99 region of the Central Valley hosts several jails and prisons, including federal, state, and local institutions. Almost every city or county has a holding cell, and many were very simple. The city of Tracy—its jail and town hall seen here—was incorporated in 1910 after being a railroad hub for several decades.

Three

Main Street of California

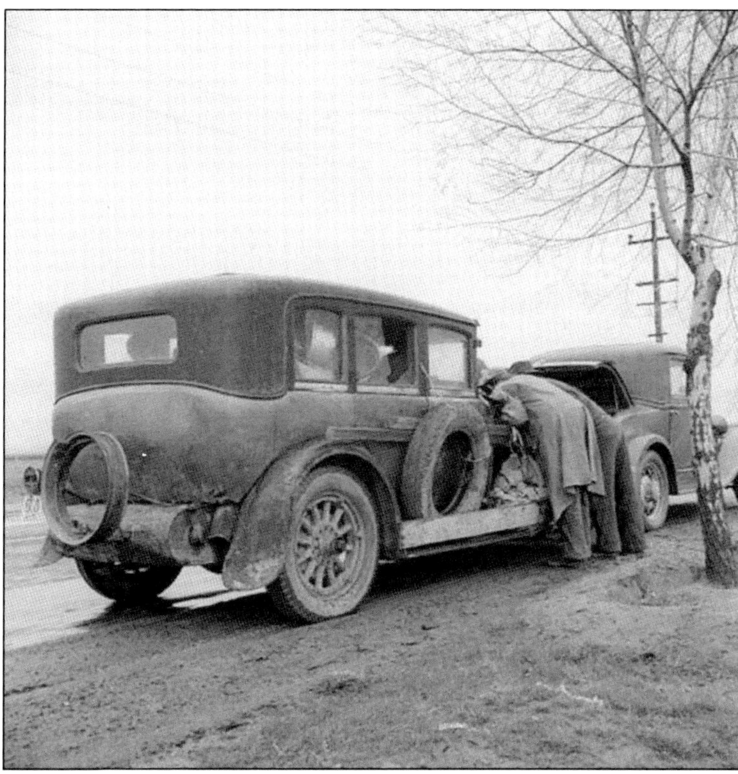

This photograph, taken along Highway 99 in the 1930s, shows two individuals repairing their car—likely trying the jump the battery. At that time, there was little or no commercial road service available. The engine's life and the level of an automobile's reliability were significantly lower than they are today. (Courtesy of the Library of Congress.)

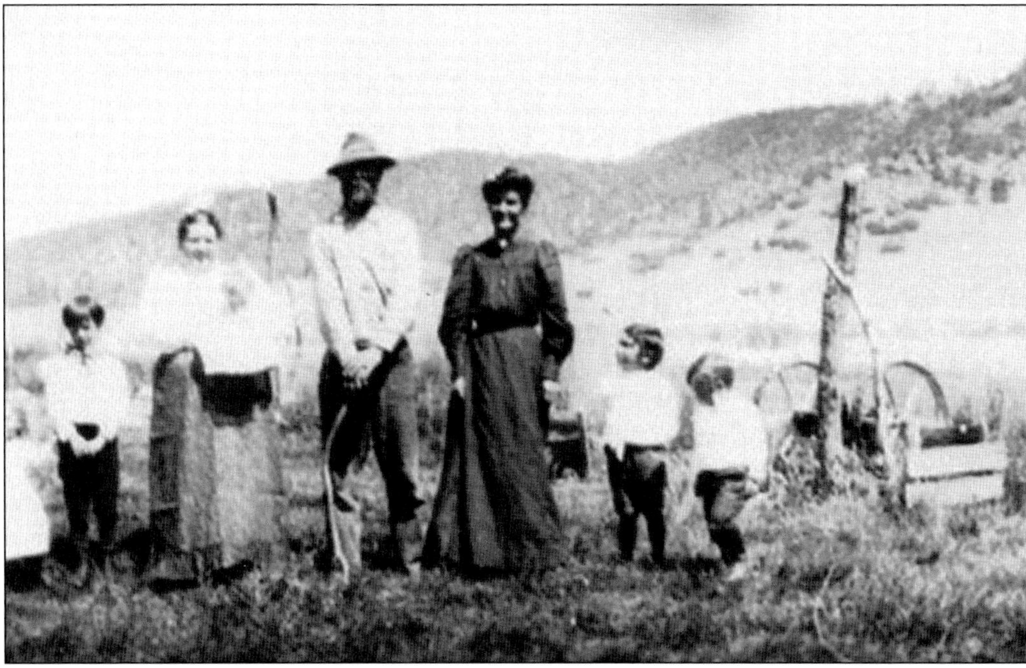

A Kern County family poses on their property in this photograph. It was individuals such as these who needed the north-to-south route provided by State Route 4 for business and personal travel. (Courtesy of the Kern County Library.)

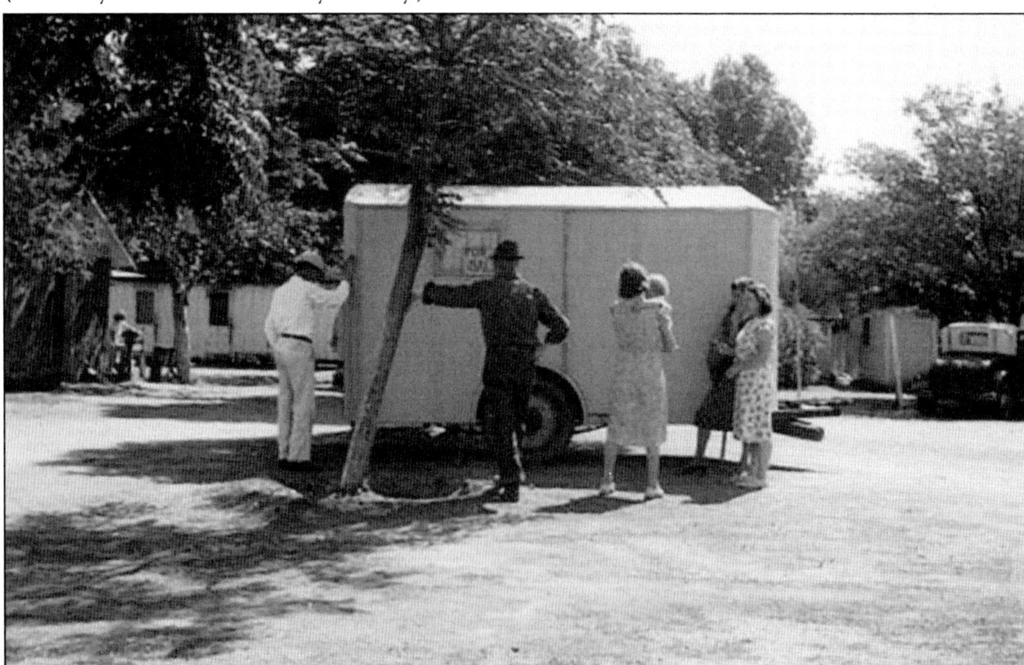

In this photograph, a family from Kern County appraises a trailer that they are thinking of buying. Considerations would have included the trailer's drain on gas mileage, its age, its suitability for their family, and its operating costs. (Courtesy of the Kern County Library.)

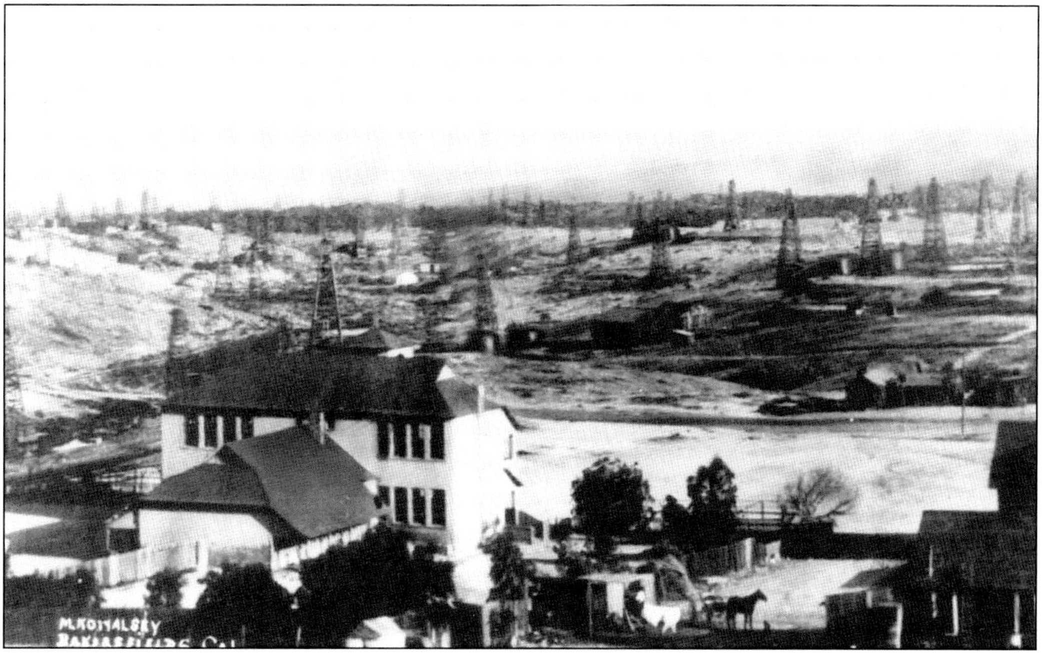

This photograph shows houses on the edge of an oil field in Bakersfield and illustrates the high density of the local oil wells. This was necessary to support the booming automobile industry and the growth of industry in California. Much of the growth in Bakersfield was driven by the need for workers in the oil fields. (Courtesy of the Kern County Library.)

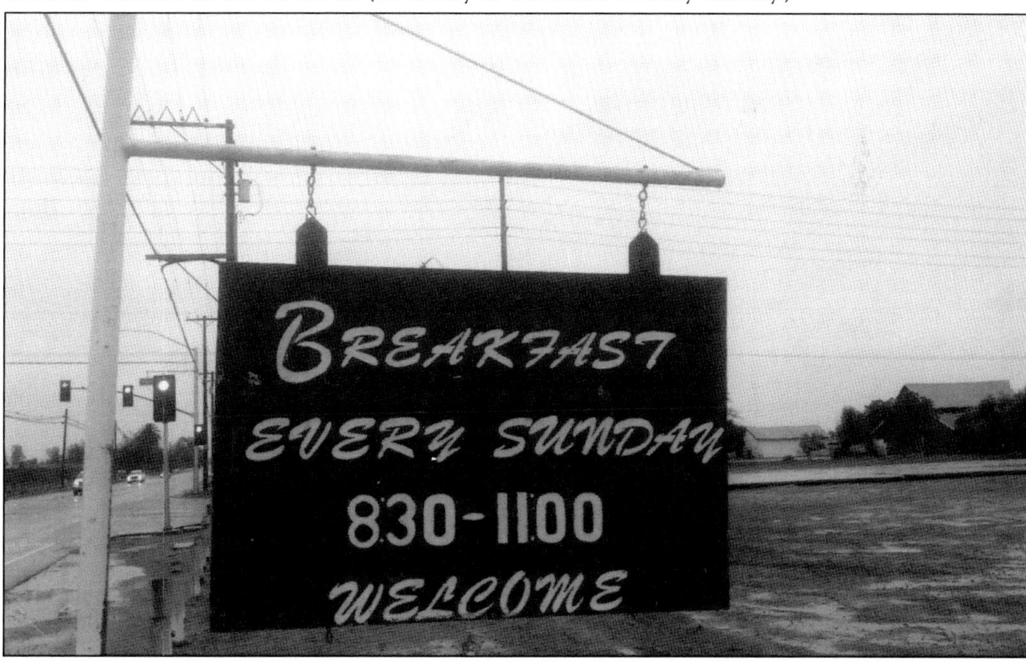

The pancake breakfast is an element of classical Americana. This photograph was taken on Main Street, west of Turlock, at the Moose Lodge. Pancake breakfasts are often sponsored by civic organizations and groups, such as fire departments, and are a part of American culture. The Loyal Order of Moose, a fraternal organization, was founded in 1888.

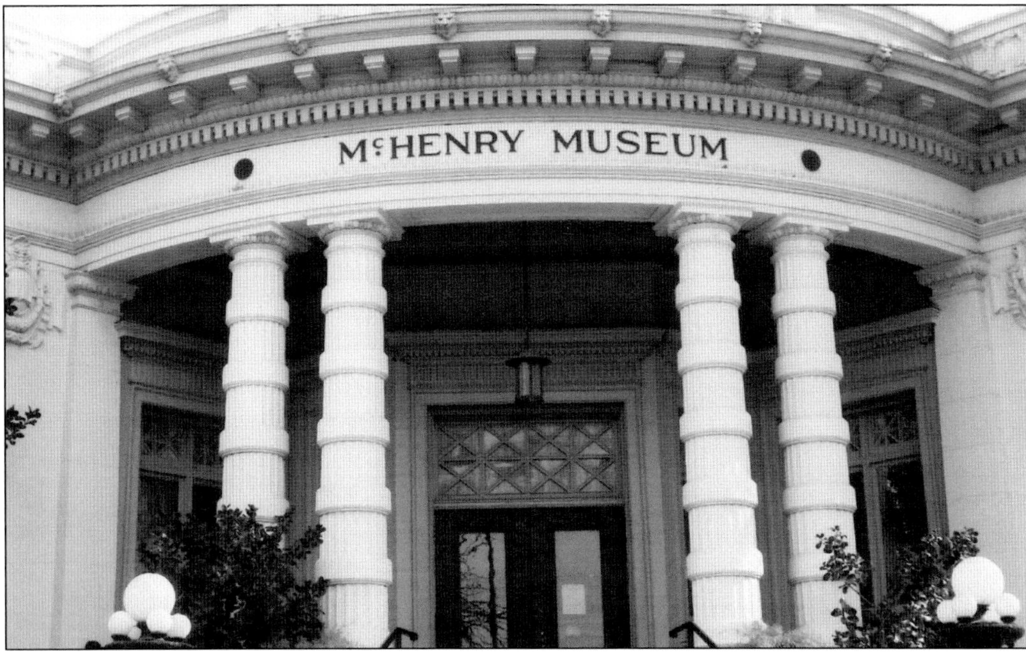

The McHenry Museum presents a description of Modesto, which is along Highway 99. Prior to the bypass being constructed, Highway 99 ran along Ninth Street. The museum has built a 1950s diner, emblematic of the teen culture. Modesto was the setting for the 1973 film *American Graffiti*, though the movie was mostly shot in San Rafael and Petaluma. (Courtesy of the McHenry Museum.)

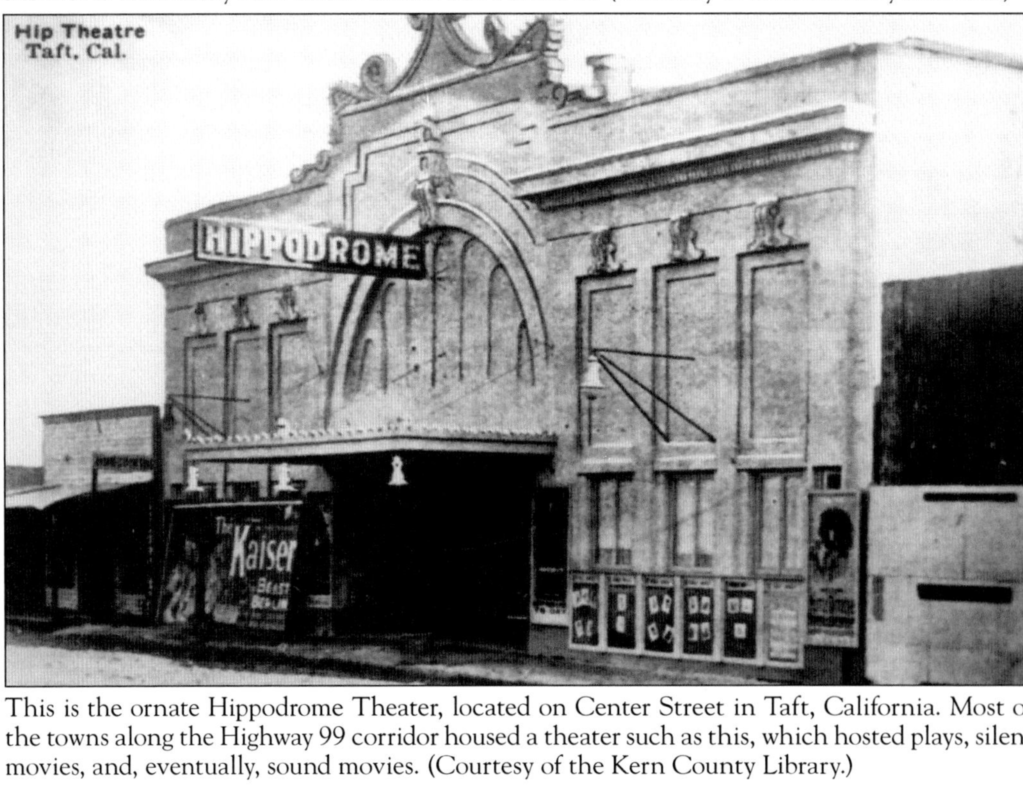

This is the ornate Hippodrome Theater, located on Center Street in Taft, California. Most of the towns along the Highway 99 corridor housed a theater such as this, which hosted plays, silent movies, and, eventually, sound movies. (Courtesy of the Kern County Library.)

This image shows an orderly building that houses a milk producer in Tulare. Dairy was, and still is, an important part of the Highway 99 corridor's agricultural base. Tulare has been an agricultural center since the inception of Highway 99. The city's current population is about 60,000. (Courtesy of the Library of Congress.)

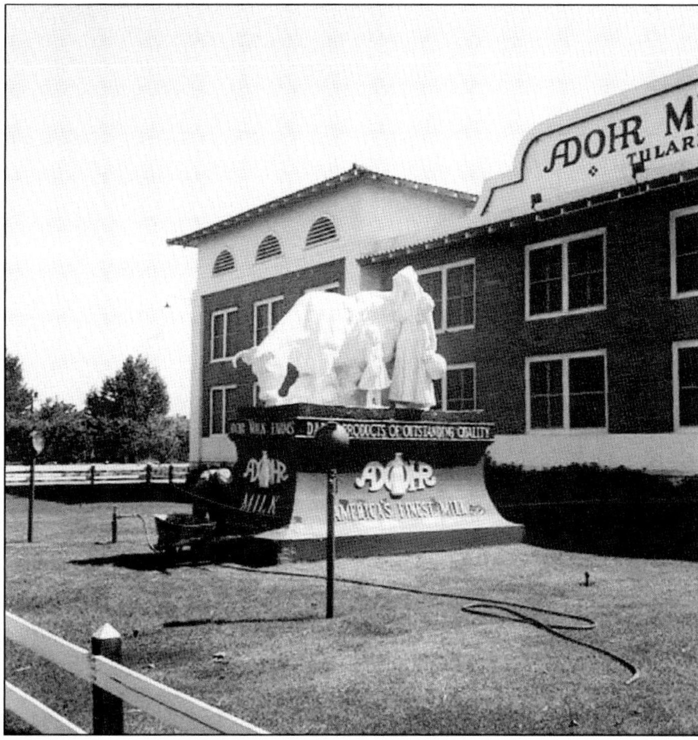

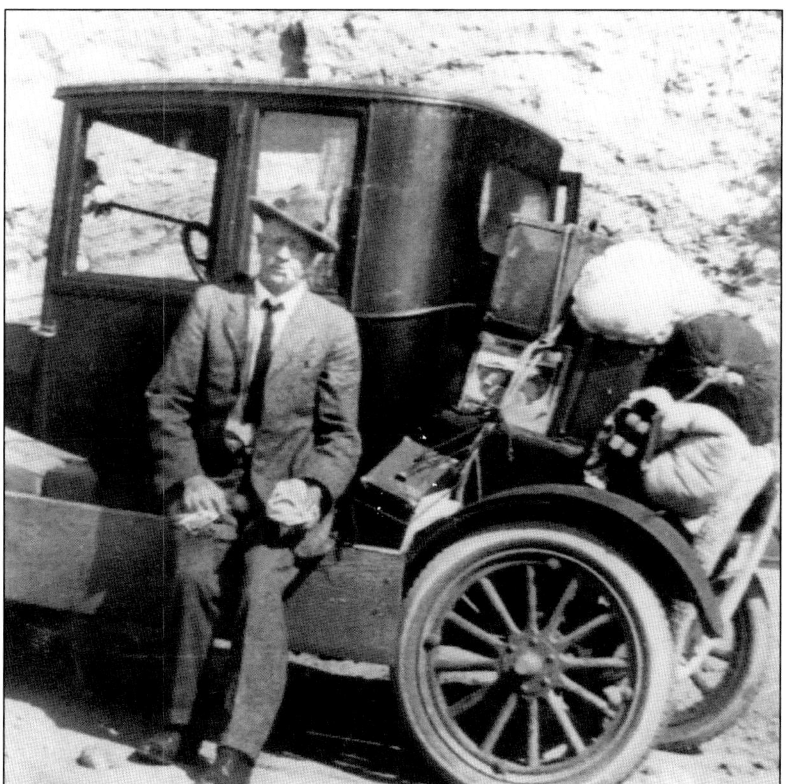

This photograph shows a Kern County man moving his possessions in an early-model car. Brakes of the period were not very reliable, and he has had to place a large rock behind the rear tire to prevent the vehicle from rolling down this dirt road. (Courtesy of the Library of Congress.)

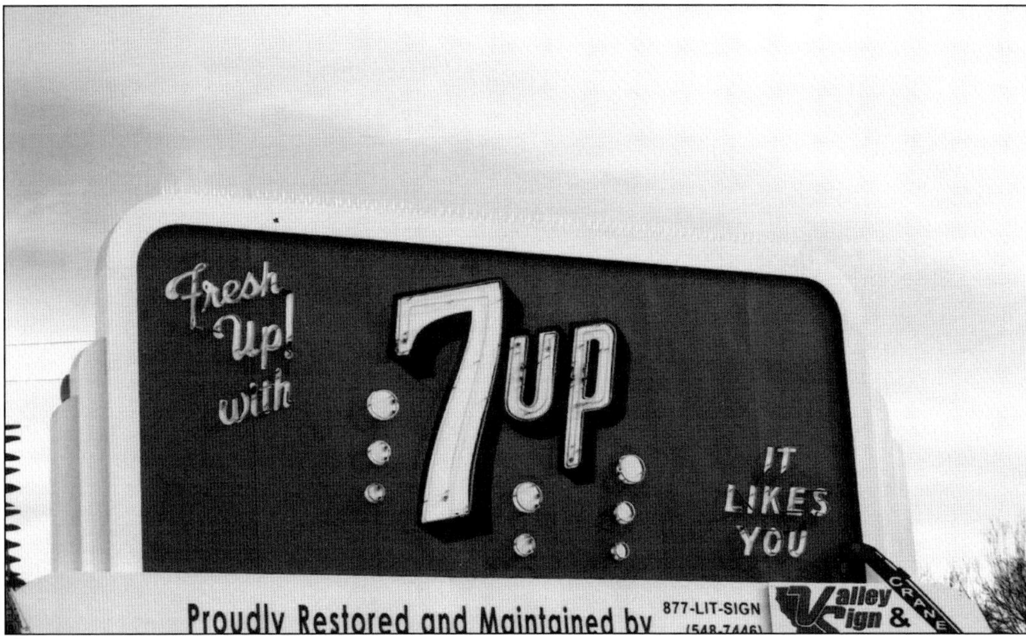

This is a nostalgic 7 Up sign, located on Main Street in Merced—which parallels the old route of Highway 99. Signs like this were common along Highway 99, and in the cities and towns that it travelled through. A 7 Up was refreshing, because traveling on Highway 99 in the summer was hot and uncomfortable, as most vehicles did not have air conditioning until the 1960s or later.

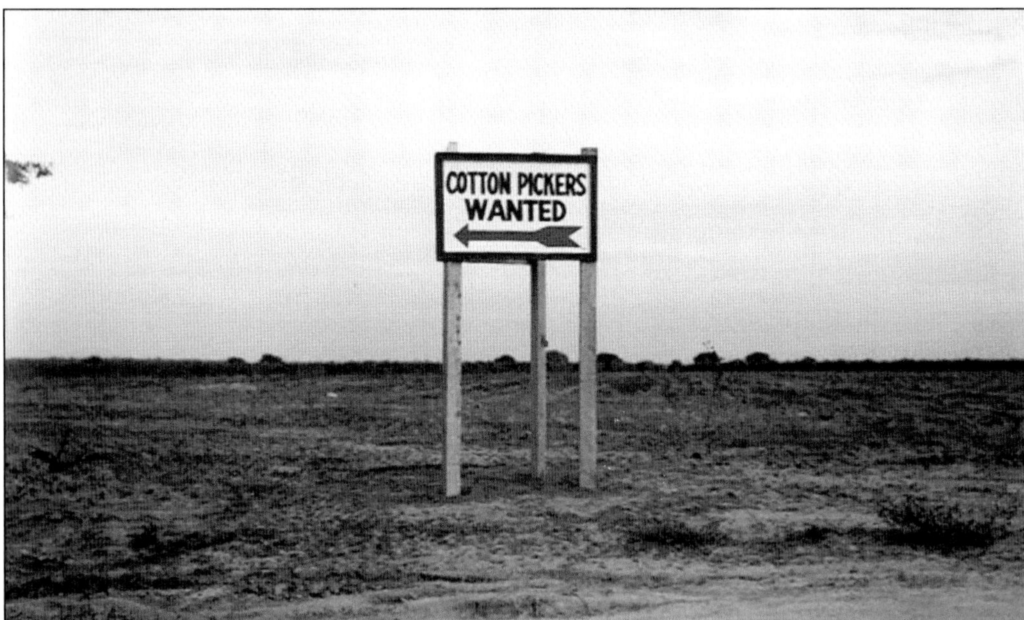

This sign advertises the need for cotton pickers along Highway 99. Many Depression-era workers relocated to California from Oklahoma and surrounding states in order to seek work and a more stable life. Simple signs like this were a welcome sight for would-be hardworking Americans. Unemployment in the United States during the Depression exceeded 25 percent. (Courtesy of the Library of Congress.)

The city of Turlock, which is known for its grape and strawberry production, has grown significantly since it was first connected to Modesto and other cities by Highway 99. The fact that it warrants five different exits from Highway 99 shows that it is now a city of significant size. In 2014, the population of Turlock was nearly 70,000. (Courtesy of the Turlock Historical Society.)

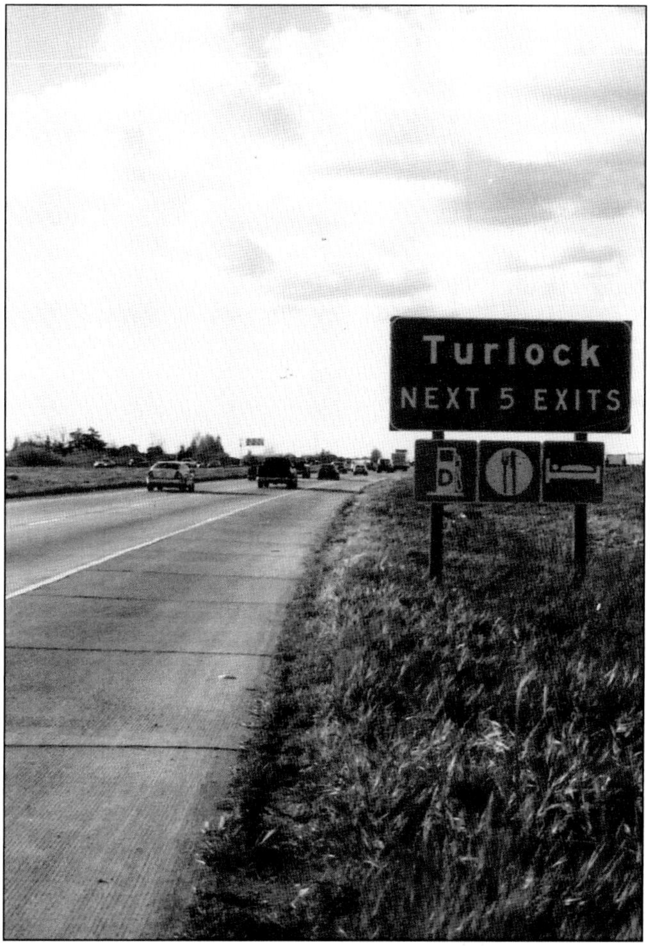

This photograph shows people unloading lumber from railroad car in Turlock onto horse-drawn wagons. In many places, the railroad ran parallel to Highway 99. Note that one individual set up an umbrella above the cart to protect himself from the heat. The Central Pacific Railroad once traveled through the town. (Courtesy of the California State Library, Sacramento.)

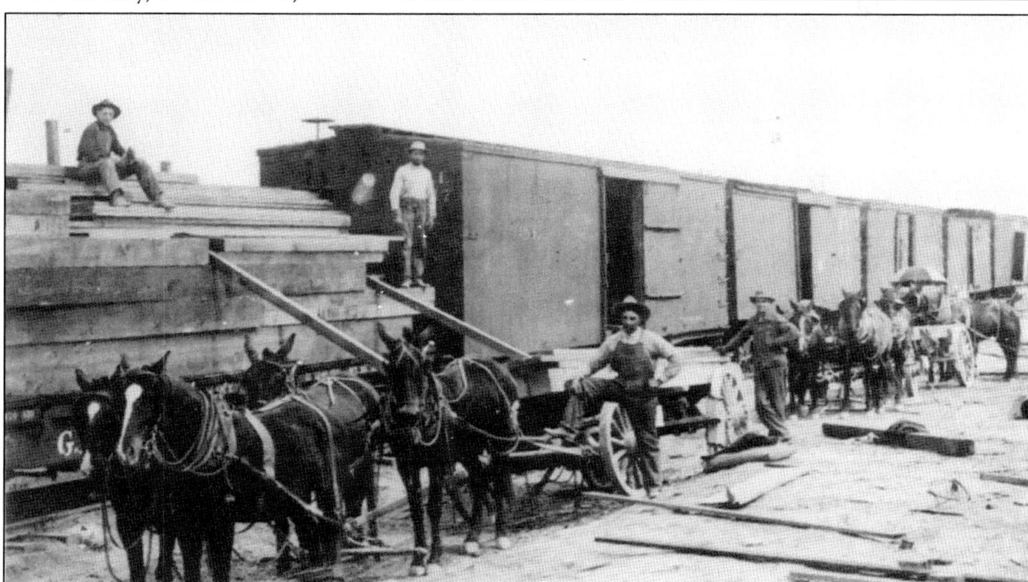

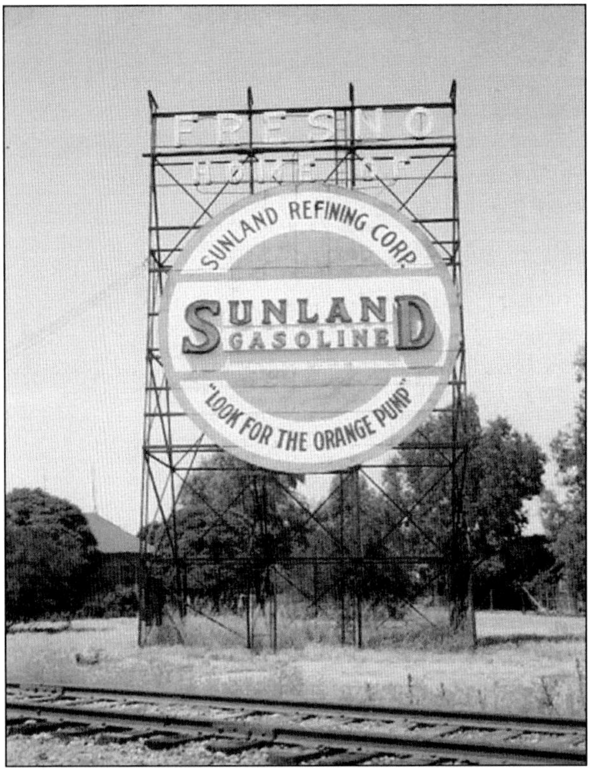

This photograph shows a large sign advertising Fresno's Sunland Gasoline somewhere along Highway 99. One of the charms of travelling on Highway 99 were the billboards themselves. The messages were typically simple and reflective of classical Americana. The Sunland Refining Corporation was established prior to 1929. (Courtesy of the Library of Congress.)

The Banta Produce Company is on Eleventh Street in Tracy, which is a section of the Lincoln Highway. The Lincoln Highway was established in 1913—about the same time that Highway 99 was first being paved. Banta, located along the Central Pacific Railroad, is actually a small, unincorporated area to the east of Tracy.

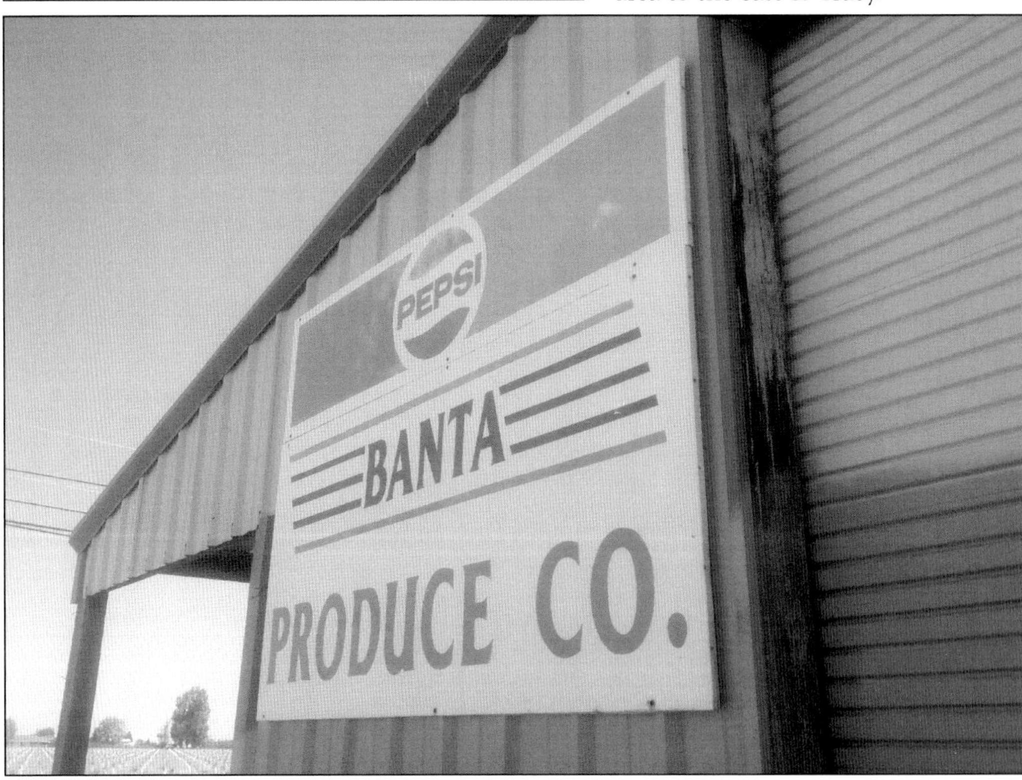

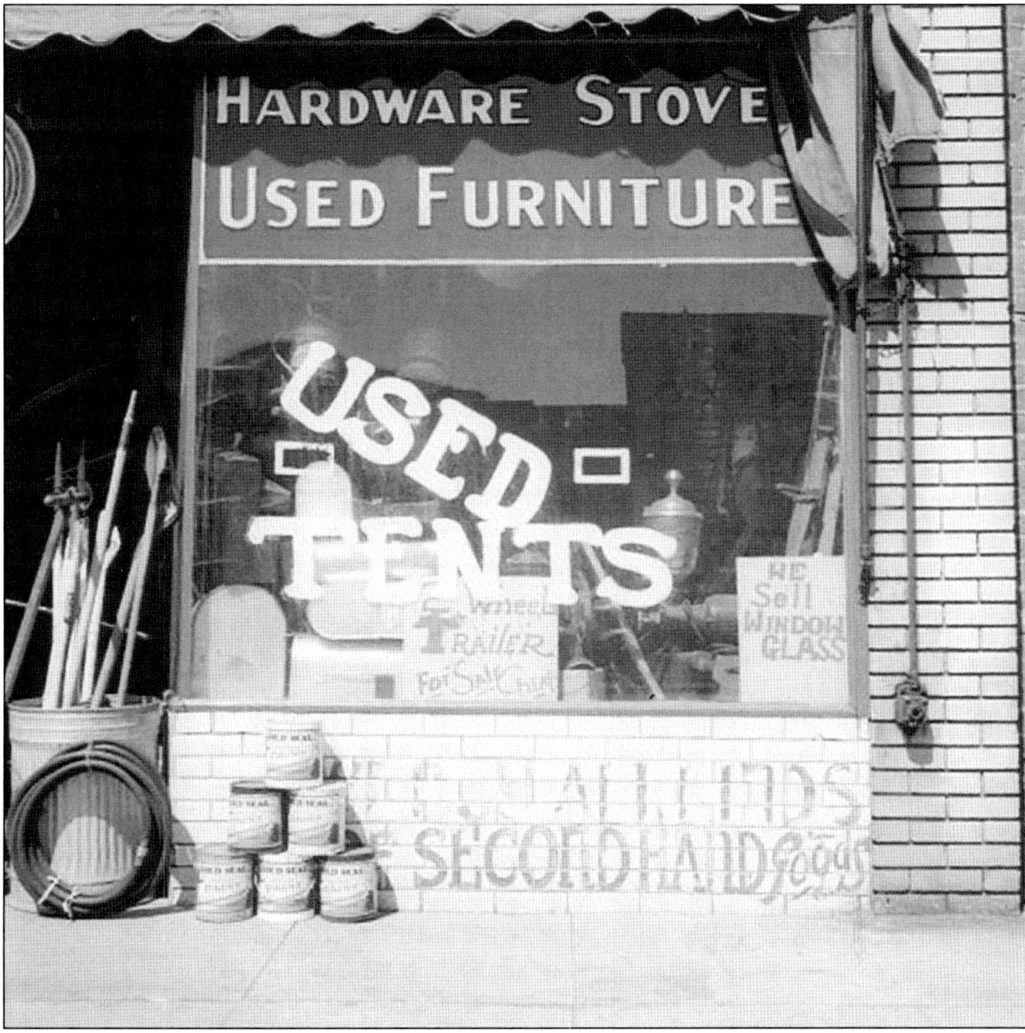

This 1930s photograph shows a simple hardware store that was built along Highway 99. It sold a variety of items, including tools, building supplies, and window glass. It purchased and sold used goods as well as new materials. (Courtesy of the Library of Congress.)

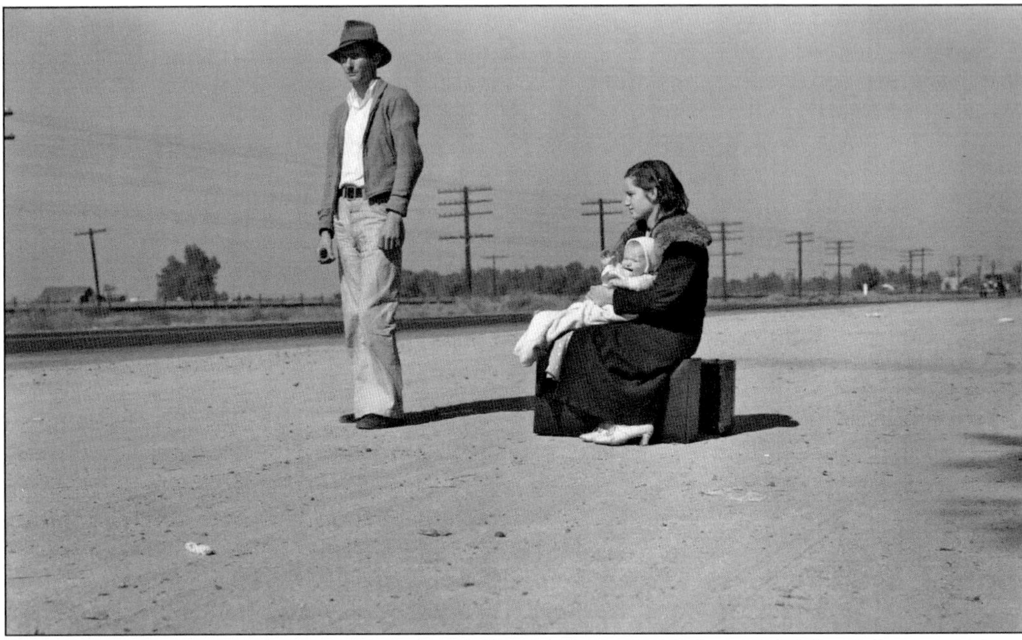

This 1930s photograph shows a young family hitchhiking on Highway 99. The father was 24 and the mother was 17. They came to California from Winston-Salem, North Carolina. Their baby was born in 1935 in the Imperial Valley, California, where they were working as field laborers. (Courtesy of the Library of Congress.)

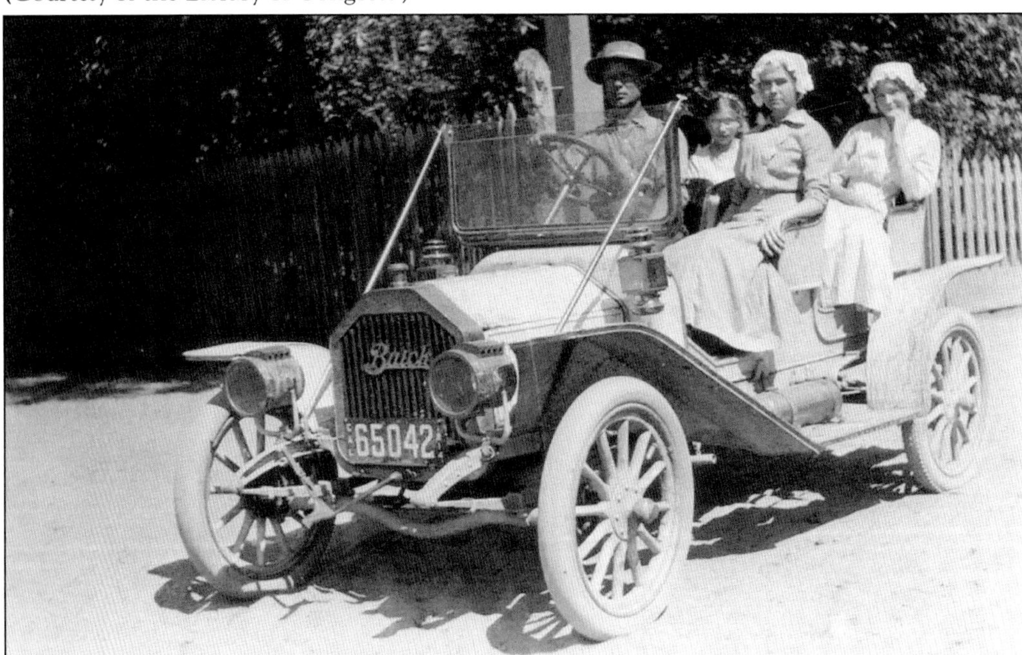

This image is of a Kern County family ready for a ride in an early-model Buick. These early cars had open tops, which made travel difficult on roads that were often in poor condition. Buick, formed in 1899, was one of the earliest automobiles driven in the United States. (Courtesy of the Kern County Library.)

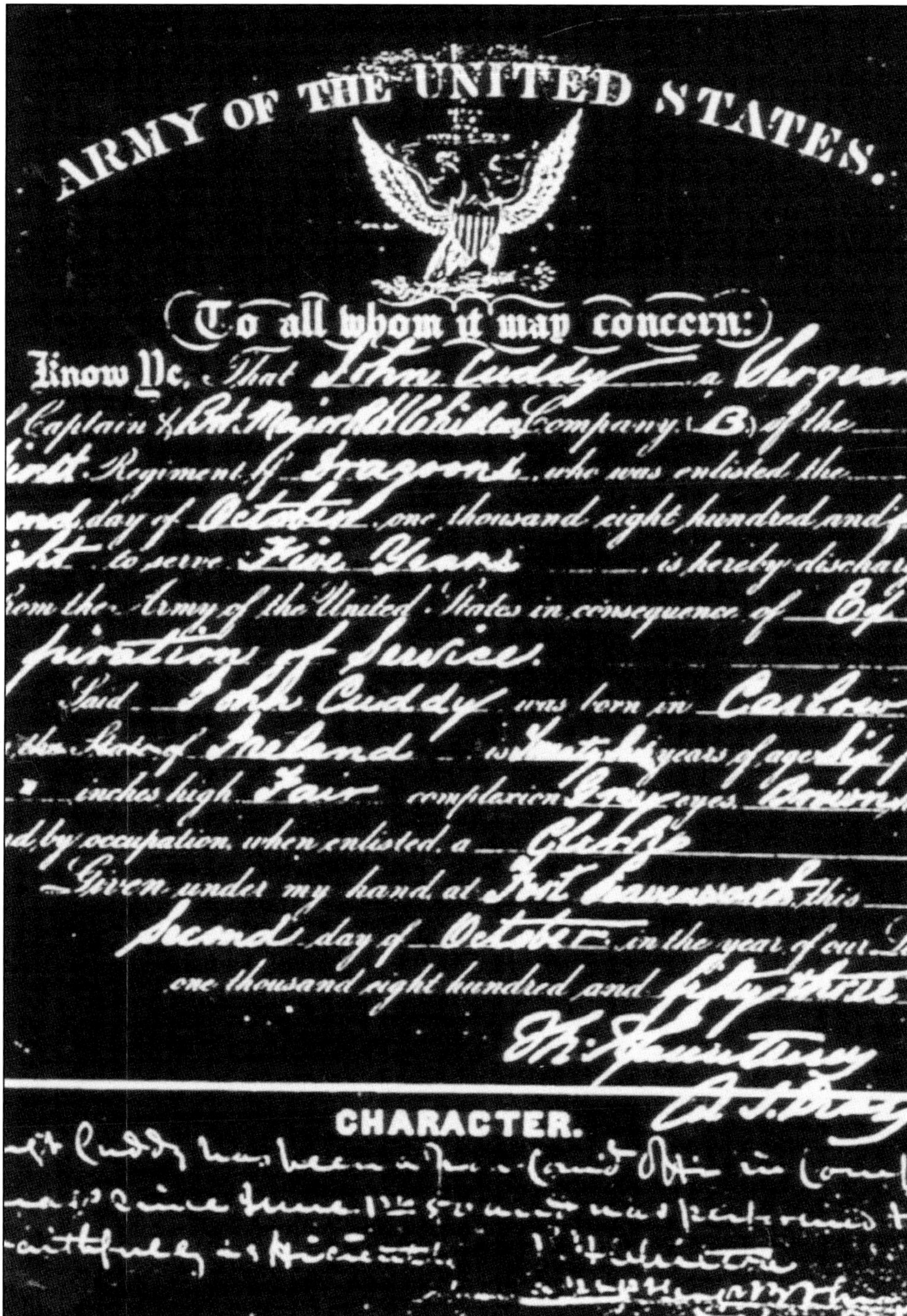

ARMY OF THE UNITED STATES.

To all whom it may concern:

Know Ye, That John Cuddy a Sergean[t] [of] Captain & Bvt. Major [illegible] Company (B) of the [F]irst Regiment of Dragoons who was enlisted the [seco]nd day of October one thousand eight hundred and f[orty] [e]ight to serve Five Years is hereby discharg[ed] [f]rom the Army of the United States in consequence of Expiration of Service.

Said John Cuddy was born in Carlow [in] the State of Ireland is twenty-six years of age, [illegible] inches high Fair complexion Grey eyes Brown [hair] and, by occupation, when enlisted, a Clerk.

Given under my hand at Fort Leavenworth this Second day of October in the year of our Lo[rd] one thousand eight hundred and fifty three.

CHARACTER.

[illegible]

This is a copy of a military discharge form, dating from 1853. It reflects the patriotism often found in California's Central Valley. The cities and towns along Highway 99 regularly recognize and honor those who have served in the US military through plaques in their historic downtown areas as well as parades and celebrations. (Courtesy of the Kern County Library.)

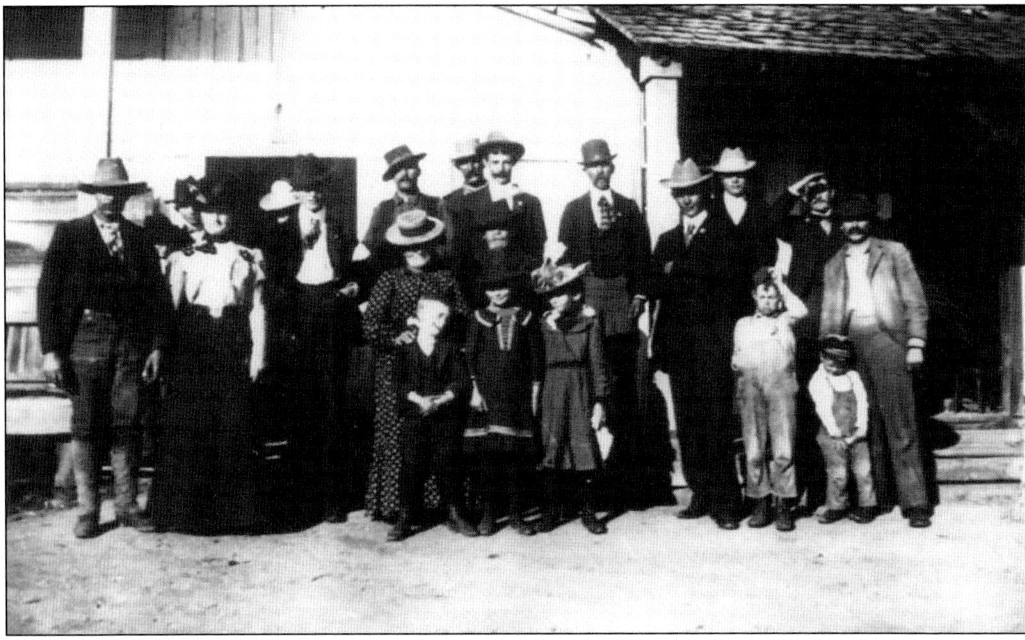

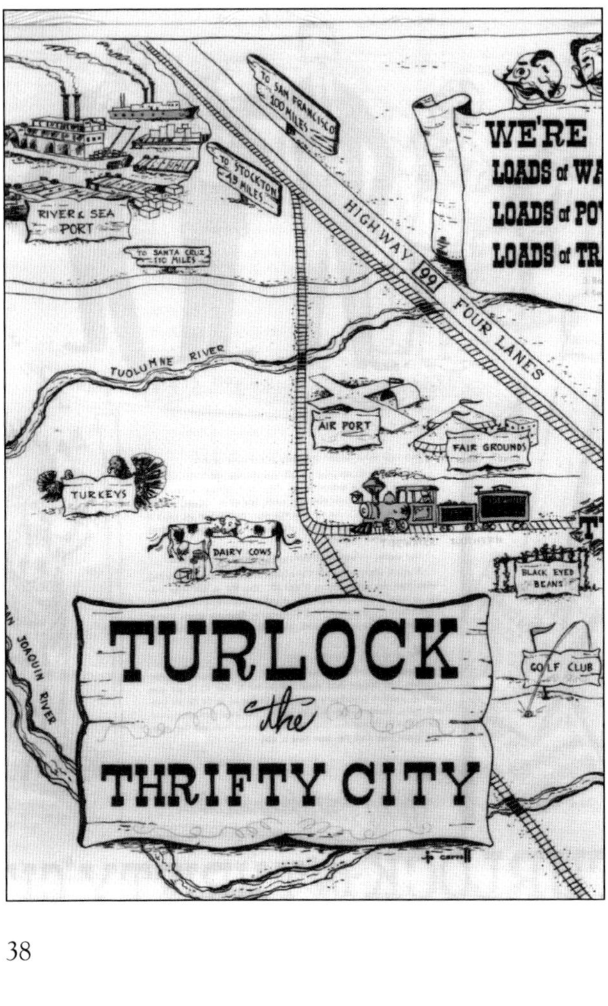

This photograph shows a family posing near a grocery store in Kern County. In addition to groceries, the store sold building supplies, plumbing fixtures, tools and other hardware, and household goods. At this time, owner-operated grocery stores—as opposed to corporate-owned establishments—were the norm. Today, the population of Kern County is about 850,000. (Courtesy of the Kern County Library.)

This map identifies Turlock as "the thrifty city." It seems to have paid off, as Turlock's historic downtown is thriving, its agricultural sector is strong, and it has a commercial and industrial base. Turlock was founded on December 22, 1871, by John William Mitchell. (Courtesy of the Turlock Historical Society.)

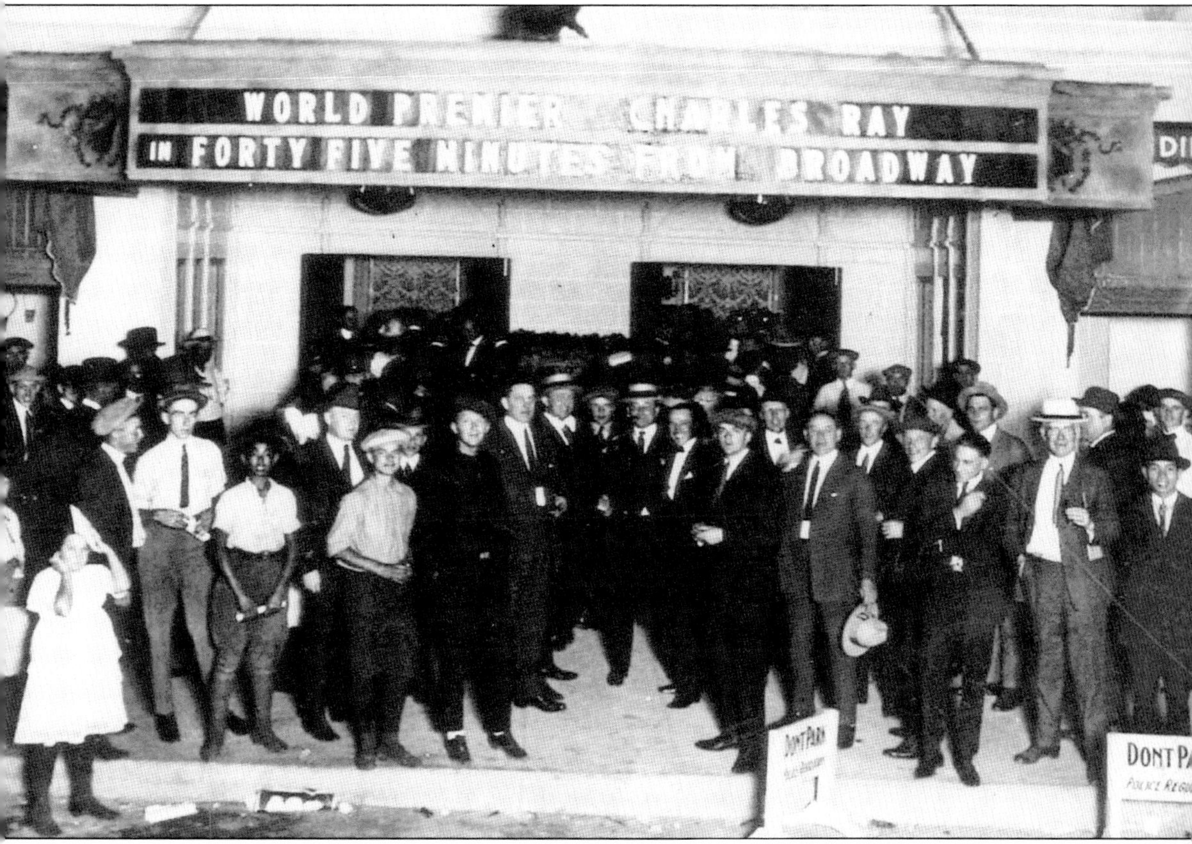

This photograph shows individuals gathered for a screening of *45 Minutes from Broadway*, starring Charles Ray. Note the formal attire worn by the patrons at this cultural event. Theaters such as this one in Kern County were often ornate. This 1920 film was based on a three-act play that was written in 1905 and ran until 1912. (Courtesy of the Kern County Library.)

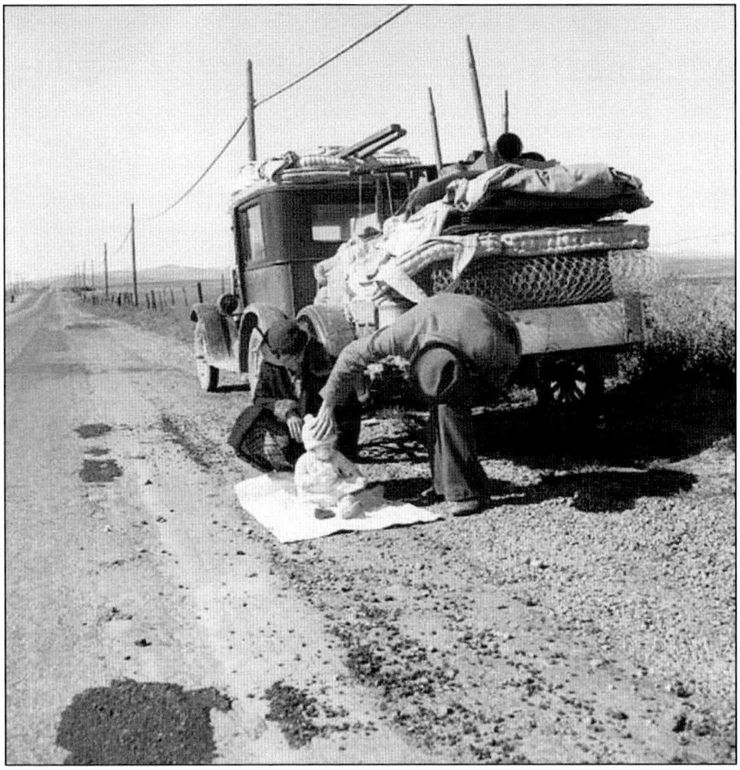

This 1930s immigrant farm family is seen giving their infant a chance to play and rest from their uncomfortable journey. It was common to see whole families travelling in cars or trucks that were loaded beyond the vehicles' rated capacity. The population of California was growing rapidly in this period. In 1920, the population of California was about three and a half million, but it doubled to about seven million by 1940. (Courtesy of the Library of Congress.)

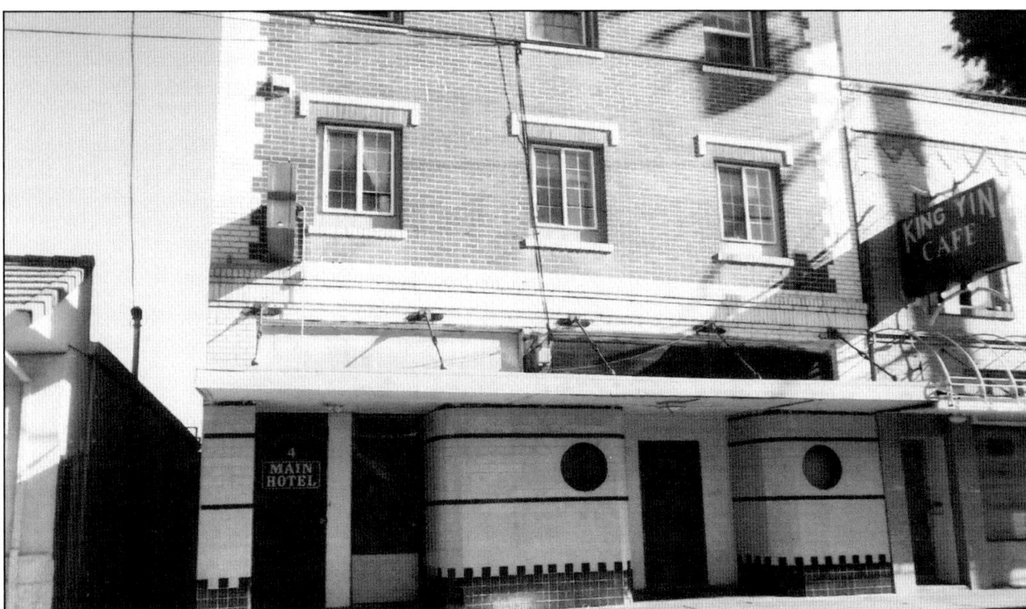

This is Main Street in Lodi. At one time, this section of Main Street was the hub of Lodi—and even included a small Chinese sector—but now it is largely a forgotten few blocks between the prosperous, newer section of Lodi and the older section of town. This section of Main Street houses a portion of society that has fallen out of the mainstream of American life but still maintains its dignity. Lodi was incorporated in 1906 but has been inhabited since the 1860s.

Four

Roadside Businesses

This heavily loaded, older-model car is traveling on an overpass on Highway 99. This multilane section of the highway is paved, designed to drain, and has safety barricades to either side. Typical horsepower ratings for these older small vehicles were much lower than the typical passenger sedans produced in 2014. (Courtesy of the Library of Congress.)

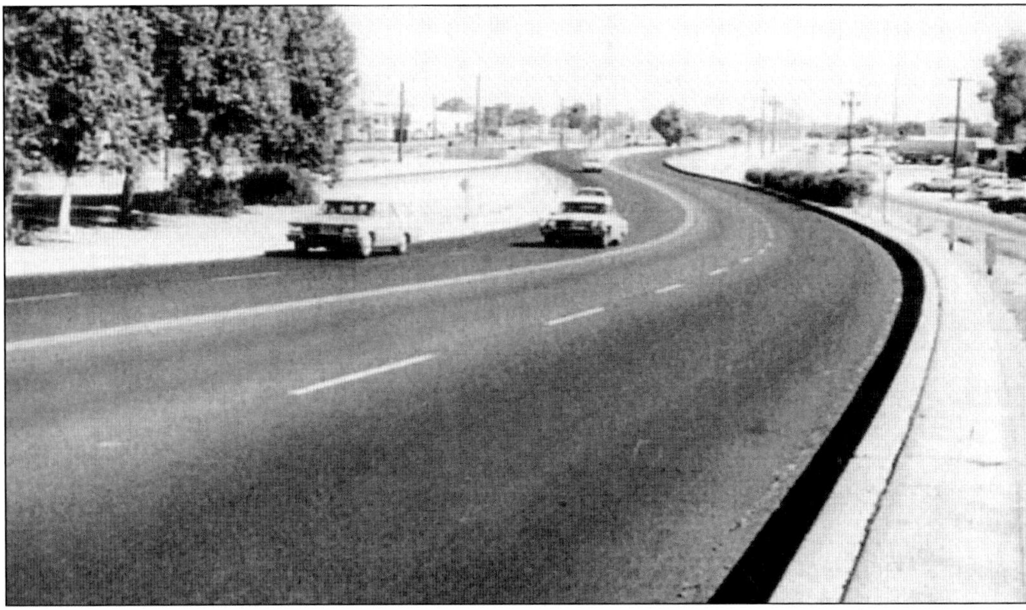

Golden State Boulevard in Turlock was previously a route of Highway 99. Highway 99 is often referred to as the Golden State Highway. The Golden State is an appropriate designation for California and is the state's official nickname. California's modern development can be traced back to the discovery of gold in 1848. (Courtesy of the Turlock Historical Society.)

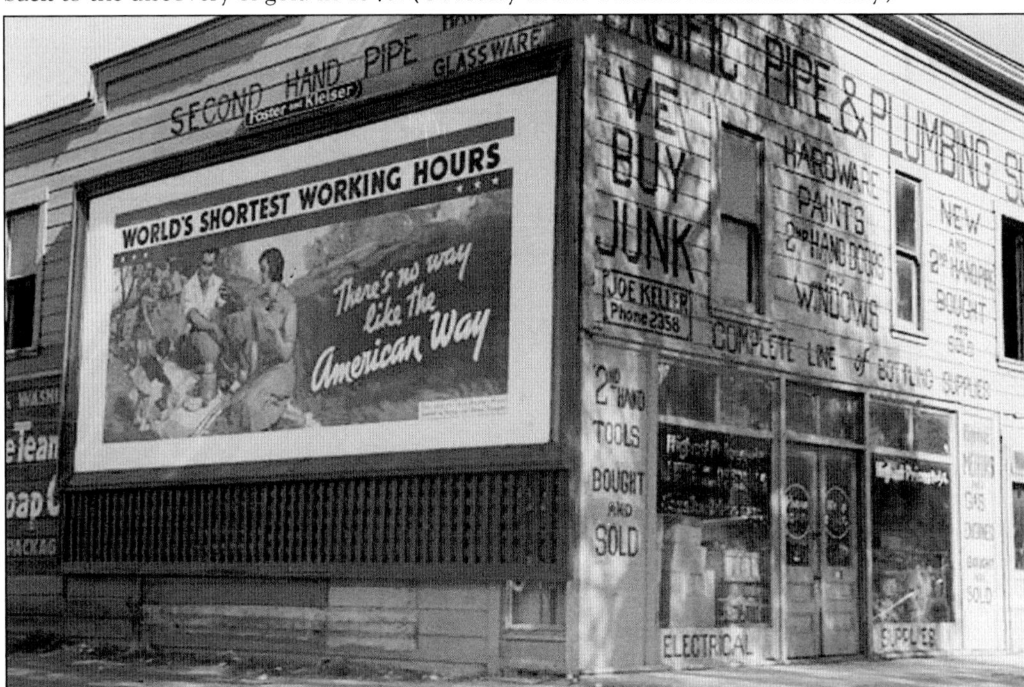

Pacific Pipe & Plumbing Supply supplied both new and used goods. Many goods were expensive to manufacture, so it was worth the time and expense to repair certain pieces of equipment rather than dispose of them. A billboard from the 1930s and 1940s is prominently displayed on the wall and extols the "American Way." (Courtesy of the Library of Congress.)

This simple sign, advertising potatoes, was easy to see from Highway 99. The area was relatively uncongested and did not suffer from "sign pollution." Potatoes—including russet, red, white, yellow, purple/blue, fingerling, and petite—are the leading vegetable crop in the United States, with an annual production of about 40 billion pounds. (Courtesy of the Library of Congress.)

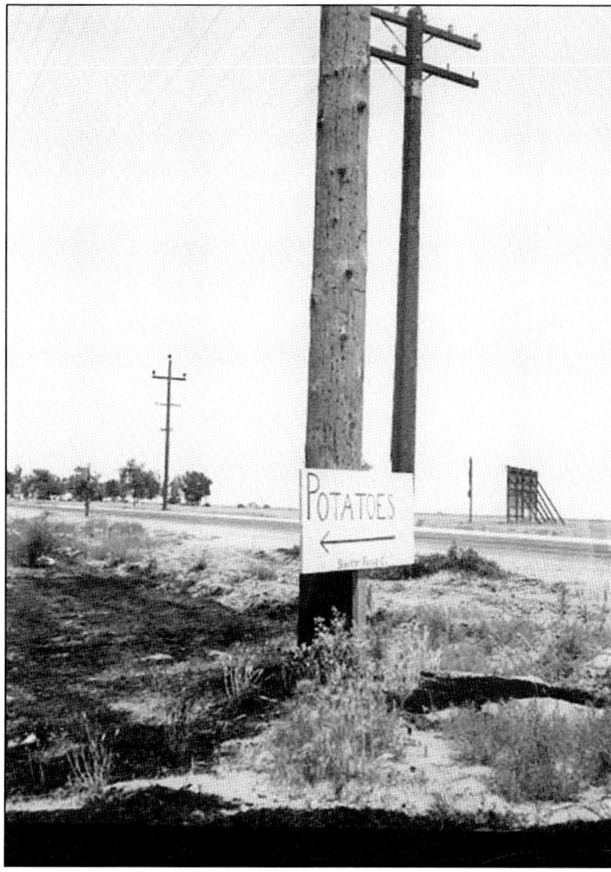

Since the 1950s, this motel has operated along what is now Business 99 in Merced. The motel's sign and architectural style were typical of that seen in the Central Valley in the 1950s and 1960s. The lettering of the sign evokes a certain sense of this time and place.

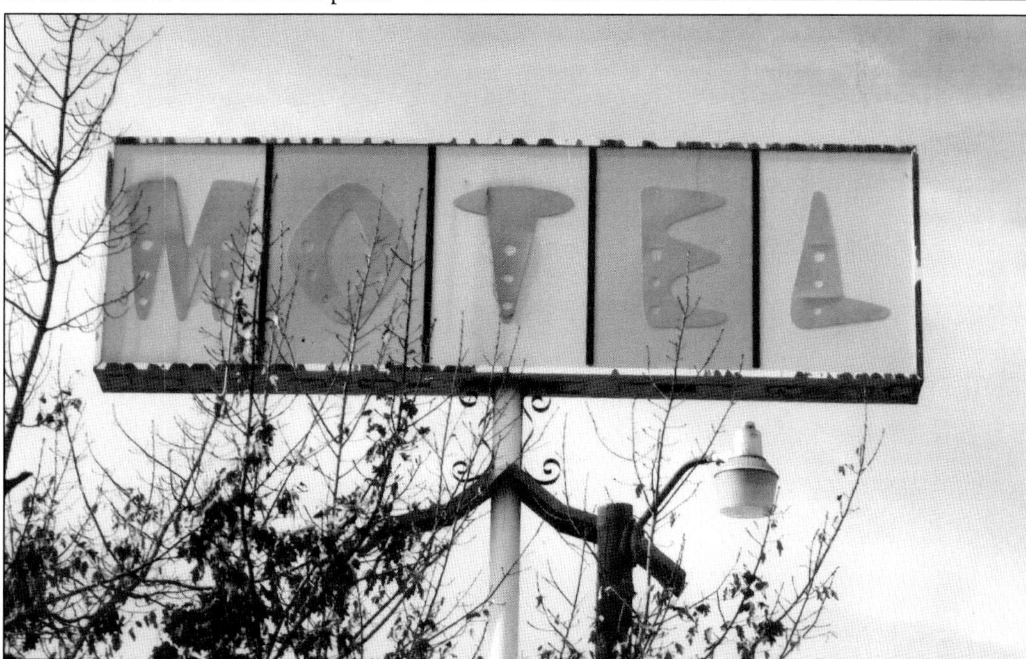

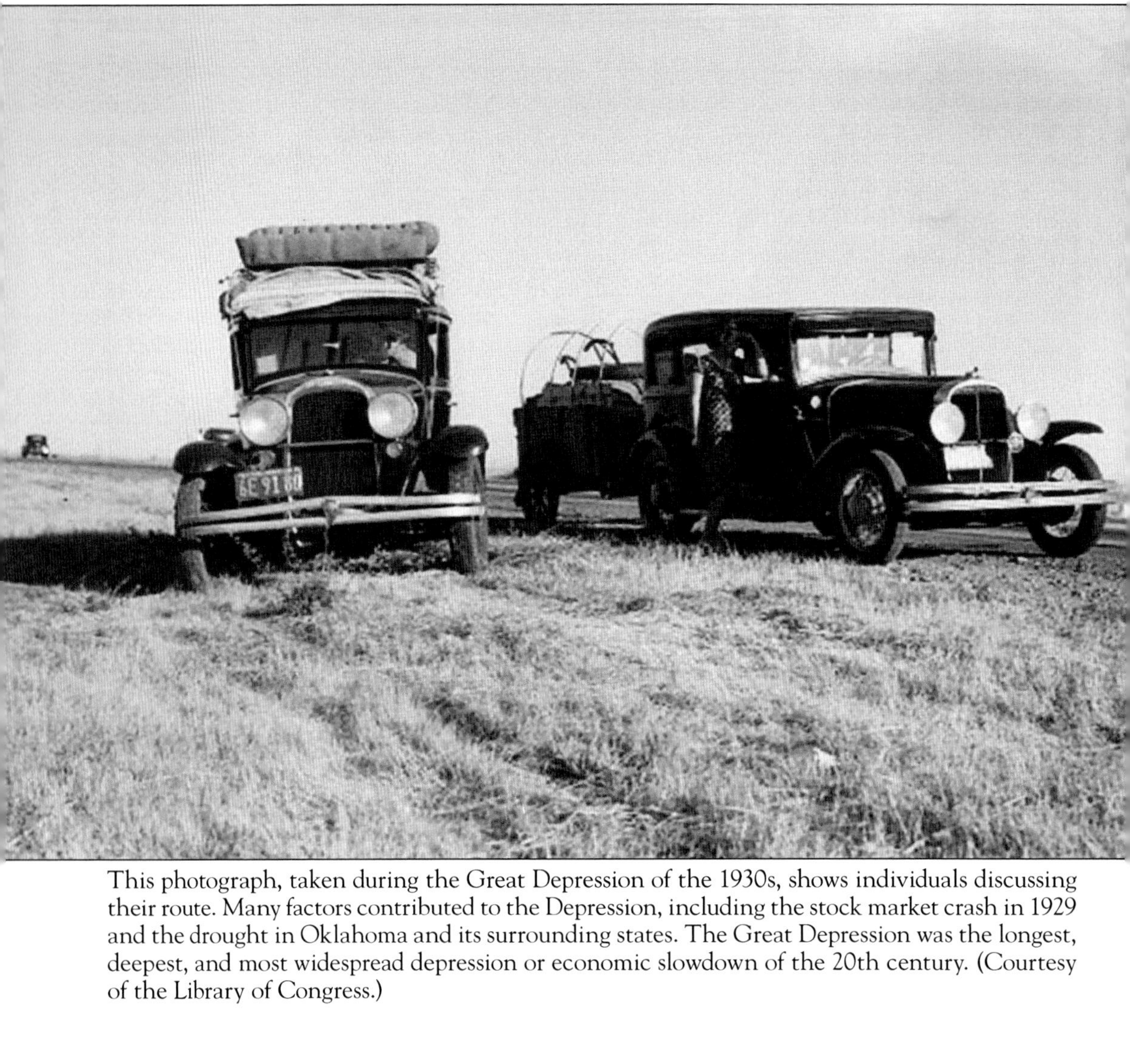

This photograph, taken during the Great Depression of the 1930s, shows individuals discussing their route. Many factors contributed to the Depression, including the stock market crash in 1929 and the drought in Oklahoma and its surrounding states. The Great Depression was the longest, deepest, and most widespread depression or economic slowdown of the 20th century. (Courtesy of the Library of Congress.)

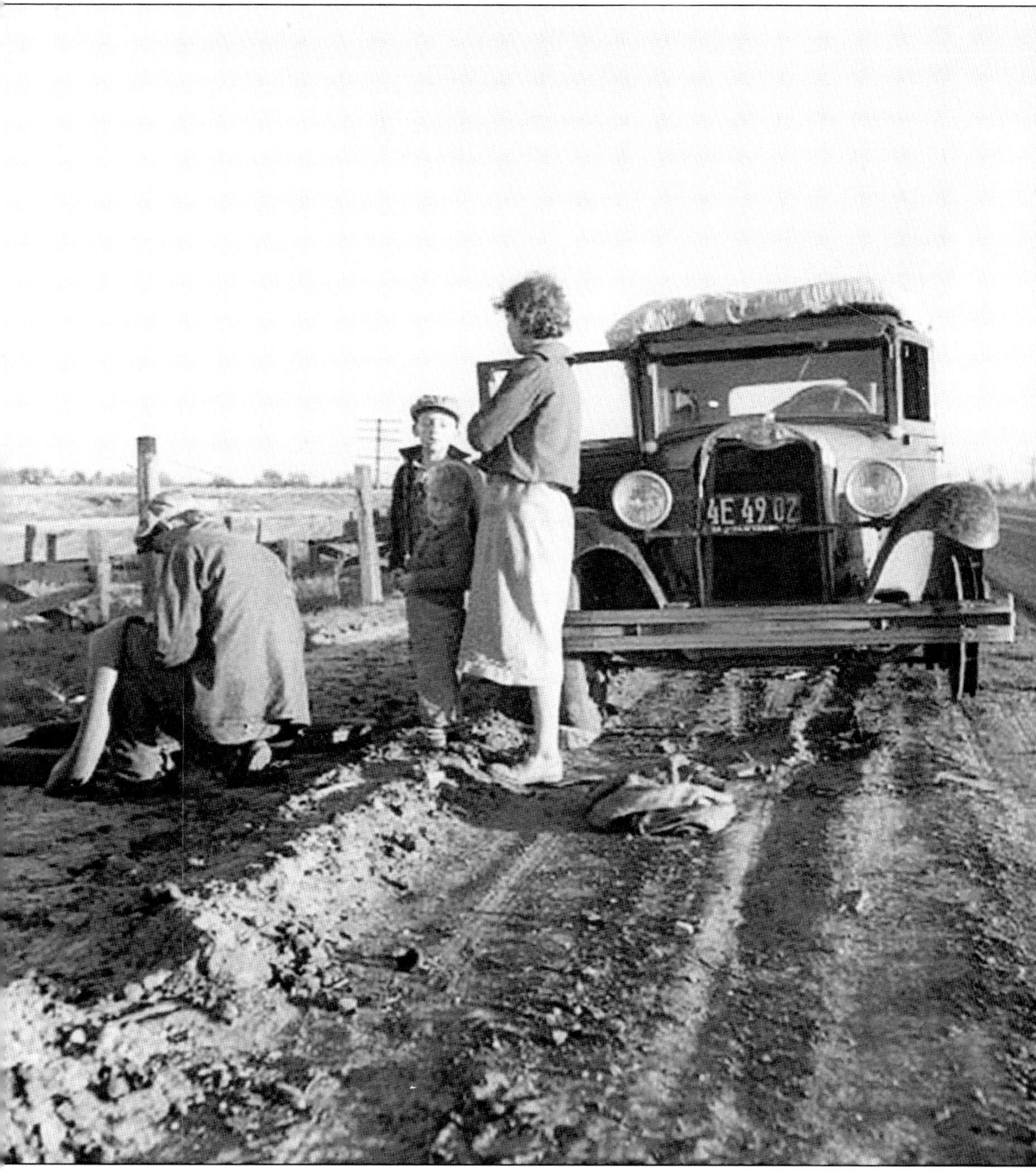

Due to the design of the vehicles and the condition of the roads in the 1930s, changing tires and repairing cars were common occurrences along Highway 99. The tires and wheels of the cars were very thin and required an interior tube to be operable. (Courtesy of the Library of Congress.)

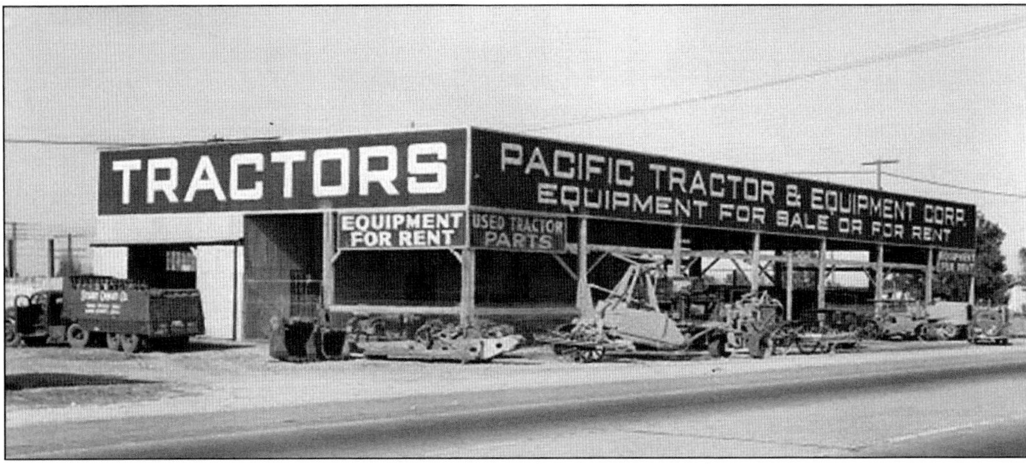

The Pacific Tractor & Equipment Corporation, which was founded prior to 1939, was a typical Highway 99 roadside business. Establishments such as this reflected the rich agricultural heritage of the Highway 99 corridor. The owner sold or rented new and used agricultural equipment and tools. (Courtesy of the Library of Congress.)

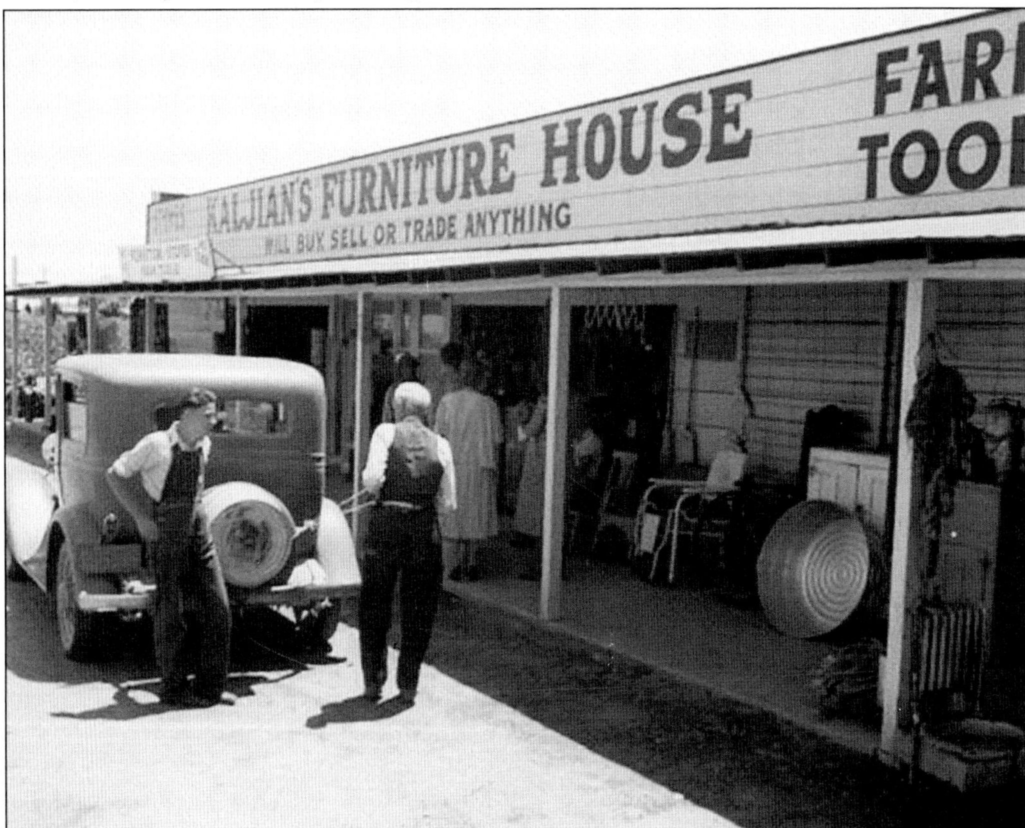

Kaljian's Furniture House, which was also established prior to 1939, was a roadside business along Highway 99 that would buy, sell, or trade anything, including farm tools, stoves, and medical equipment. The economy was poor at the time, so merchants and customers would obtain goods by any means that was available to them. (Courtesy of the Library of Congress.)

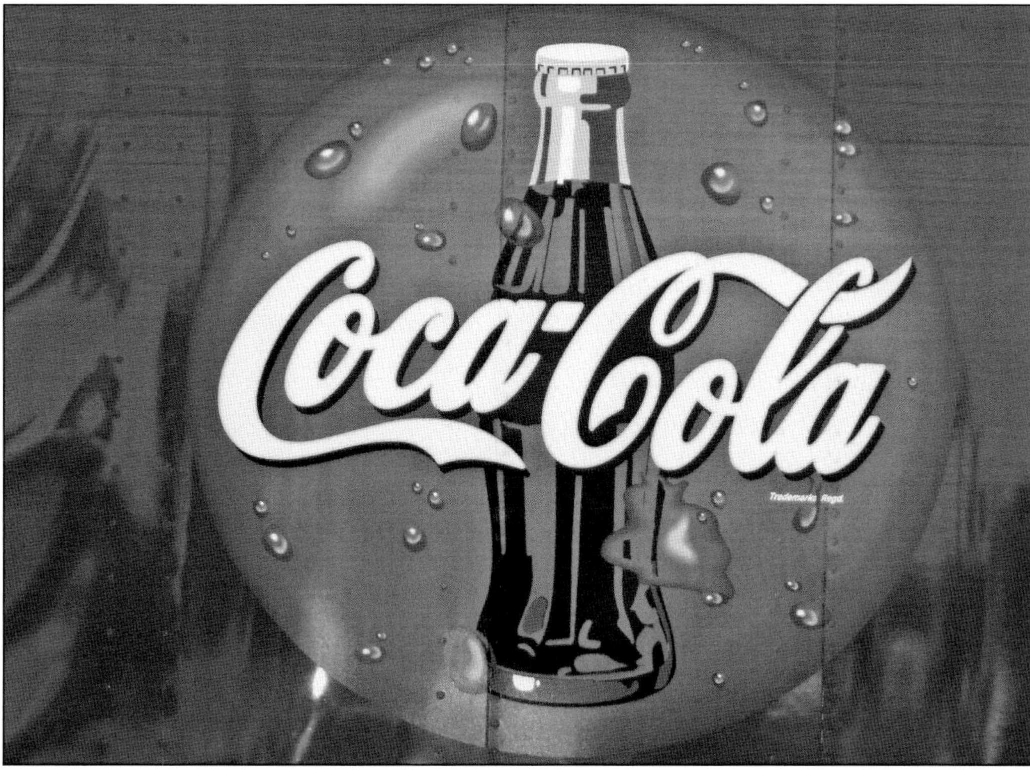

Coca-Cola is a part of American culture that connects the generations. The bright red logo is recognized by all and has not changed in decades. It is a vintage logo that is used widely today. From bottle caps to large semis, it is seen at many locations.

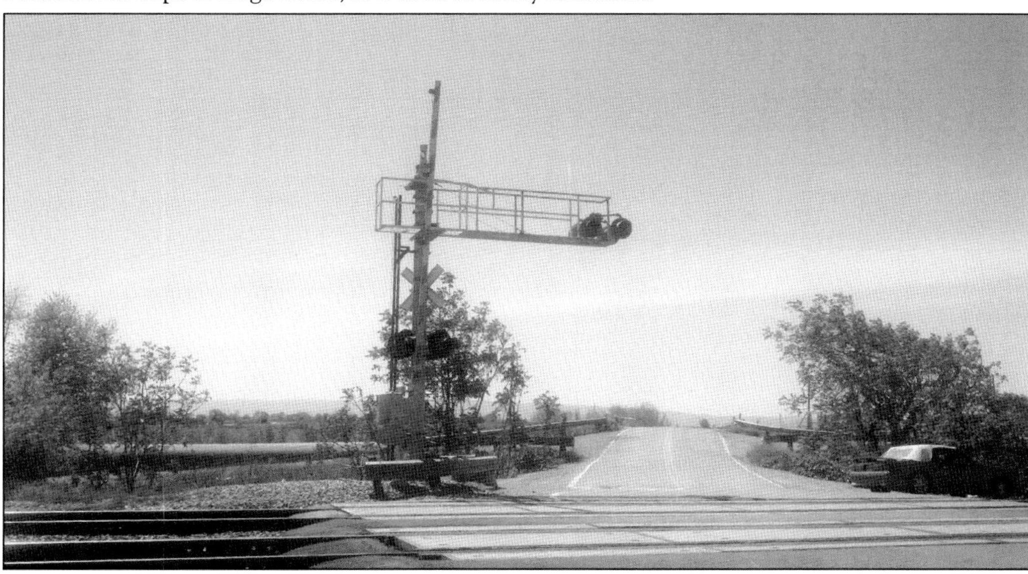

This railroad crossing, which is located about 50 yards from the railroad depot in Holt, is located at the intersection of Whiskey Slough Road (or Lower Jones Road) and West Lower Jones Road. This is in the old section of Holt, where the Japanese American and Chinese American populations lived from the 1880s until the 1930s.

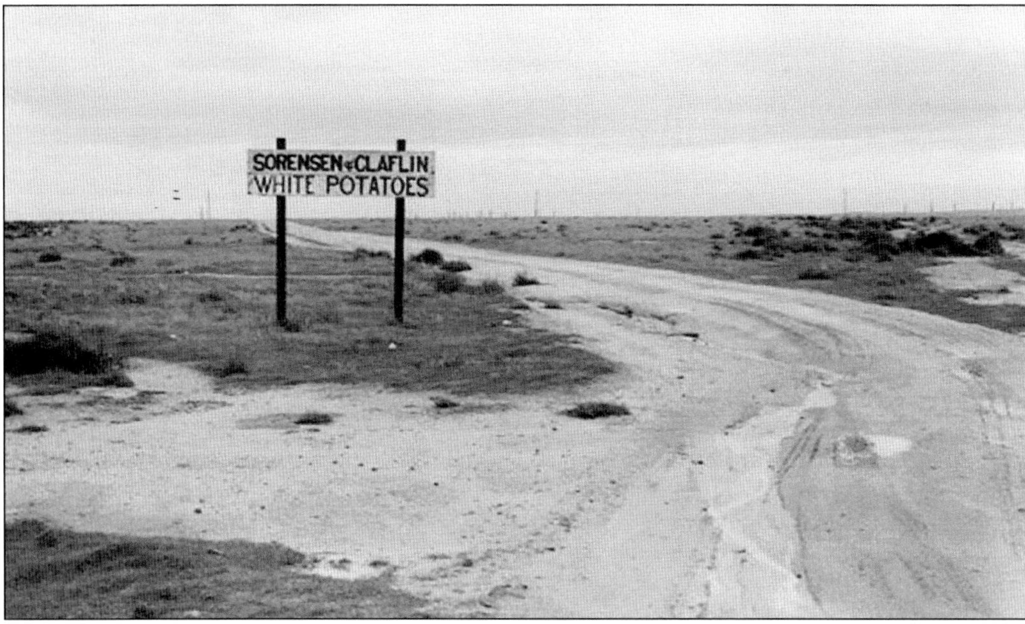

From Highway 99, travelers could observe this private roadway—which was a barely passable dirt road. Following a storm, vehicles or equipment that tried to use this roadway would have been impeded. Individuals named Sorensen and Claflin grew white potatoes along this stretch of Highway 99. (Courtesy of the Library of Congress.)

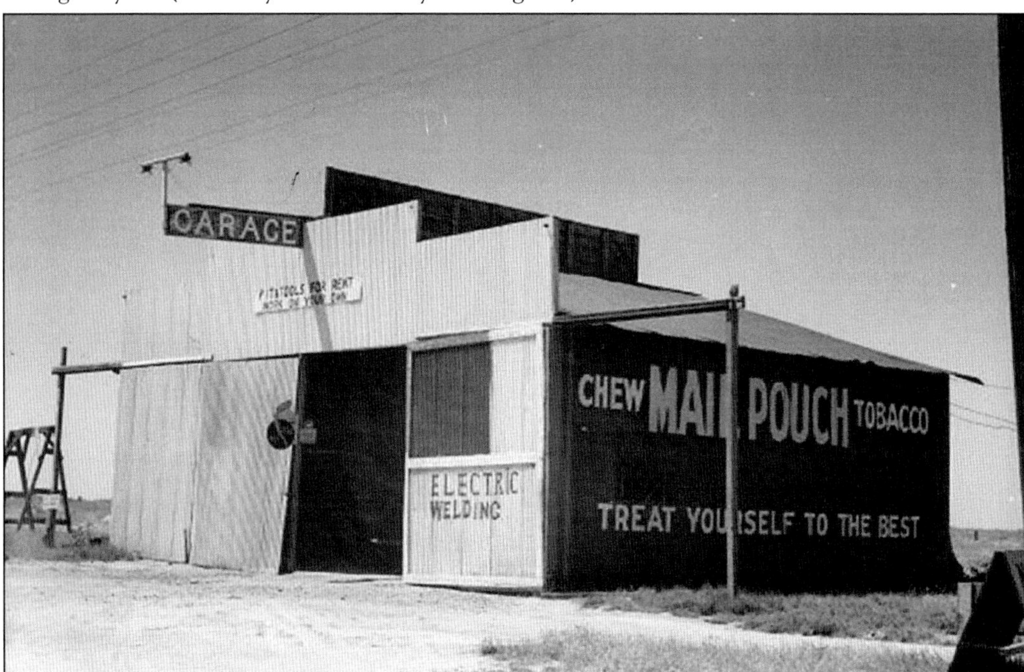

This garage on Highway 99 advertised tools for rent and welding services. The owner was paid by the Mail Pouch Tobacco Company to advertise on his building, which was considered a Mail Pouch Tobacco Barn. Starting in the 1890s, the Mail Pouch Tobacco Company paid barn owners about $2 per year to use their barn. (Courtesy of the Library of Congress.)

Cattle ranching was, and still is, a major industry along Highway 99. An example is the 31,000-acre Rankin Ranch in the Tehachapi Mountains south of Bakersfield. It has been a working cattle ranch for over a century. It is one of the oldest and largest family-owned ranches in California. This wooden structure was used to funnel cattle. (Courtesy of the Library of Congress.)

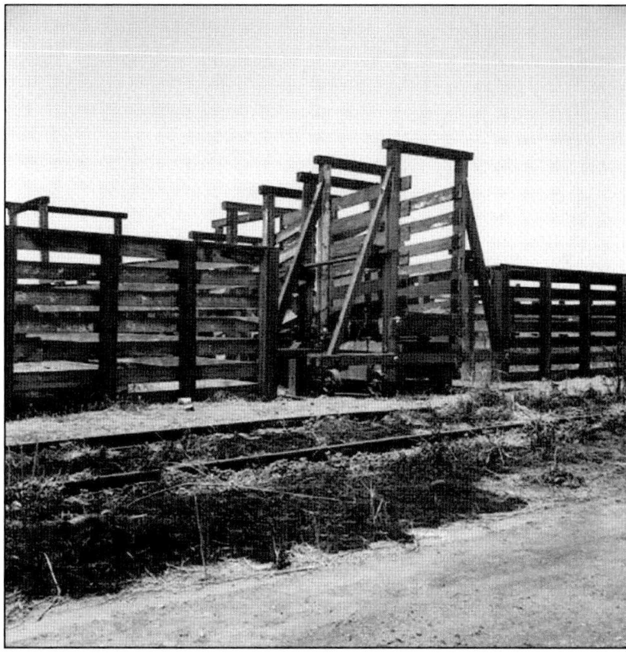

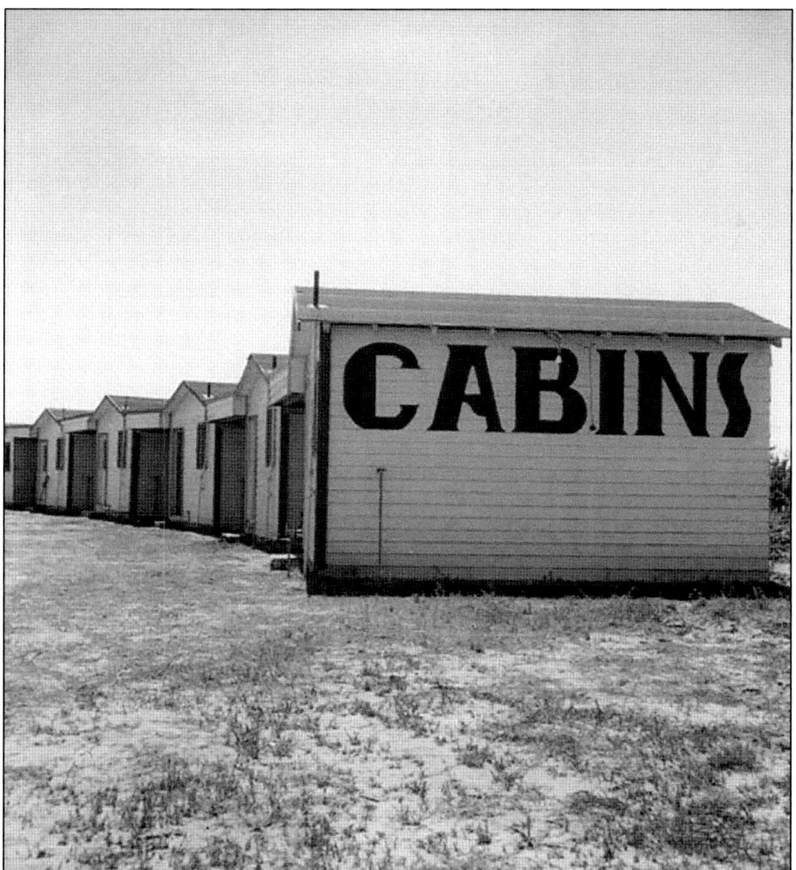

This broad sign clearly describes the row of simple, uniform cabins that were visible from the highway. They were small but adequate and had indoor plumbing. In the 1950s, motels replaced many of these cabins. (Courtesy of the Library of Congress.)

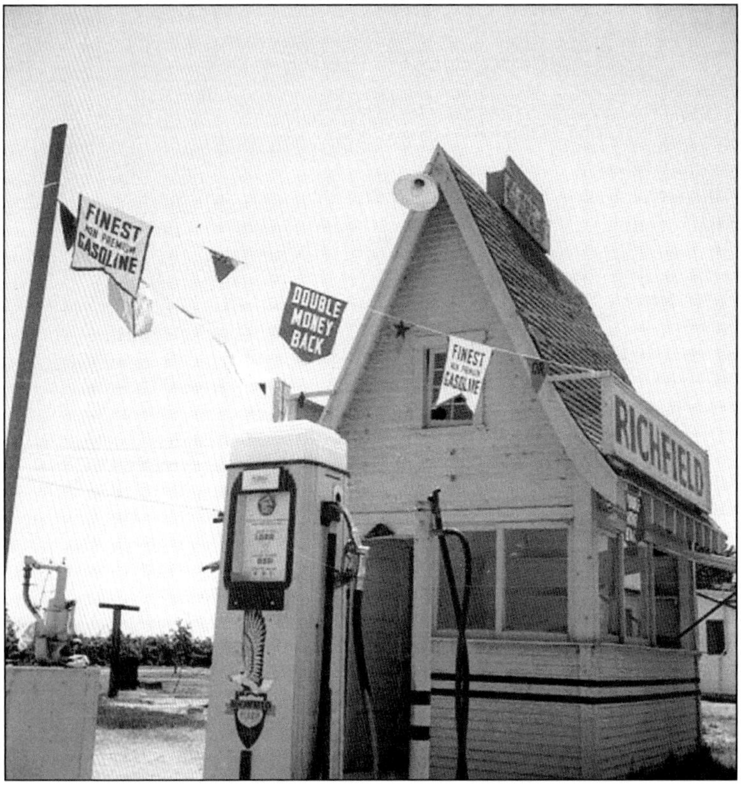

The Richfield Oil Corporation was a major brand that sold gas along Highway 99—such as at this small, unique station. It offered gas and little more. There was no vehicle repair facility or convenience store. The Richfield Oil Corporation was founded in 1905 and opened its first service station in 1917. (Courtesy of the Library of Congress.)

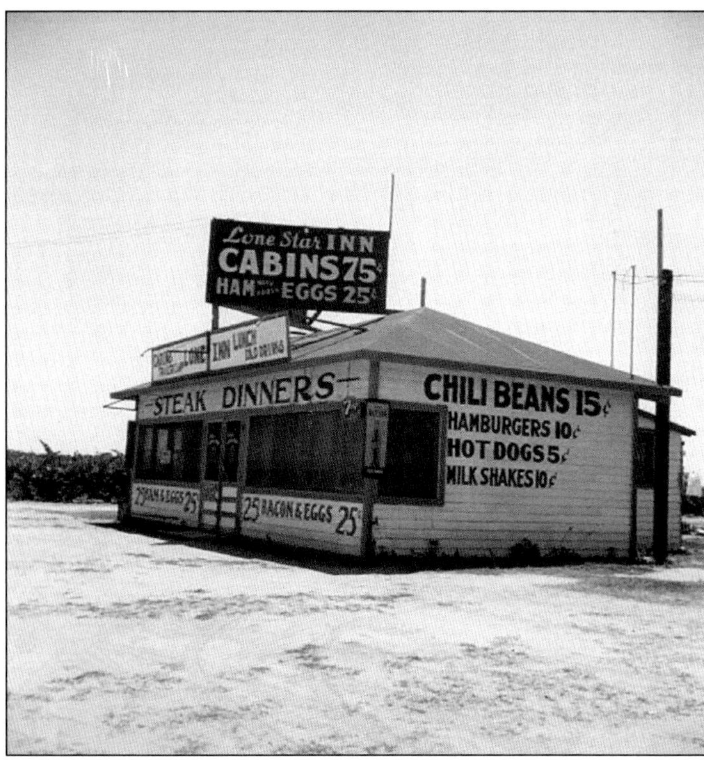

From the 1930s on, the Lone Star Inn provided fatigued travelers a place to sleep. Travel on Highway 99 from Southern to Northern California was often a multiday journey. The Lone Star Inn was an unpretentious establishment offering a night's stay in a cabin for 75¢. (Courtesy of the Library of Congress.)

This homemade sign advertised cabins for 75¢ and up. The front of the building advertised products using signage that was standard for the time but now evoke a sense of nostalgia. 7 Up was first advertised as a soft drink two weeks before the stock market crash of 1929. (Courtesy of the Library of Congress.)

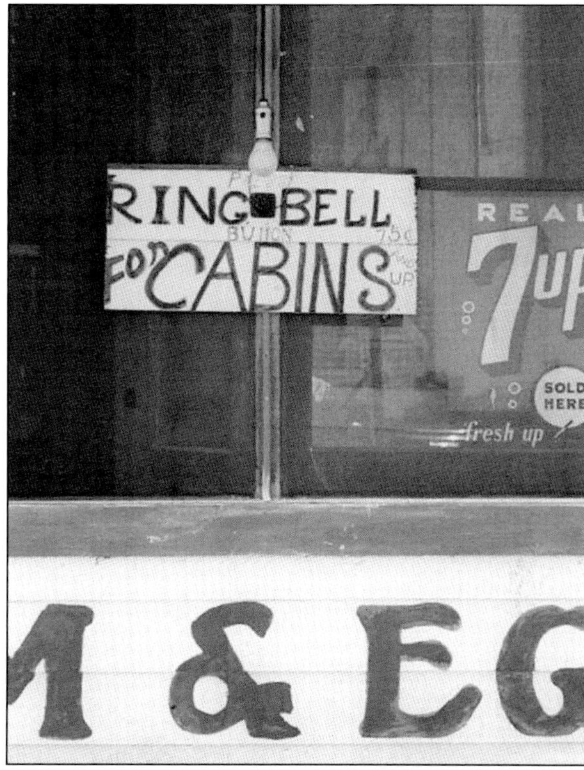

This billboard was developed by the National Association of Manufacturers in 1937. It rightfully extols the American way of life and alludes to the American dream. The National Association of Manufacturers (NAM) was founded in 1895. (Courtesy of the Library of Congress.)

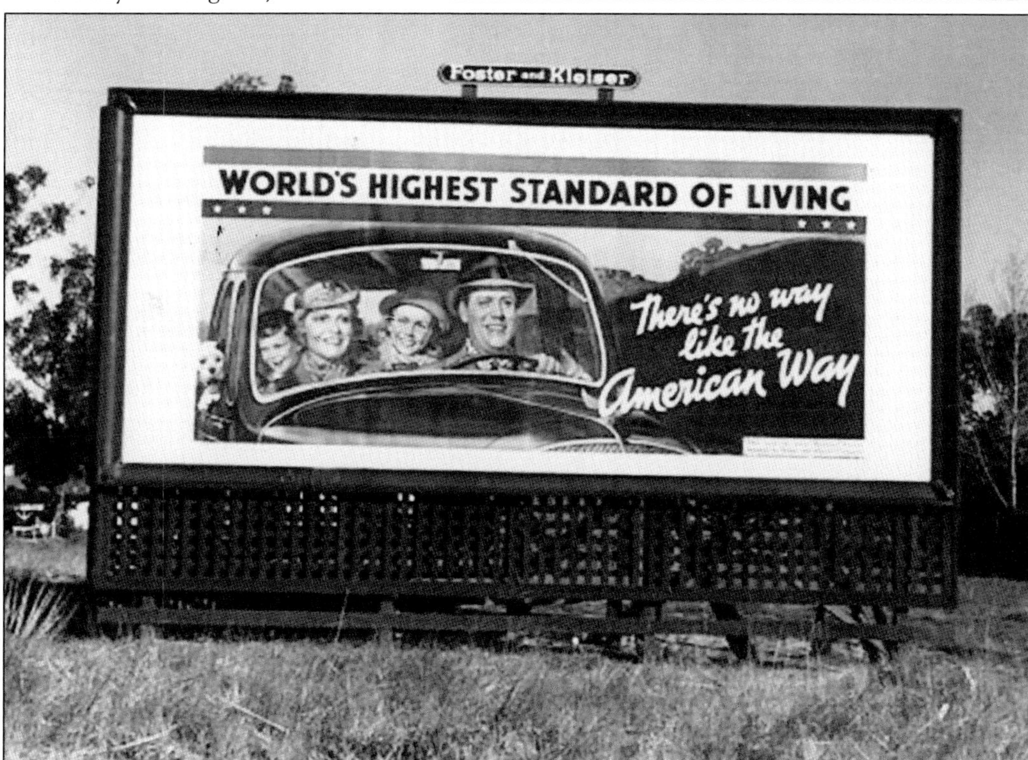

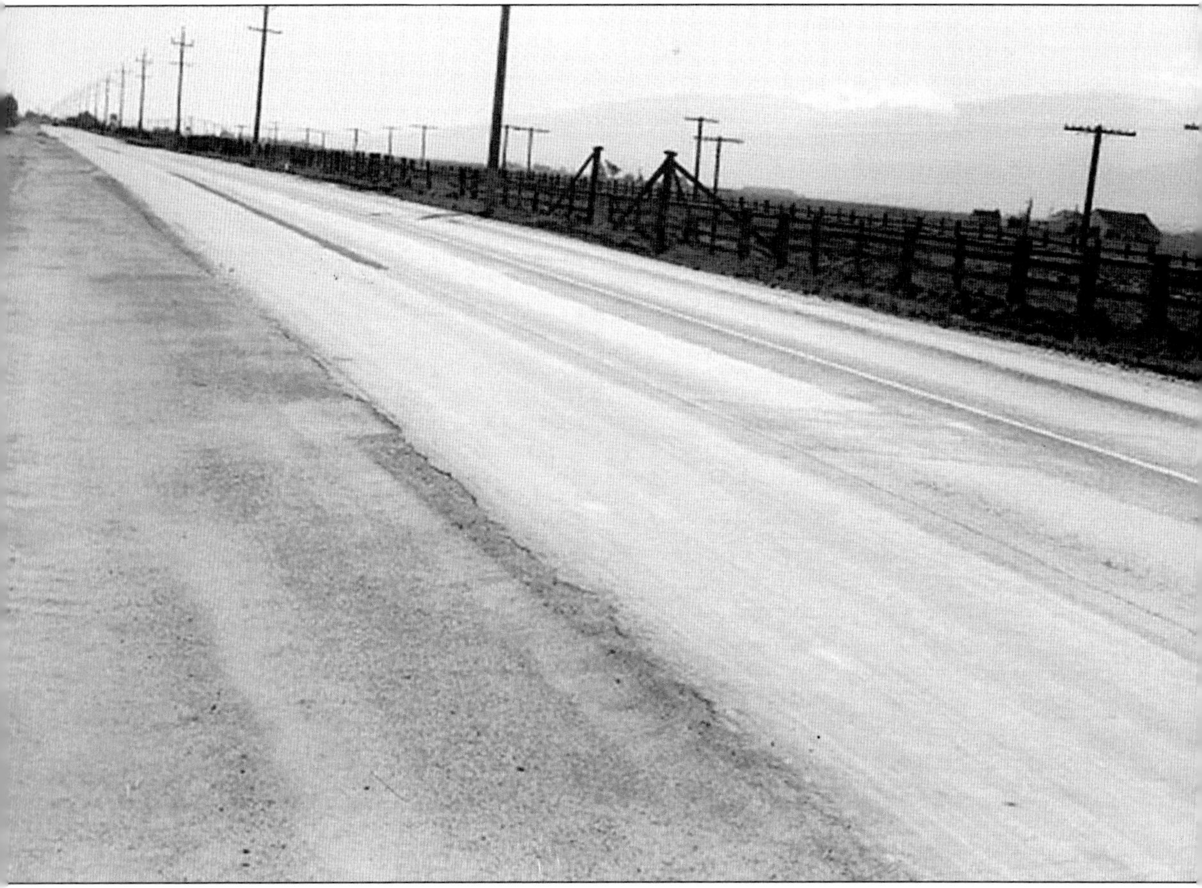

Ranchers built fencing of wood or barbed wire to keep the cattle from wandering onto Highway 99. One prominent ranch is the Tracy Ranch, which is a partnership of three families: the Freys, Selvedges, and Tracys. This organization farms as well as raises cattle. (Courtesy of the Library of Congress.)

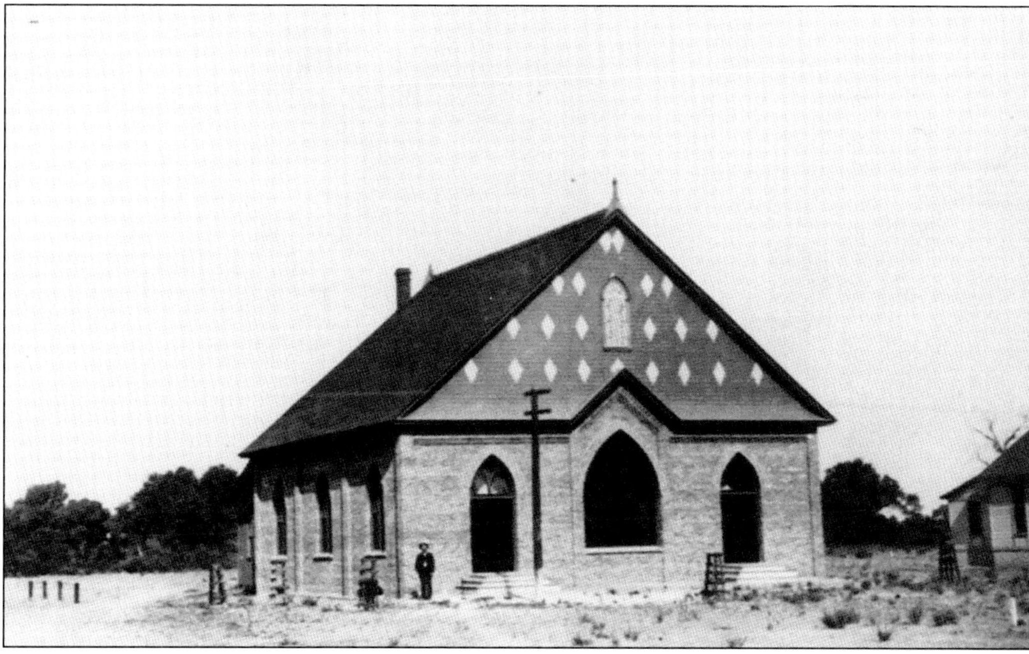

The First Baptist Church, which was located at the northwest corner of Twenty-Second and I Streets in Bakersfield, was dedicated in April 1890. It was sold in 1904 and replaced by a new building. A member of the church is seen standing outside. (Courtesy of the Kern County Library.)

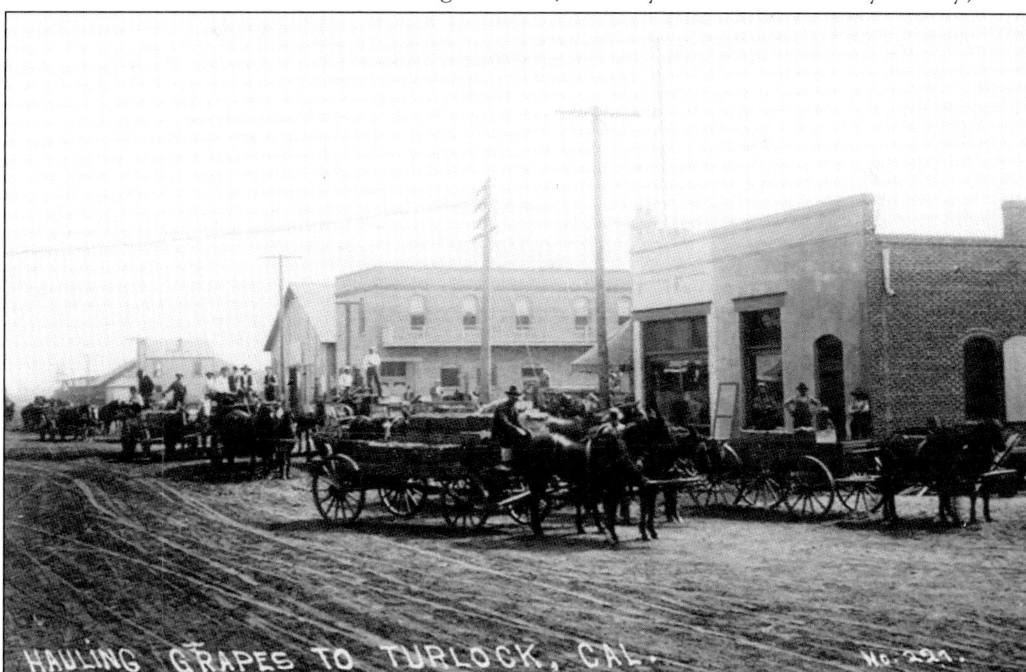

Turlock was a major producer of grapes, which—before the advent of the automobile—were hauled to market on horse-drawn wagons. California's wine history dates back to the 18th century, when missionaries planted vineyards to produce wine for communion. (Courtesy of the California State Library, Sacramento.)

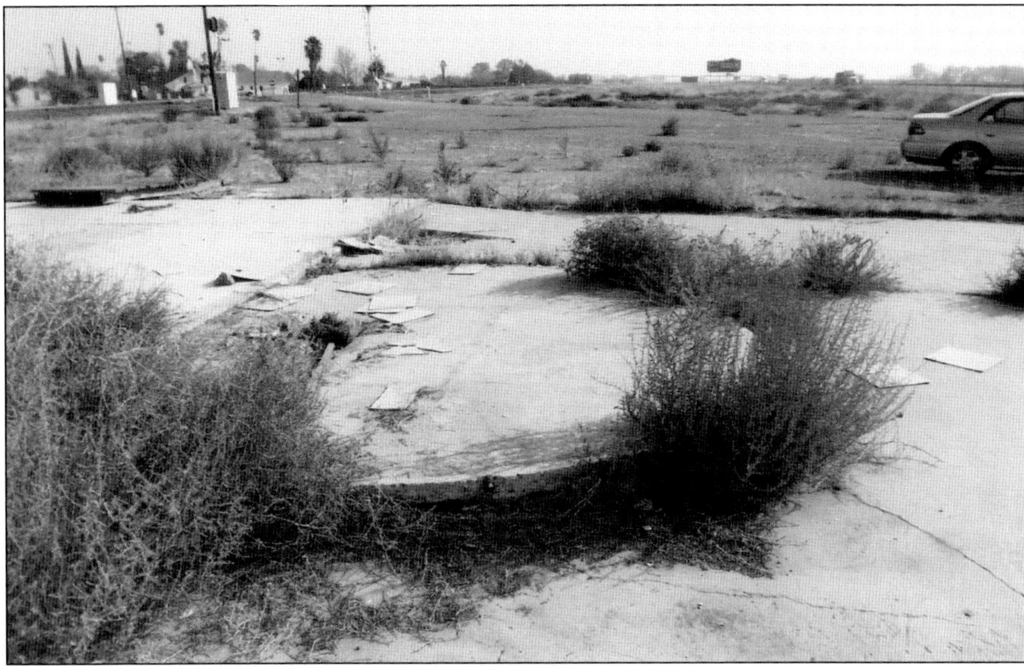

This is the foundation of the last Giant Orange juice stand, which was located along a stretch of 99. The raised portion of the foundation—where the giant orange was situated—is about 10 feet in diameter. Between 2000 and 2010, the orange was collected by the City of Chowchilla so that it could be established as a museum exhibit.

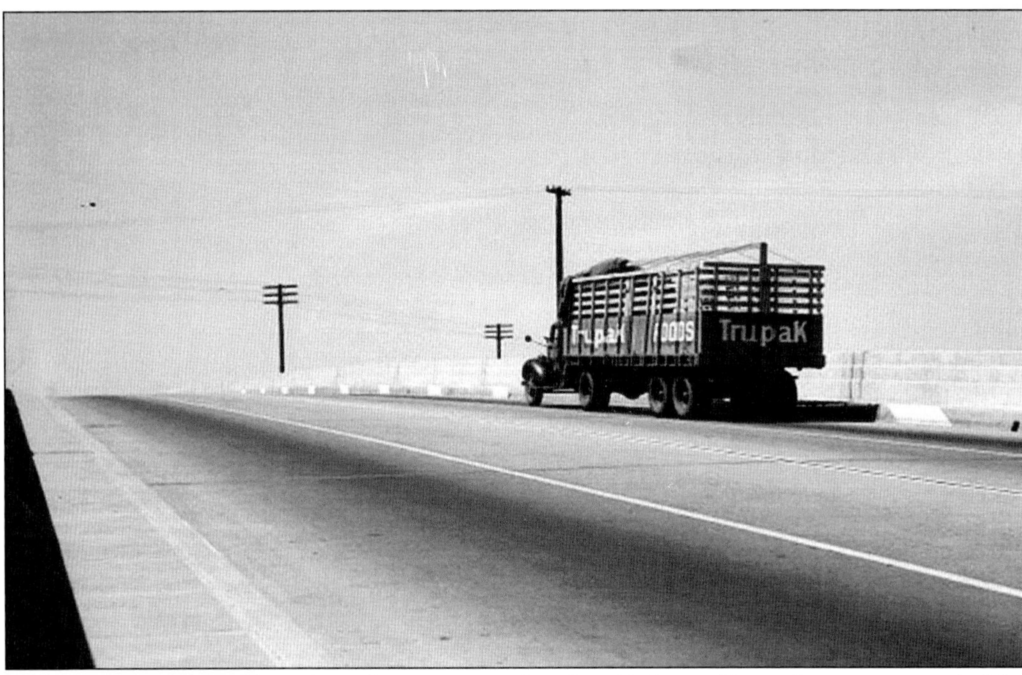

Highway 99 is still used heavily and continues to develop. Highway 99 was first constructed of dirt roads and then of asphalt. It becomes hot enough in the Central Valley that thin tires and small pieces of metal equipment can sink into the asphalt. (Courtesy of the Library of Congress.)

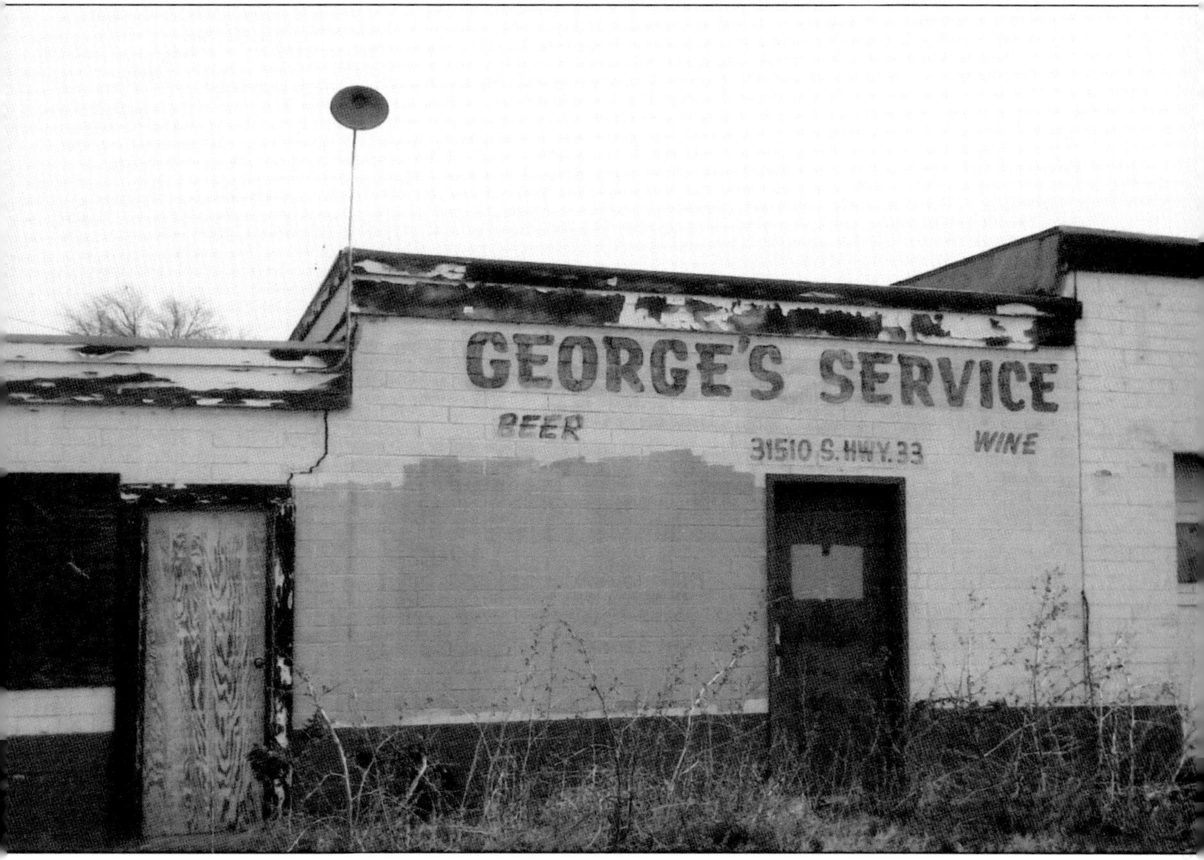

George's Service, on Highway 33, recently closed after decades of service. Highway 33 extends from Tracy to Gustine. Gustine was established in 1915 and is considered a "City of Festivals"—including its Fourth of July festivities and the Wolfsen's Sausage Tasting Event in the fall.

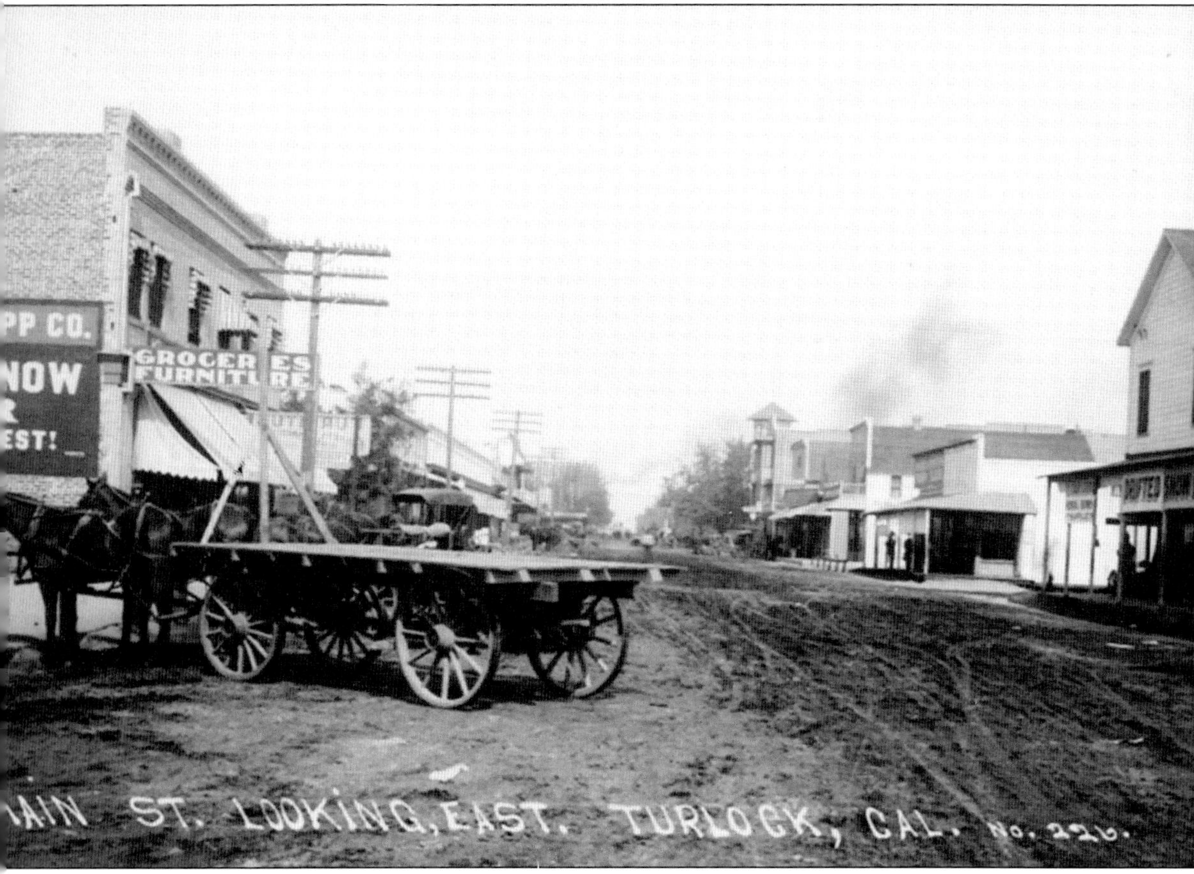

Looking east along Turlock's Main Street reveals a new frontier town in this photograph. It was established near the Central Pacific Railroad, which was constructed in the late 1800s. Turlock is one of many agricultural centers along Highway 99. (Courtesy of the California State Library, Sacramento.)

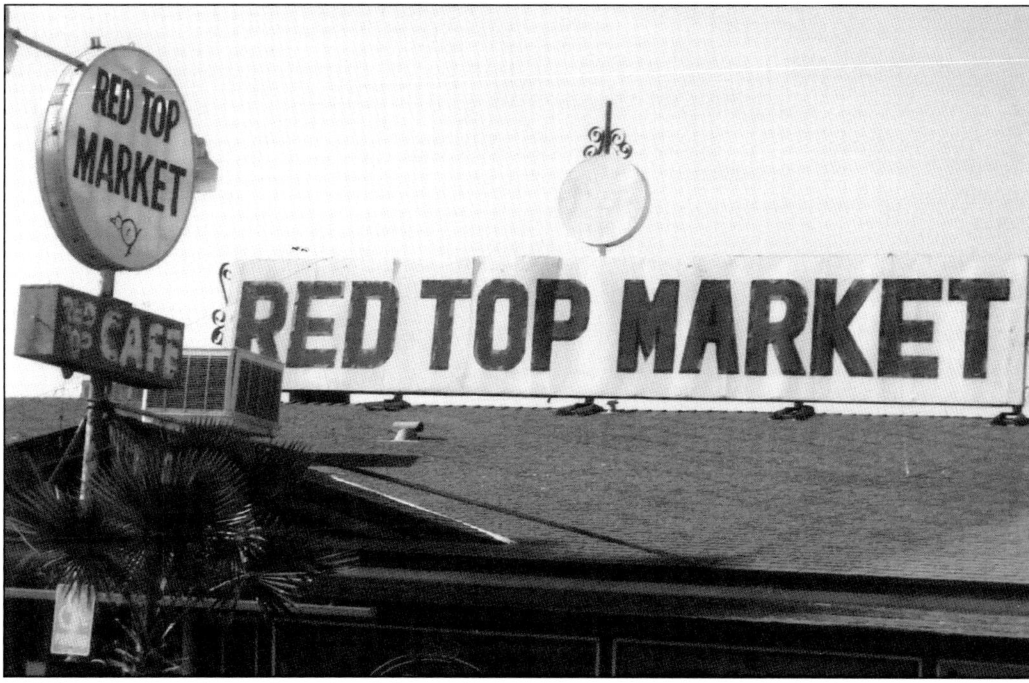

A fish museum is located inside of the Red Top Market. It is situated adjacent to a simple truck stop café, located between Chowchilla and Los Banos. The museum houses many large saltwater game fish. Highway 99 travelers often ventured a few miles off of the highway for a traditional café dinner and a look at the fish that are mounted on the wall.

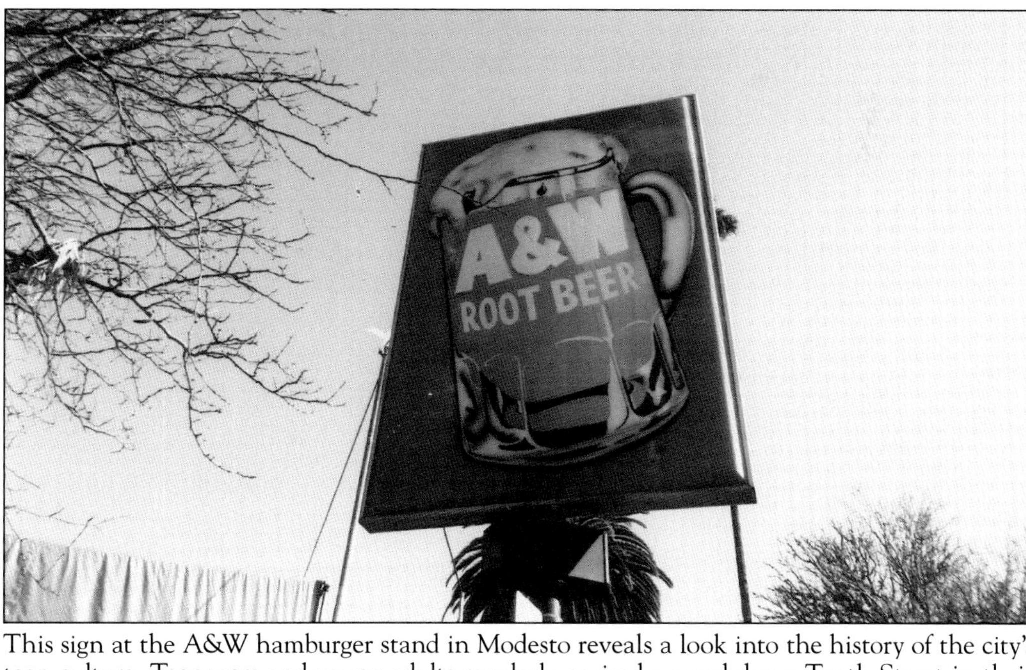

This sign at the A&W hamburger stand in Modesto reveals a look into the history of the city's teen culture. Teenagers and young adults regularly cruised up and down Tenth Street in their cars—just one block from the old route of Highway 99 on Ninth Street. This A&W restaurant has not changed much in the past few decades.

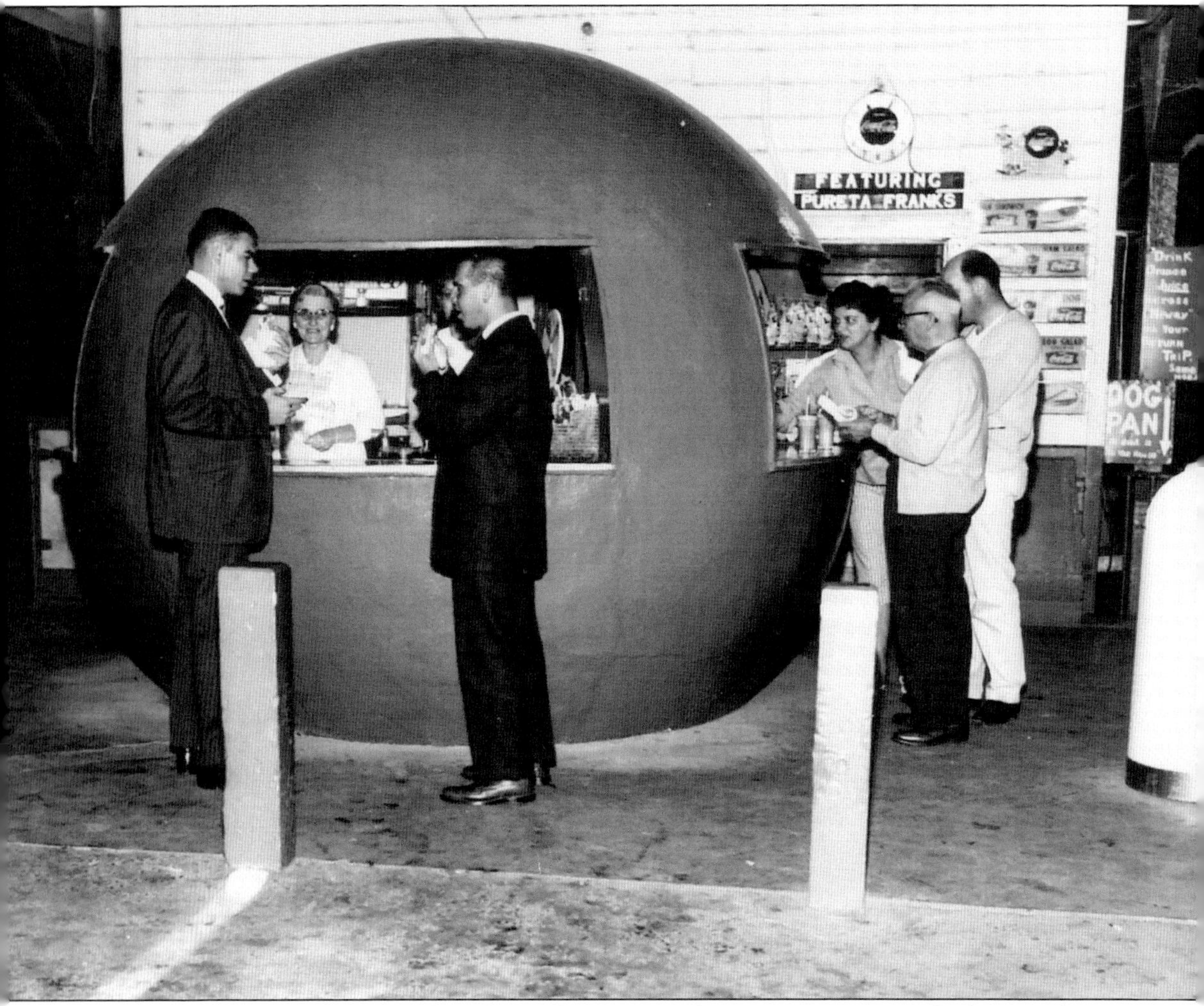

This Giant Orange juice stand was located in Dixon. The Giant Orange stands along Highway 99 serve as a symbol of the nostalgia culture that surrounds the 99 corridor. There were numerous Giant Orange stands, including one in Chowchilla called Fast Eddies. (Courtesy of Bob Schmidt.)

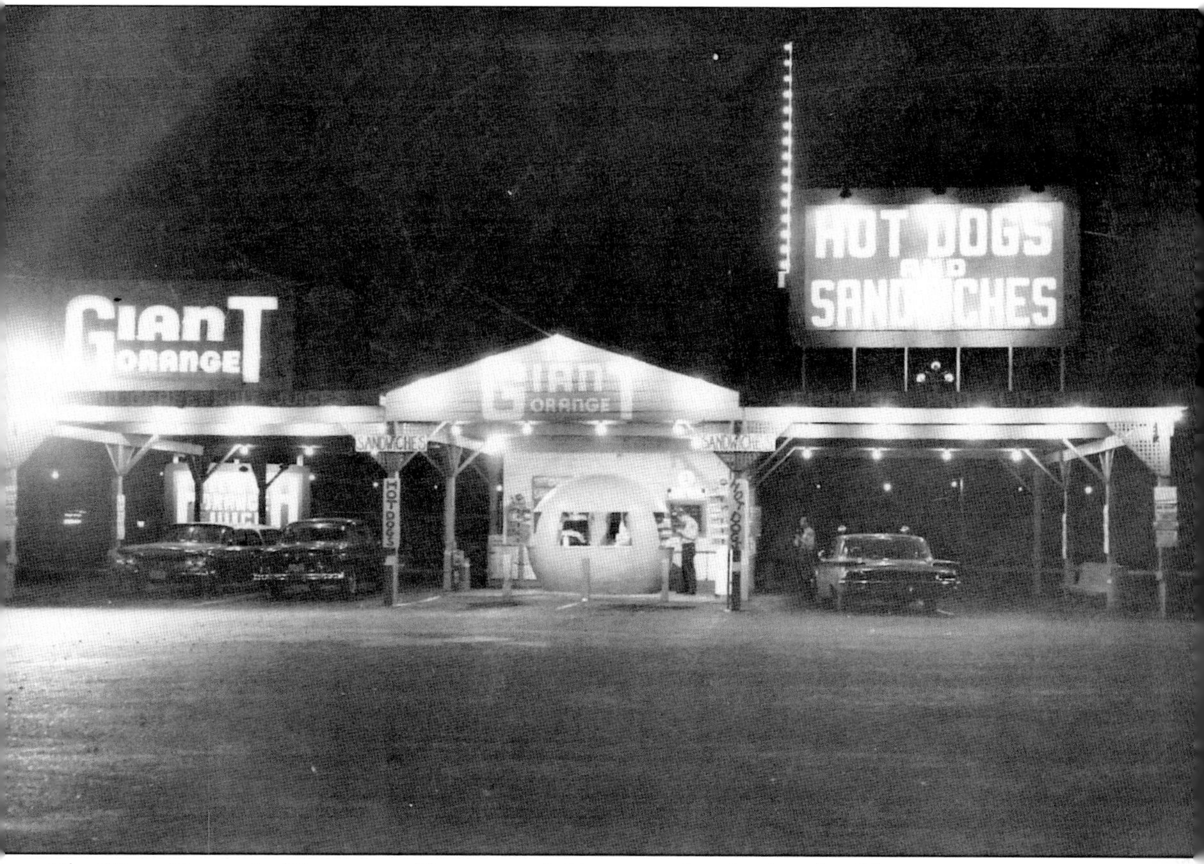

The Giant Orange in Dixon served hungry and thirsty travelers for decades. There were numerous Giant Orange stands along Highway 99, typified by the orange—which was typically about 10 feet in diameter. The first California location was in Tracy, at the intersection of Eleventh Street and Grant Line Road. (Courtesy of Bob Schmidt.)

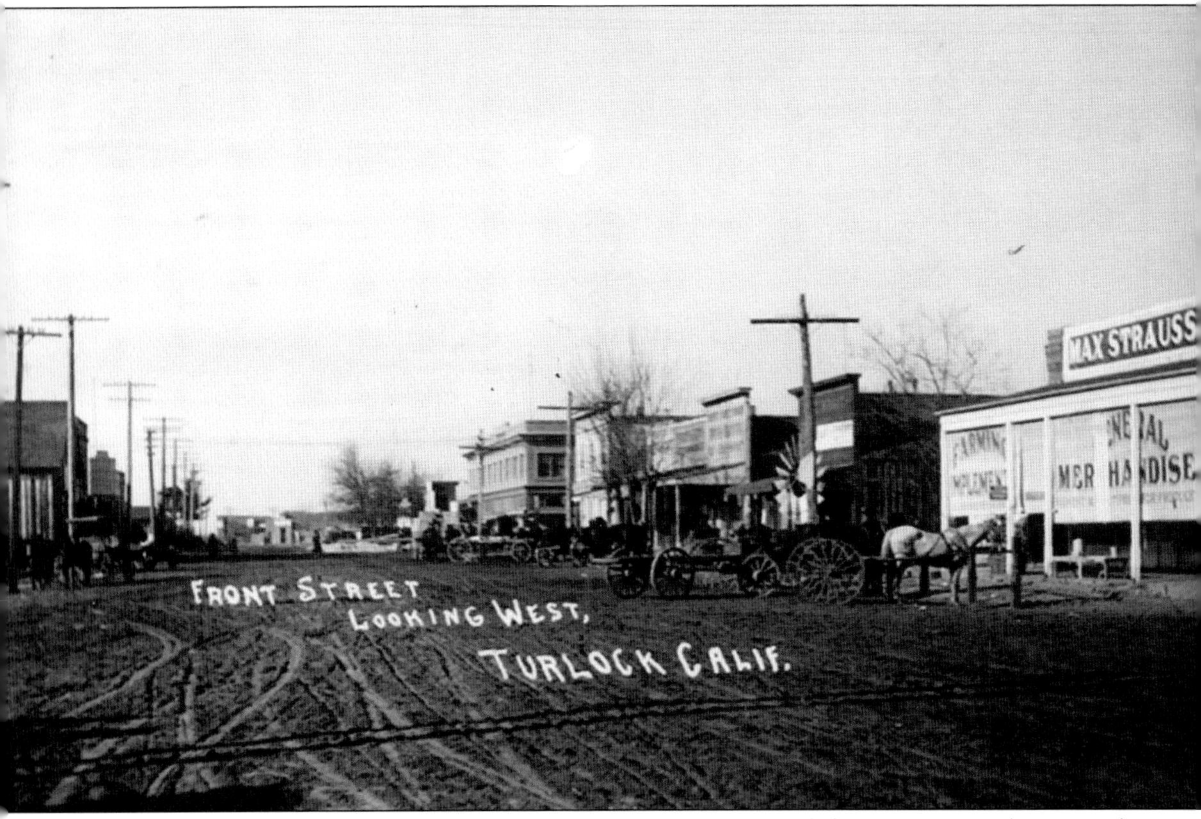

Front Street in Turlock, seen here, would develop into one of the primary roadways in the downtown area of Turlock. By the time that Turlock was incorporated, on February 15, 1908, the city's downtown was an established retail and commercial area. (Courtesy of the California State Library, Sacramento.)

Five

CHARACTER OF HIGHWAY 99

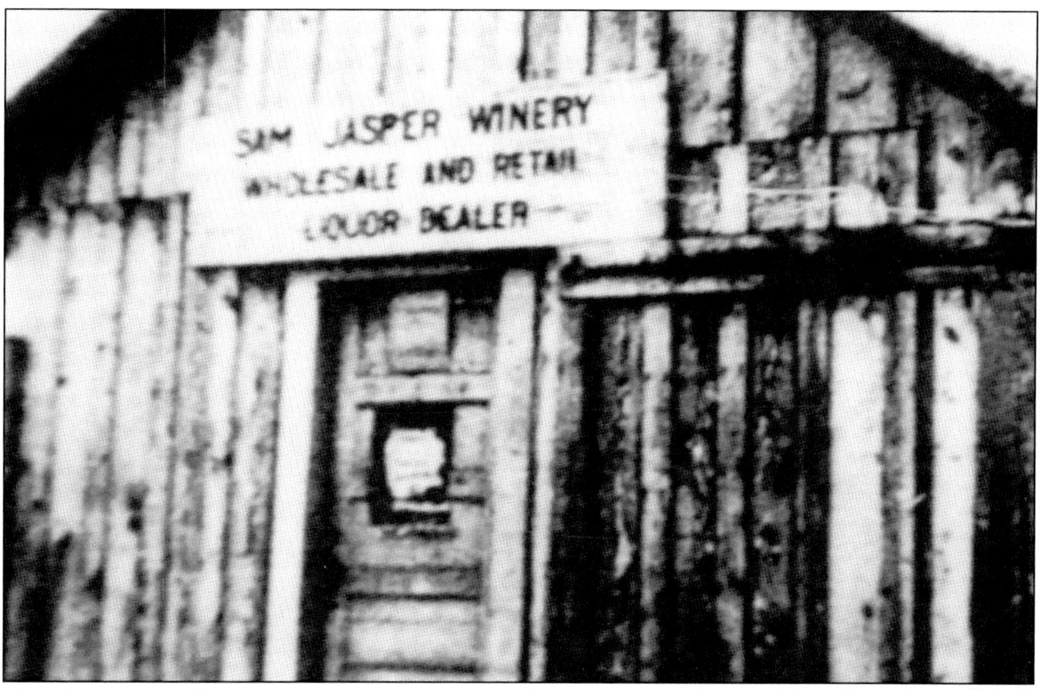

The Sam Jasper Winery was established along Highway 99 in Manteca, California. Manteca, which is located north of Modesto, was incorporated in 1918. Its first mayor was Joshua Cowell. Highway 99 passes through the city as a freeway. (Courtesy of the Manteca Historical Society.)

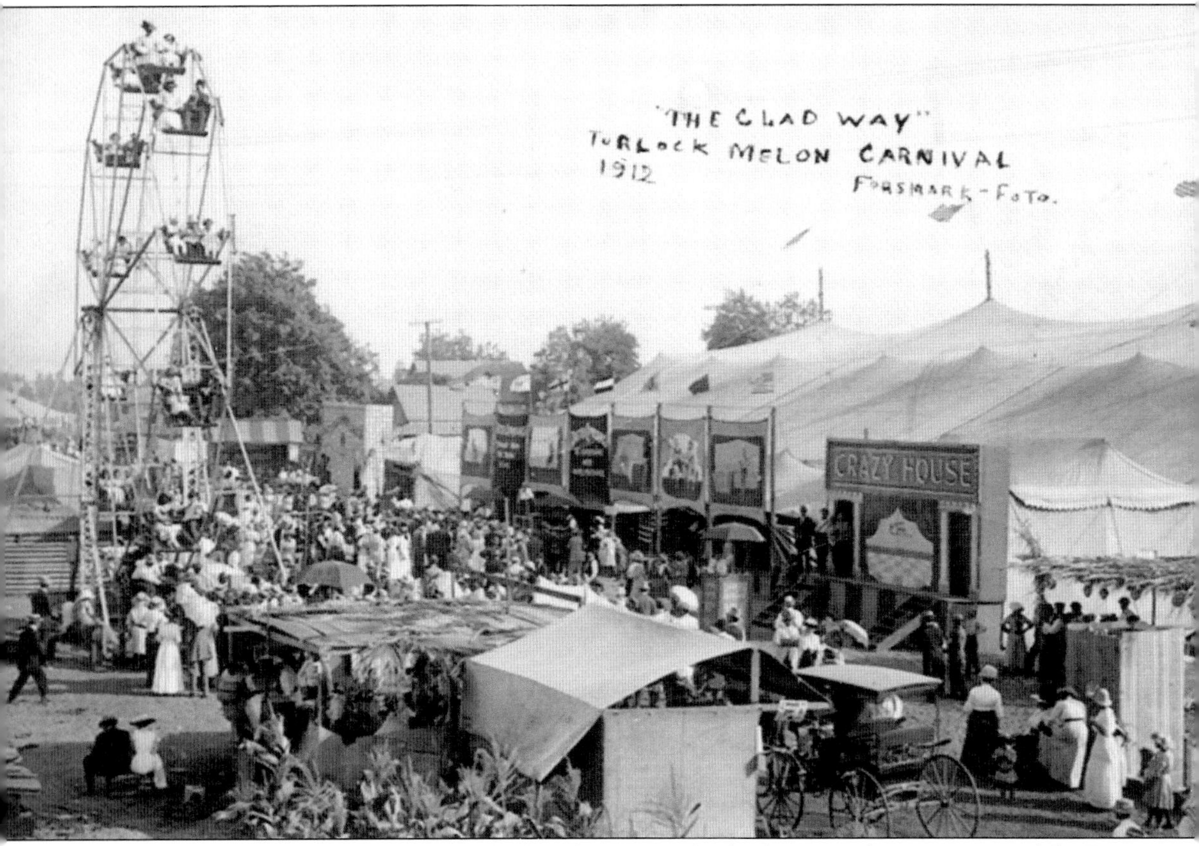

A large crowd attended the 1912 Turlock Melon Festival. The design and construction of the Ferris wheel makes it look unstable, but it apparently functioned, and the attendees enjoyed riding on it. (Courtesy of the California State Library, Sacramento.)

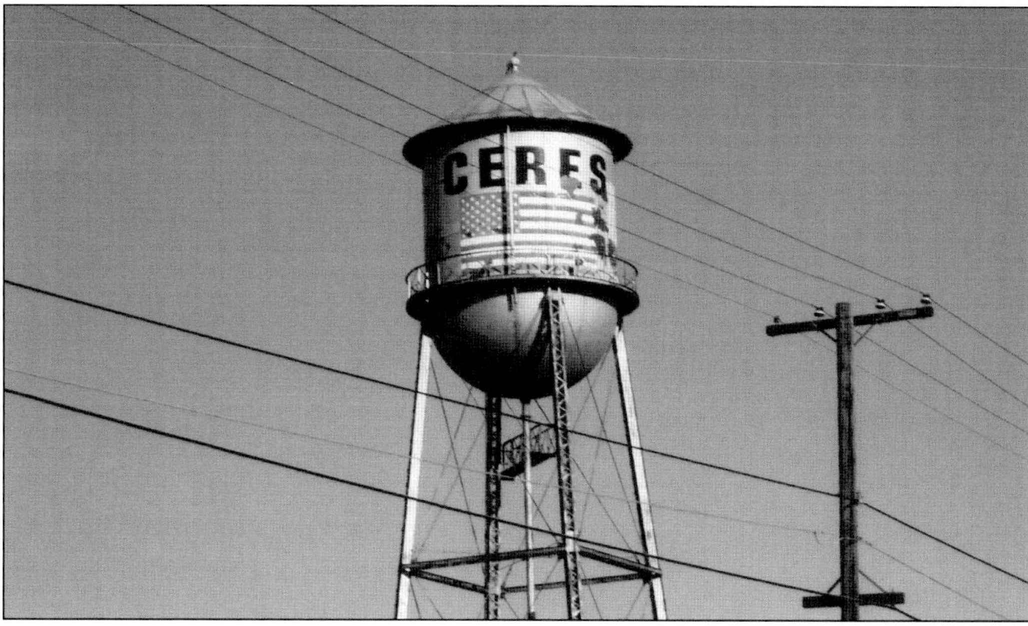

The town of Ceres, which is identified here by the traditional sign on the water tower, is located south of Modesto along Highway 99. It has modern subdivisions but maintains a charming historic downtown. Daniel C. Whitmore, along with two other founders—John Service and Cassius Warner—established Ceres in 1867. In 1870, Whitmore built a home at 2928 Fifth Street in Ceres.

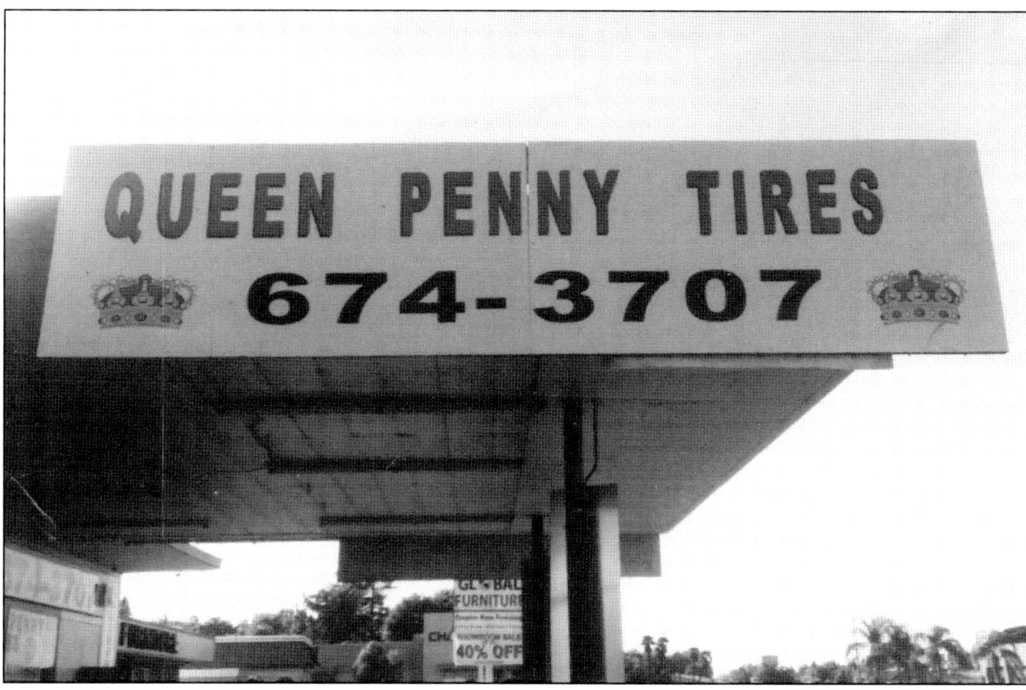

Queen Penny Tires is a unique and highly visible auto service establishment that carries on the tradition of owner-operated businesses. There are several brightly colored signs advertising this establishment. Queen Penny Tires is located at 500 Colusa Avenue in Yuba City, California.

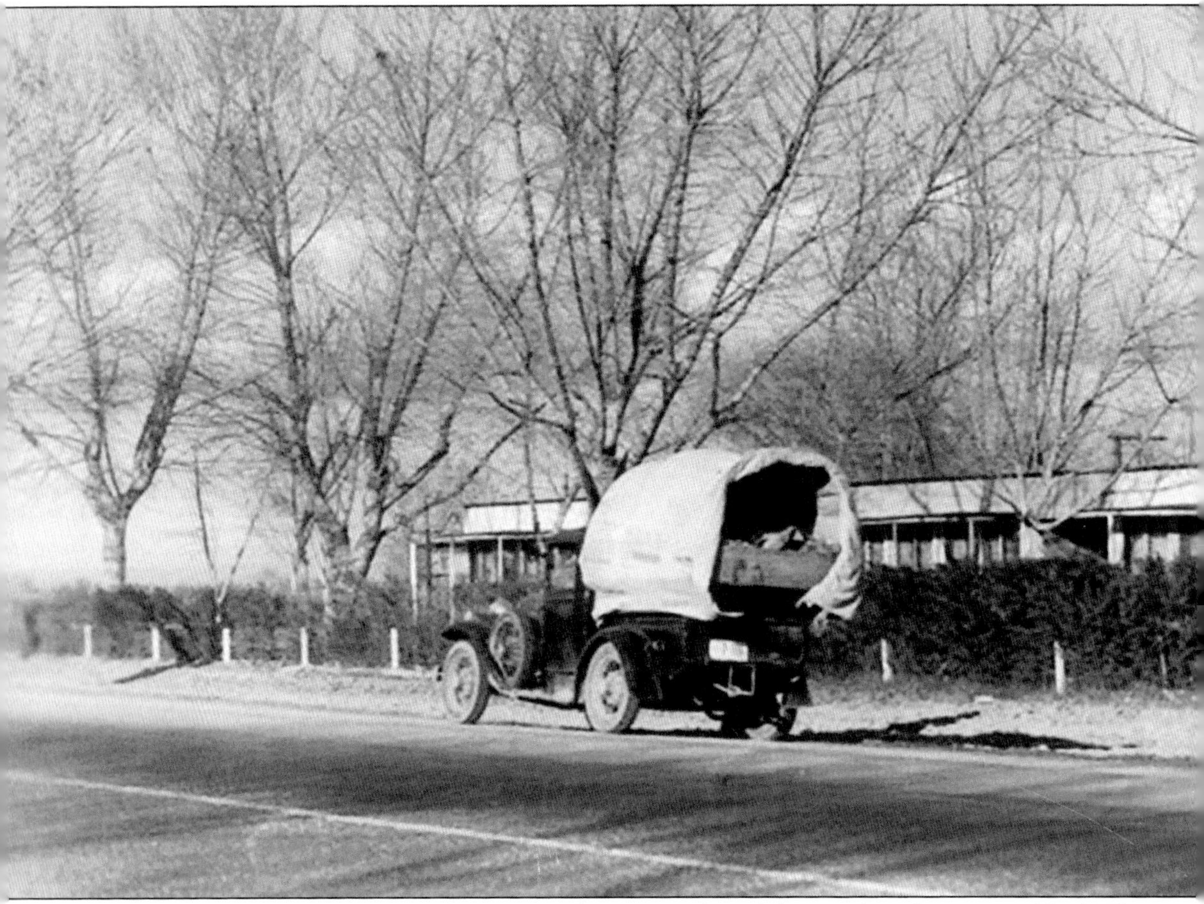

This photograph, taken in the late 1930s, shows a Ford Model T truck with a covered bed. The Model T was simple and functional but in no way luxurious. The Model T was designed so that a large number of Americans could own one. Ford mass produced Model T vehicles from the 1900s to the 1920s. This truck was typical of vehicles travelling on Highway 99 during the Great Depression. (Courtesy of the Library of Congress.)

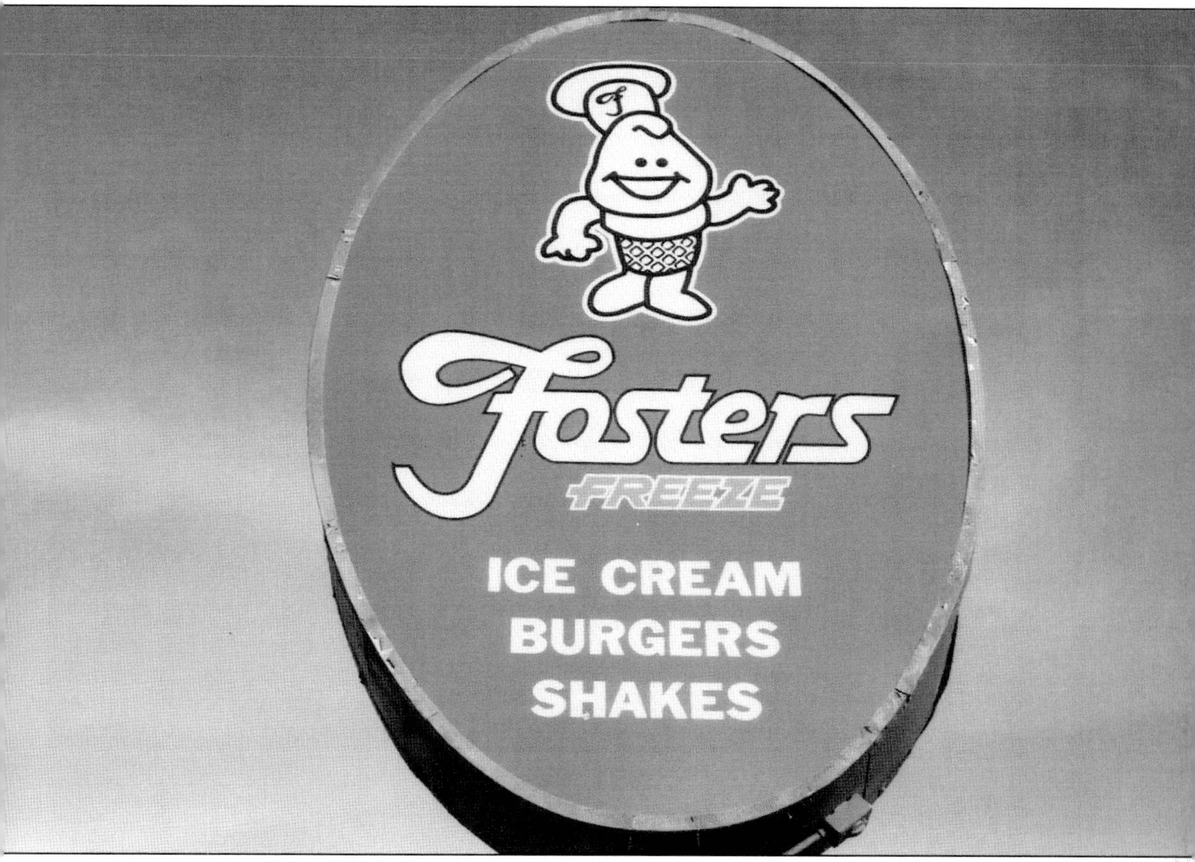

Fosters Freeze hamburger stands were common stopping points for weary and hungry Highway 99 travelers. There were, and still are, numerous Fosters Freeze restaurants on the Highway 99 corridor. George Foster opened California's first Fosters Freeze in 1946.

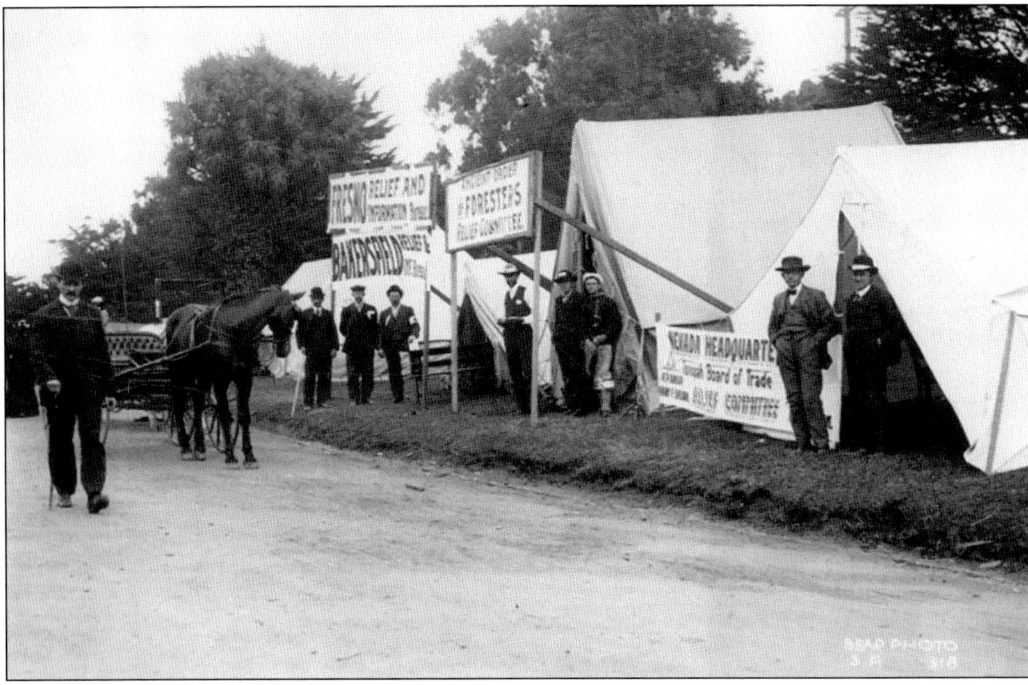

This photograph may have been taken in Golden Gate Park in San Francisco. Golden Gate Park is a large urban park consisting of about 1,000 acres of public grounds. It is 20 percent larger than Central Park in Manhattan. (Courtesy of the Kern County Library.)

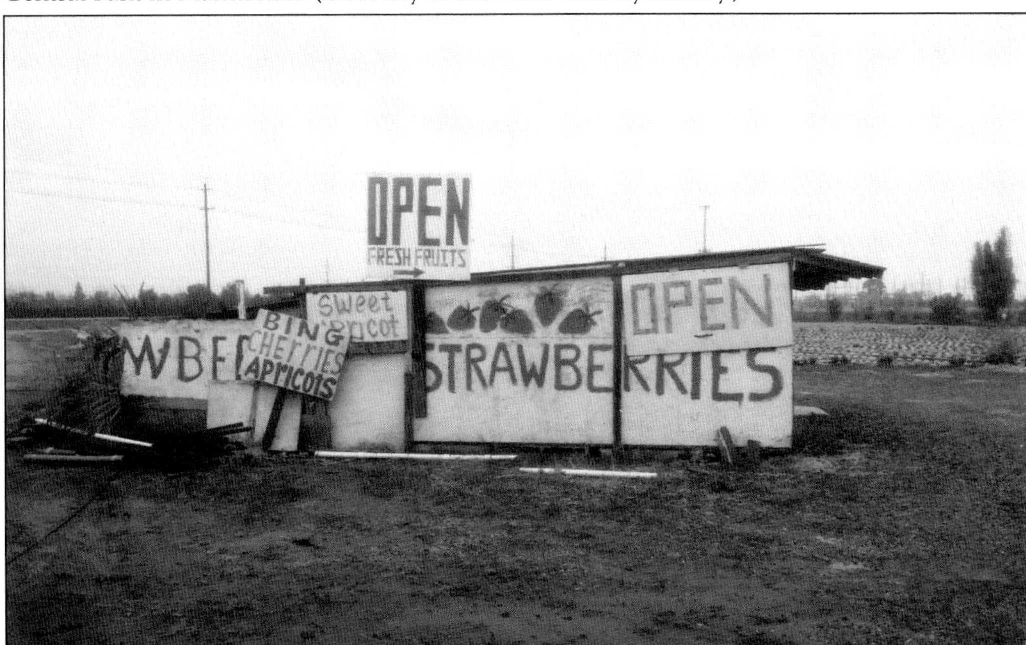

In many areas of the Central Valley—including the pictured area to the west of Turlock—strawberries and other fruits are staples of the agricultural industry. Roadside fruit stands were developed as early as the 1930s. California is the leading supplier of strawberries in the country and produces about 80 percent of the strawberries grown in the United States.

This Ford Model T was abandoned along Highway 99. It was saved so that parts could be extracted from it. Some mechanical and structural components had already been removed when this photograph was taken. Ford produced an estimated 15 million of these vehicles—which cost about $1,000—at its plants in Detroit, Michigan. (Courtesy of the Library of Congress.)

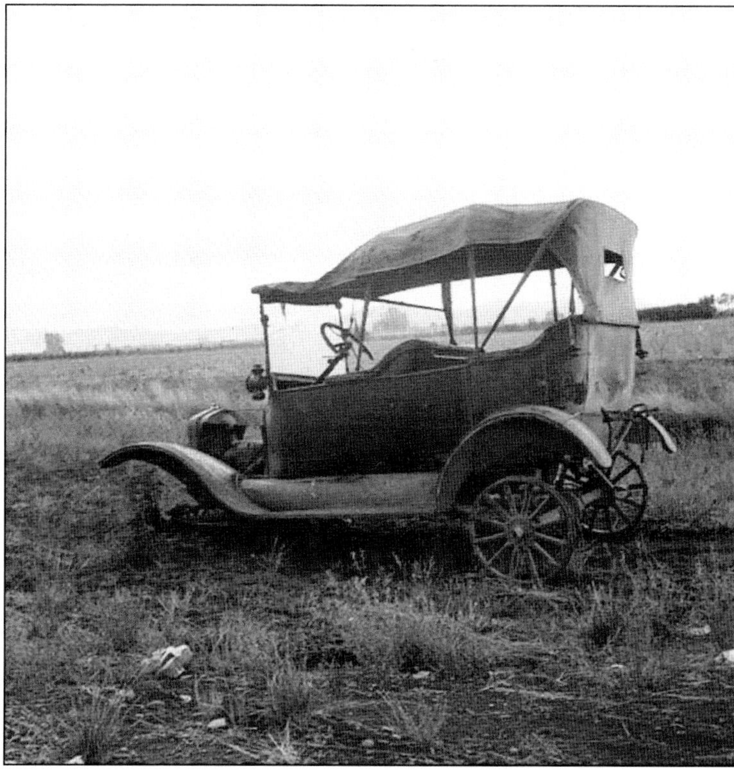

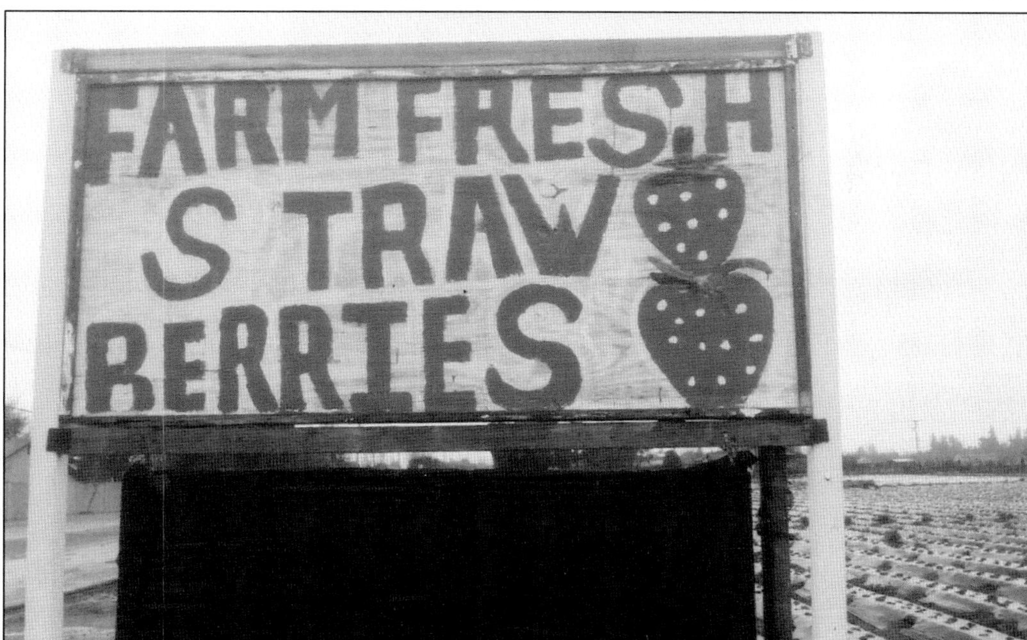

Simple, handmade signs add to the charm of the fruit and vegetable industry in the Turlock area. These stands are owner operated, as opposed to being run by a corporate farming enterprise. Much of the agricultural research about strawberry production is performed at the University of California, Davis, which was founded in 1905.

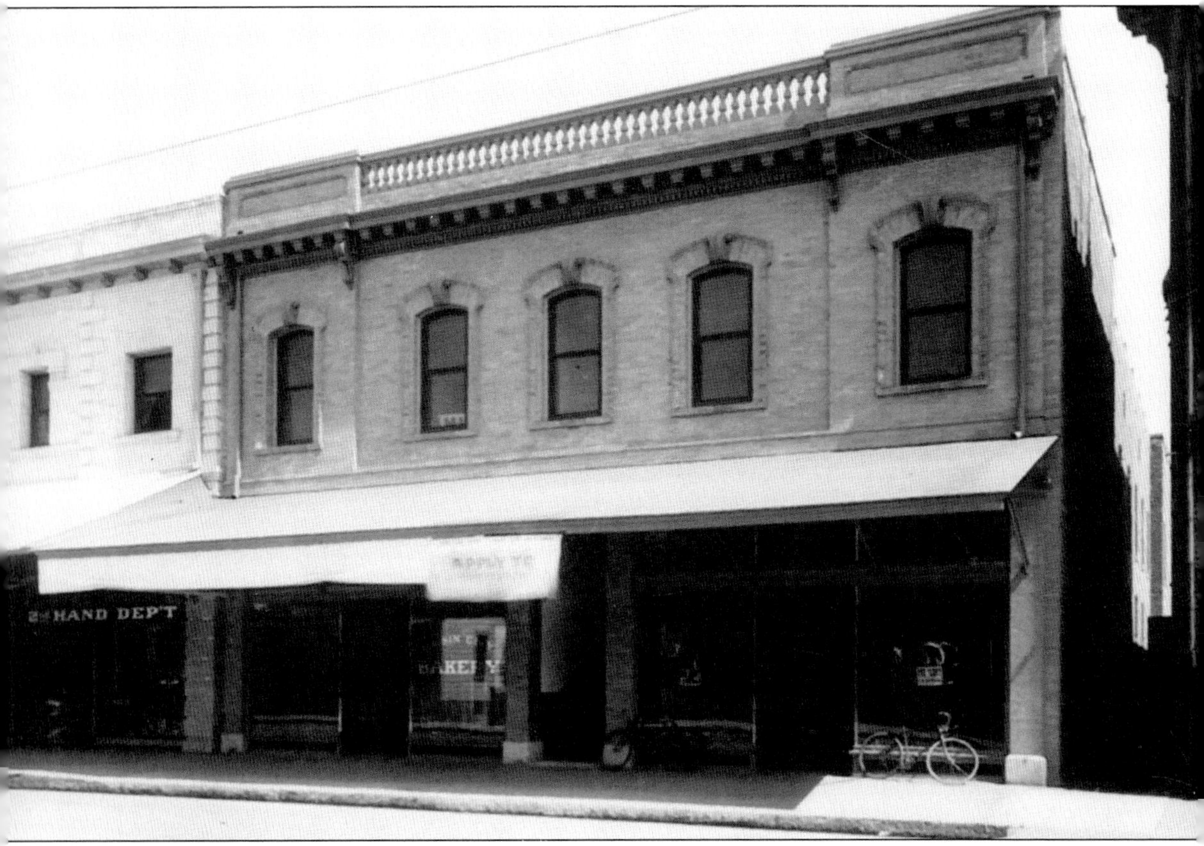

Many styles of architecture were common in the early 20th century, including the Beaux-Arts, Second Empire, Victorian, Queen Anne, Shingle, and Richardsonian Romanesque styles. Many of these styles were present in the cities along Highway 99, particularly Modesto, Fresno, and Bakersfield. (Courtesy of the Kern County Library.)

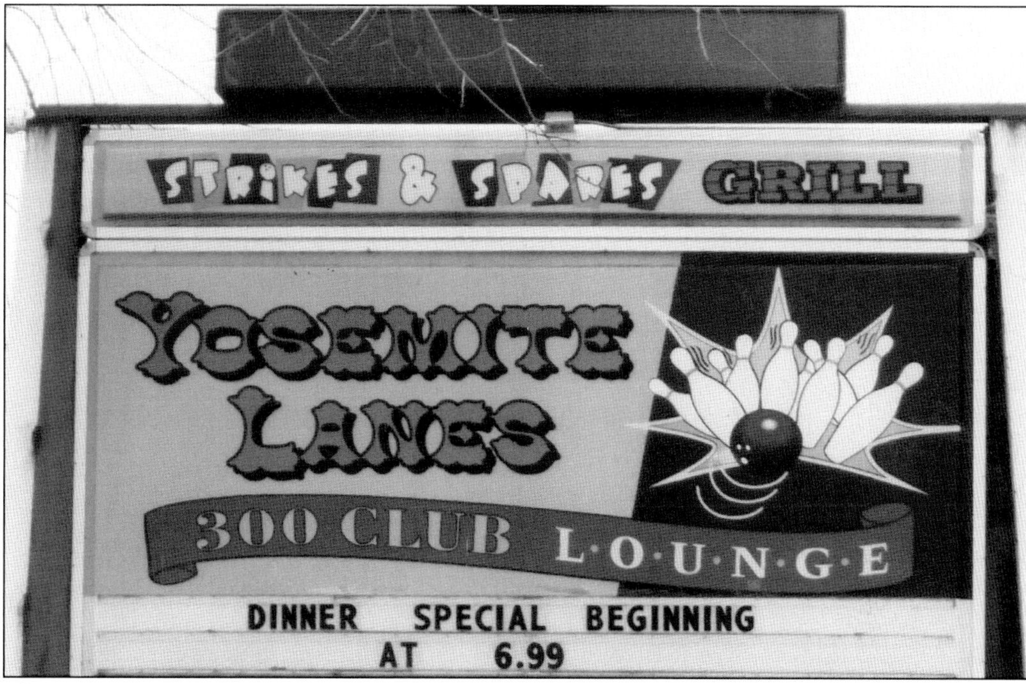

The Yosemite Lanes bowling alley and the 300 Club Lounge are situated in the same building on Yosemite Avenue, to the east of Modesto. It had become a popular recreational location by the 1960s. Bowling a 300 game, which means getting 10 strikes in a row, is accomplished by about 1 in 10,000 bowlers.

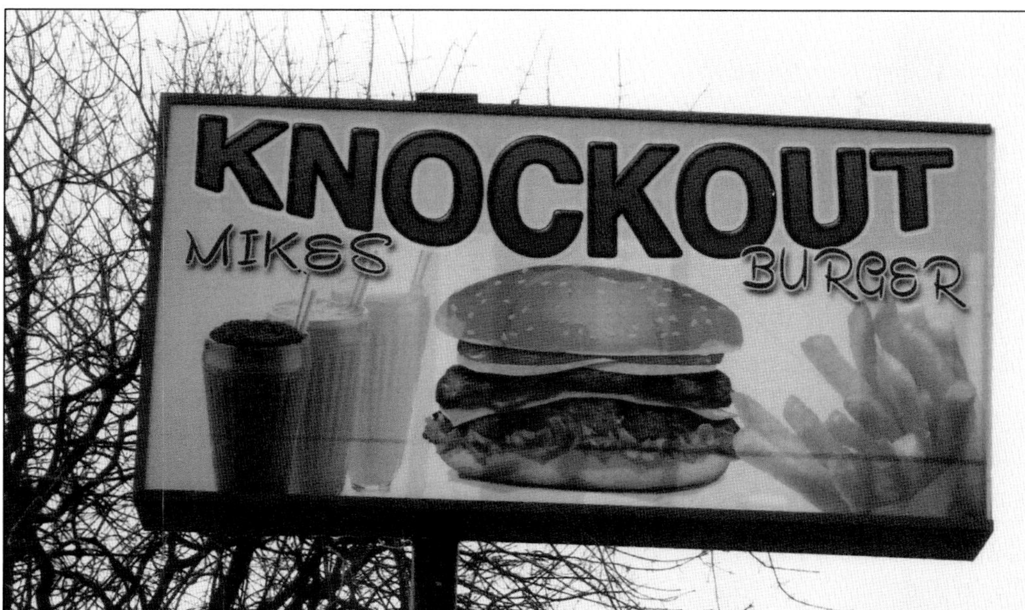

Mike's Knockout Burger is located close to the Yosemite Lanes bowling alley at 1751 Yosemite Boulevard in Modesto. Mike's Knockout Burger is typical of the 1950s-style hamburger stands that once surrounded Modesto. Such restaurants served as gathering places for teenagers, who would socialize as well as enjoy the barbecued foods.

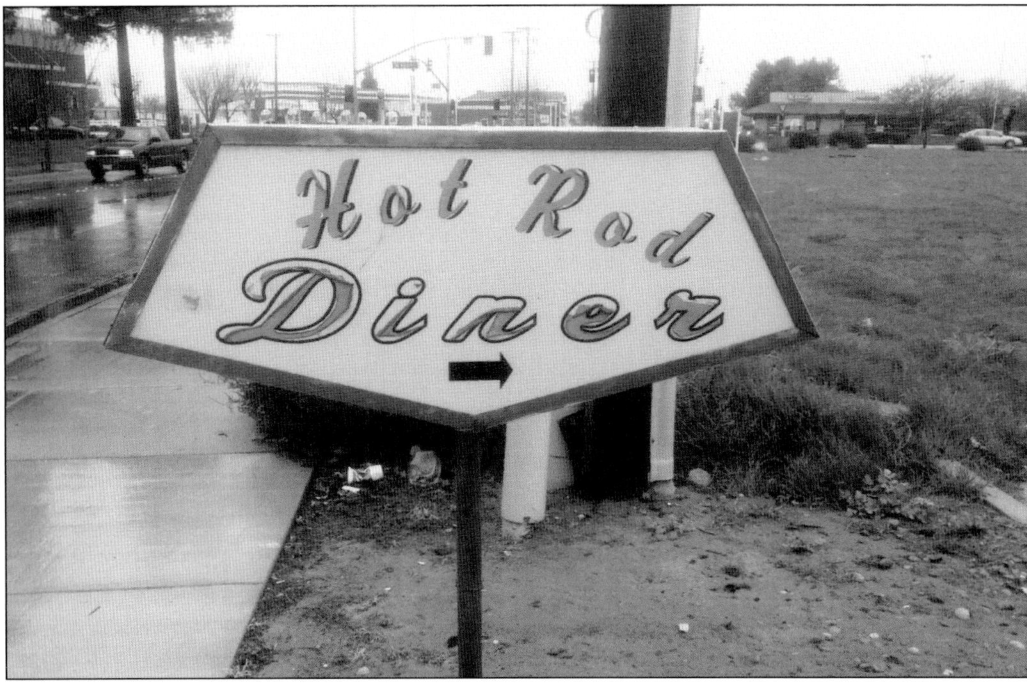

This sign in Turlock welcomes patrons to the Hot Rod Diner. Hot rods and cruising were an integral part of 1950s teen culture. A hot rod is usually an older American car that has been modified with an oversized engine. The term hot rod was commonplace in the 1930s.

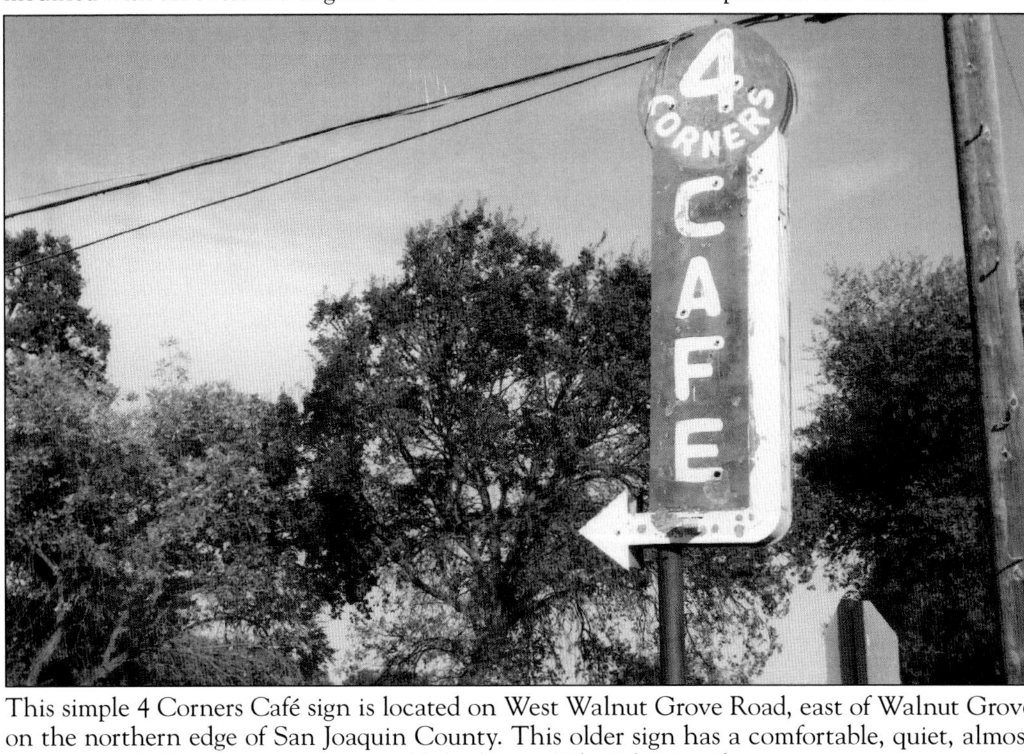

This simple 4 Corners Café sign is located on West Walnut Grove Road, east of Walnut Grove on the northern edge of San Joaquin County. This older sign has a comfortable, quiet, almost lonely appeal. Walnut Grove was established in 1850 by John W. Sharp.

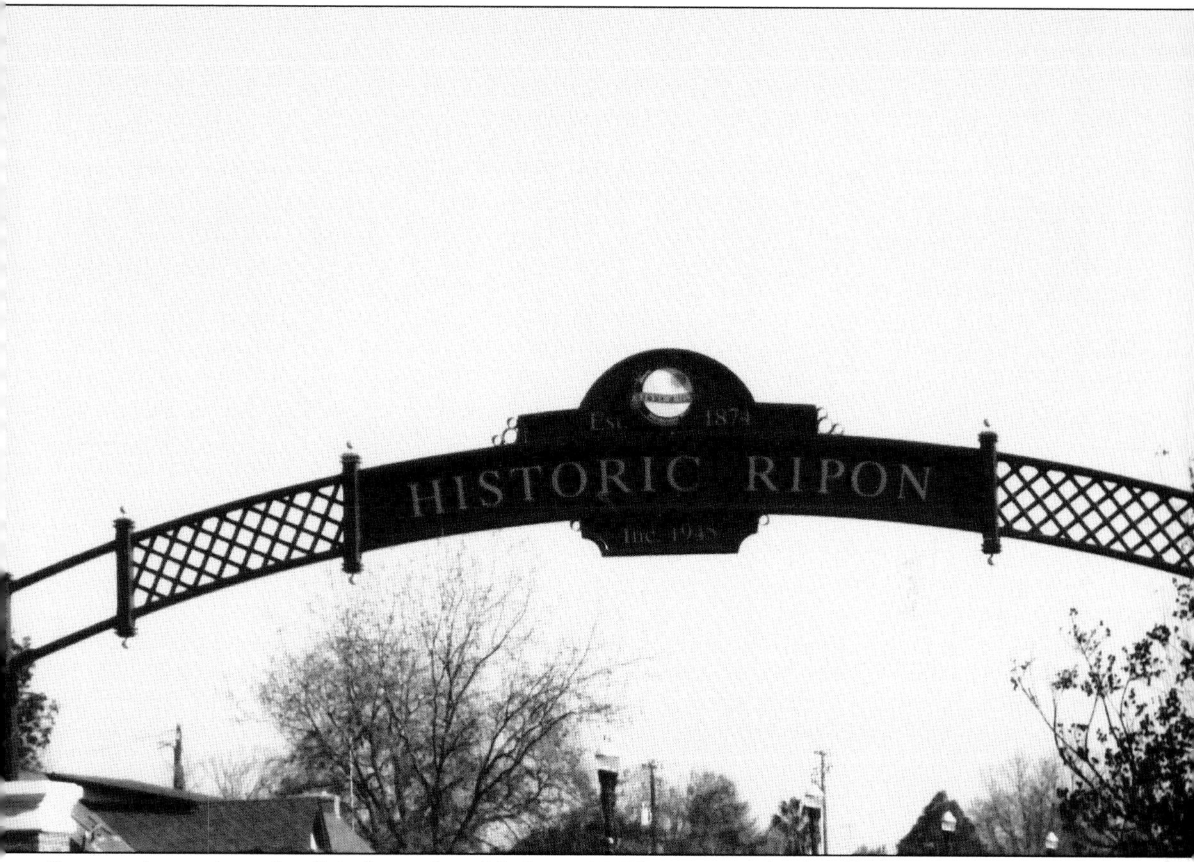

Ripon is located north of Modesto along Highway 99. There are multiple off-ramps from Highway 99 leading into the small town, which is known for its significant almond production. It was established in 1874, but it was not incorporated until 1945.

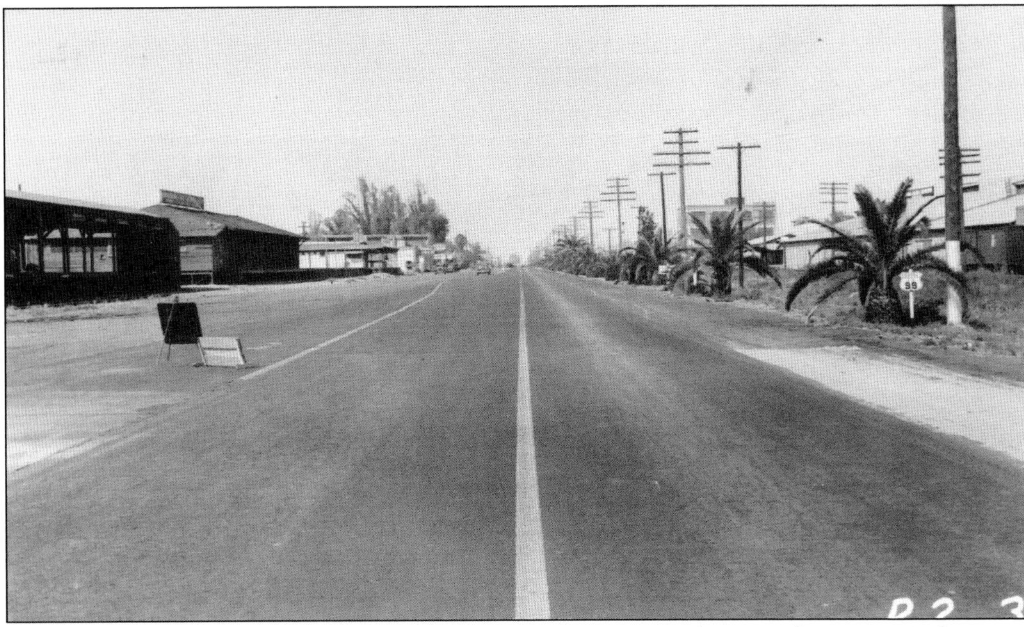

Highway 99 travels through Tulare and five other counties on the route between Modesto and Bakersfield. Tulare County contains wooded mountainous areas such as the Sequoia and Kings Canyon National Parks, as well as several Central Valley cities in the Highway 99 corridor. The major towns in Tulare County include Visalia, Tulare, and Porterville. (Copyright © California Department of Transportation.)

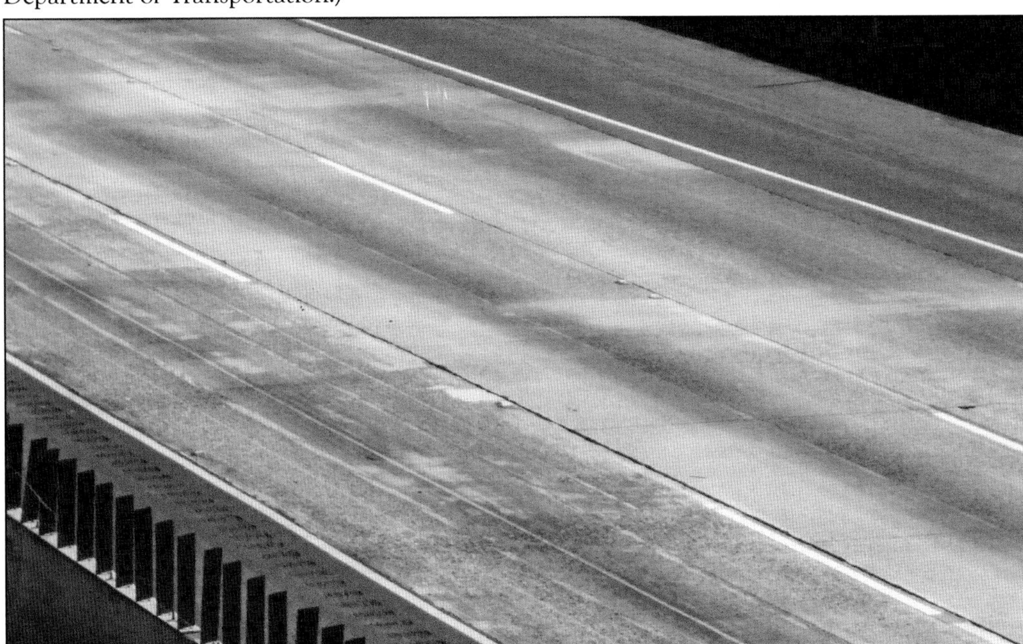

This photograph of Highway 99 was taken from an overpass in Modesto. In 2014, the average daily traffic volume on Highway 99 in the Modesto area is approximately 100,000 vehicles per day. In 1914, the average daily traffic volume in the Modesto area was estimated to be about 1,000 vehicles per day.

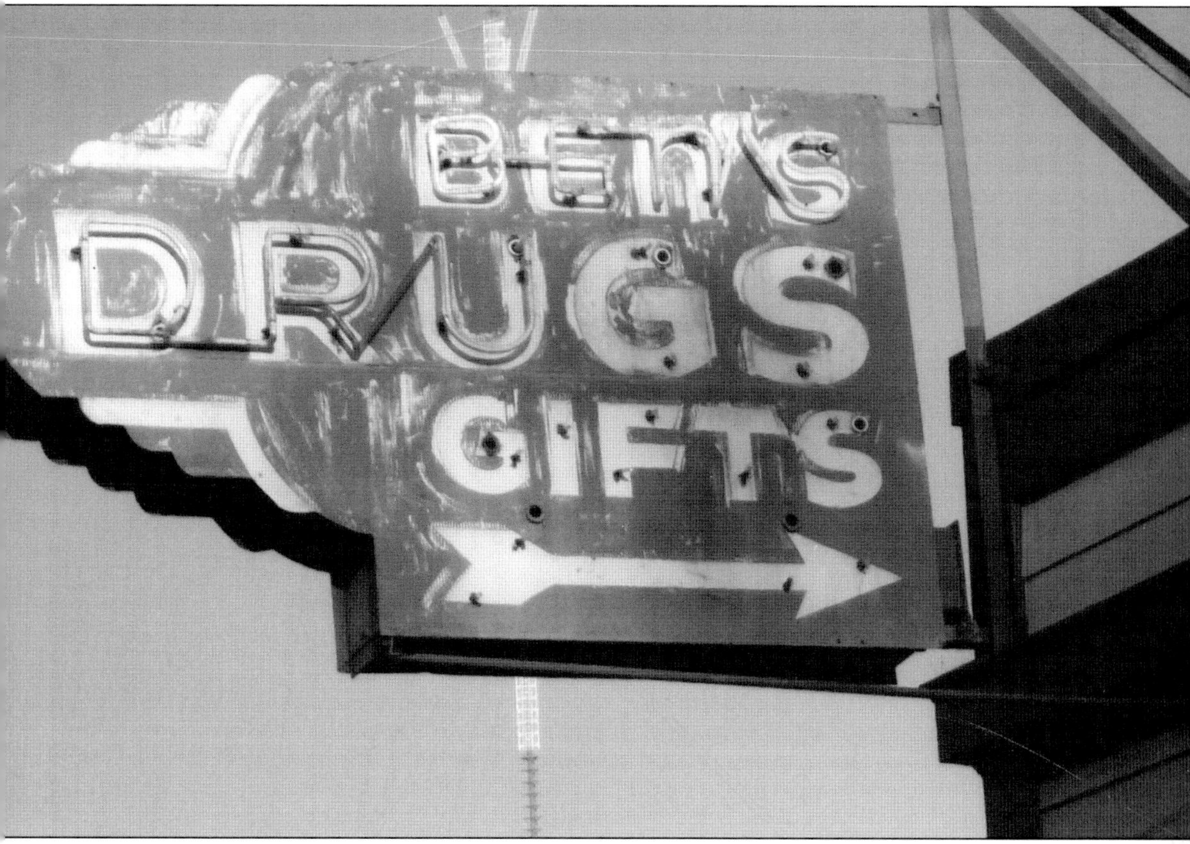

Ben's Drugs is part of the community and history of Walnut Grove. As early as 1914, a large Japanese community was living in Walnut Grove. Ben's Drugs—just down the block from Kawamura's Barber Shop—is located at 14112 Market Street, which serve's as Walnut Grove's main street.

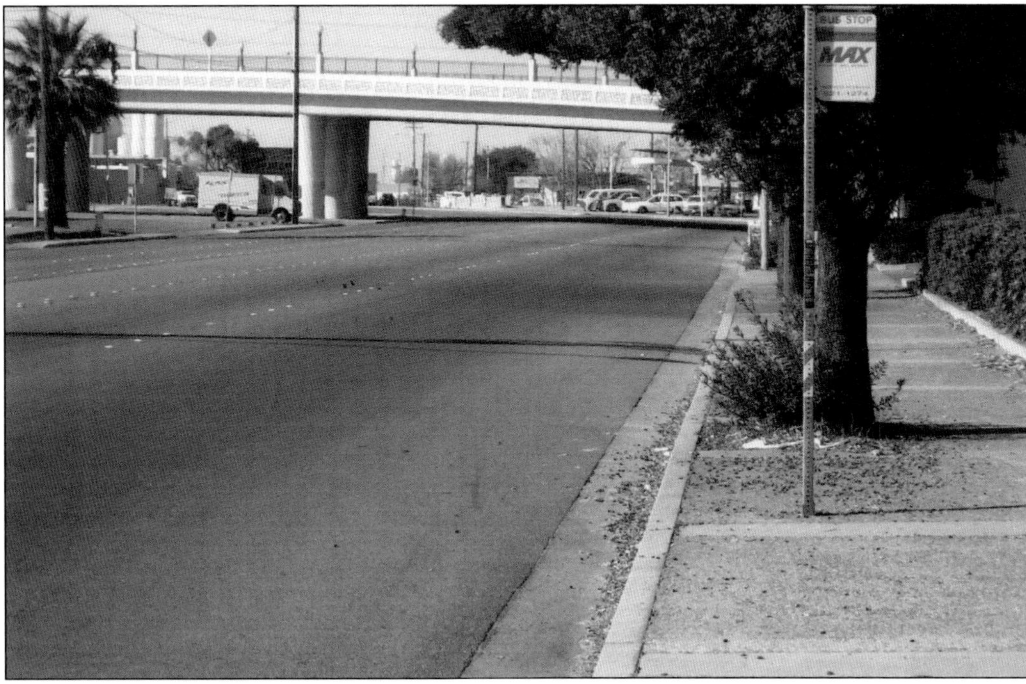

The five lanes of Business 99 in Merced are lined with industrial, commercial, and retail establishments. This street was previously a part of Highway 99 before the bypass was constructed. Merced County was established in 1855. In 2005, Merced became the home of the 10th University of California campus: University of California, Merced.

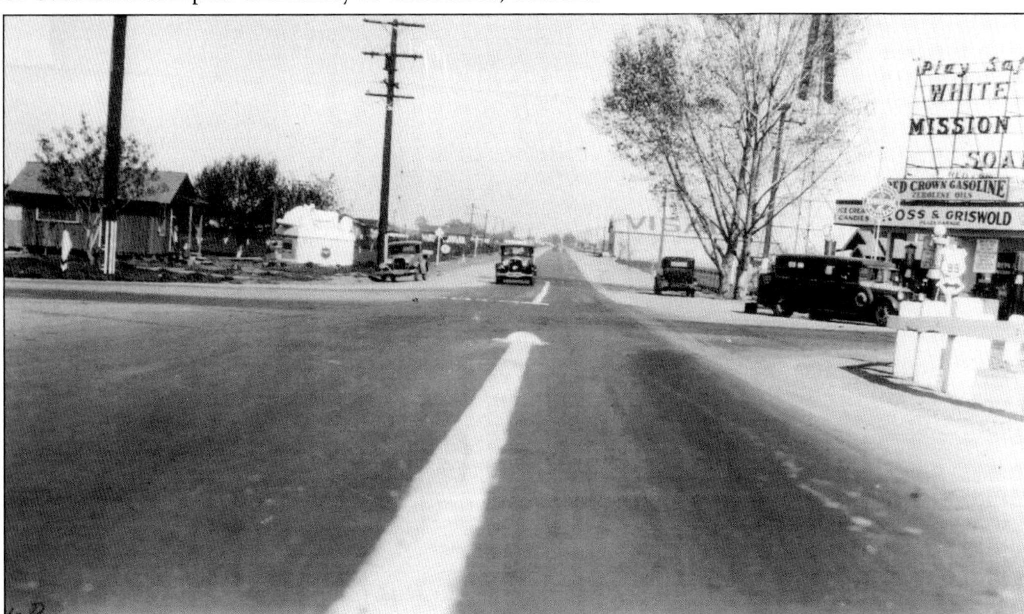

This Ross and Griswold gas station and garage, which operated during the Depression, was situated along the highway in Tulare County. It sold gasoline, soap, household goods, cold soft drinks, and groceries. The Highway 99 sign in the foreground identifies the direction of Highway 99. The photograph was taken in 1929. (Copyright © California Department of Transportation.)

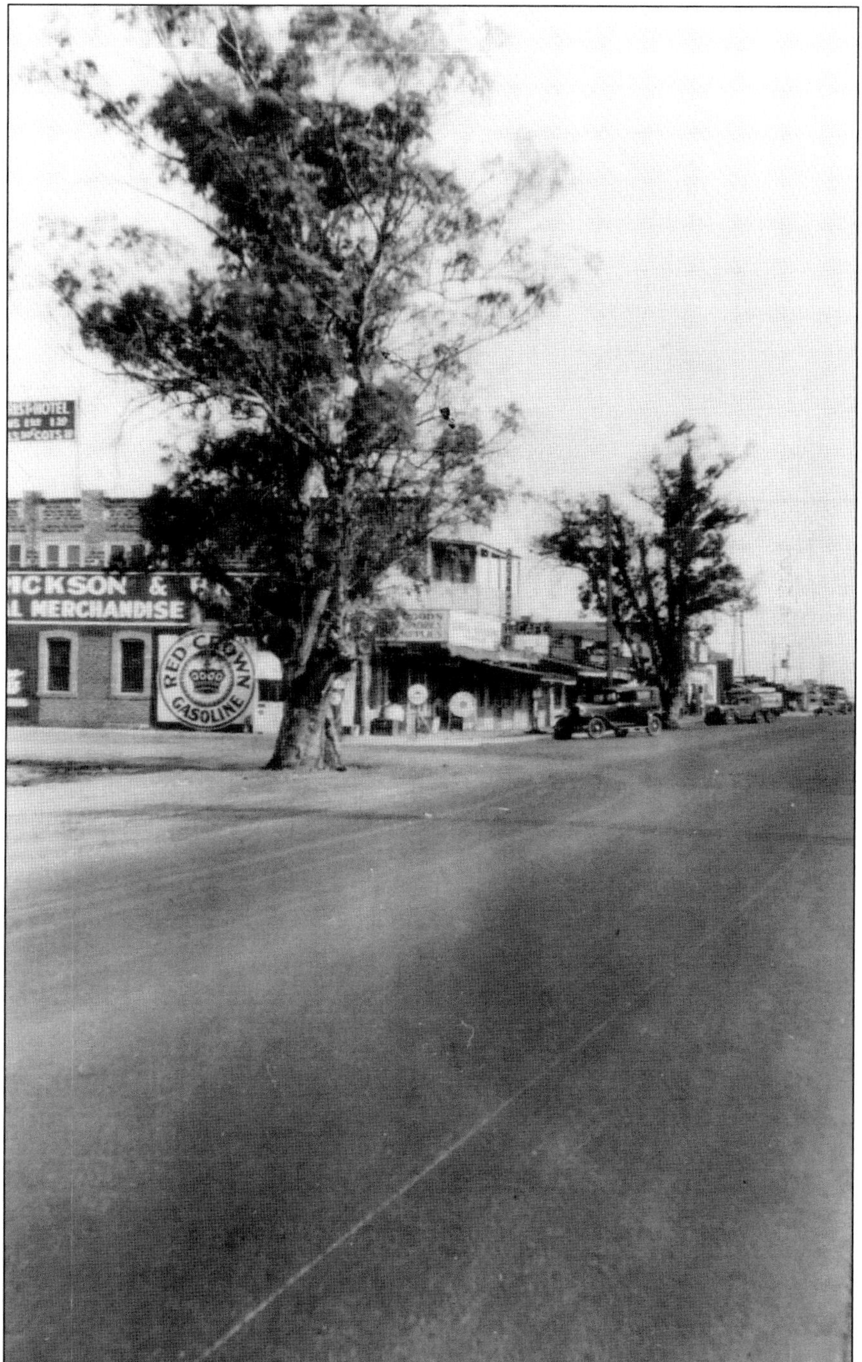

Large signage was often painted onto the sides of buildings that were visible from roadways. On this building, a merchandising sign and an advertisement for Red Crown Gasoline were present. Red Crown logos were routinely found on buildings and on the top of old-style gasoline pumps.The brand is so much a part of nostalgic American culture that it warrants a small museum located in Lafayette, Indiana. (Copyright © California Department of Transportation.)

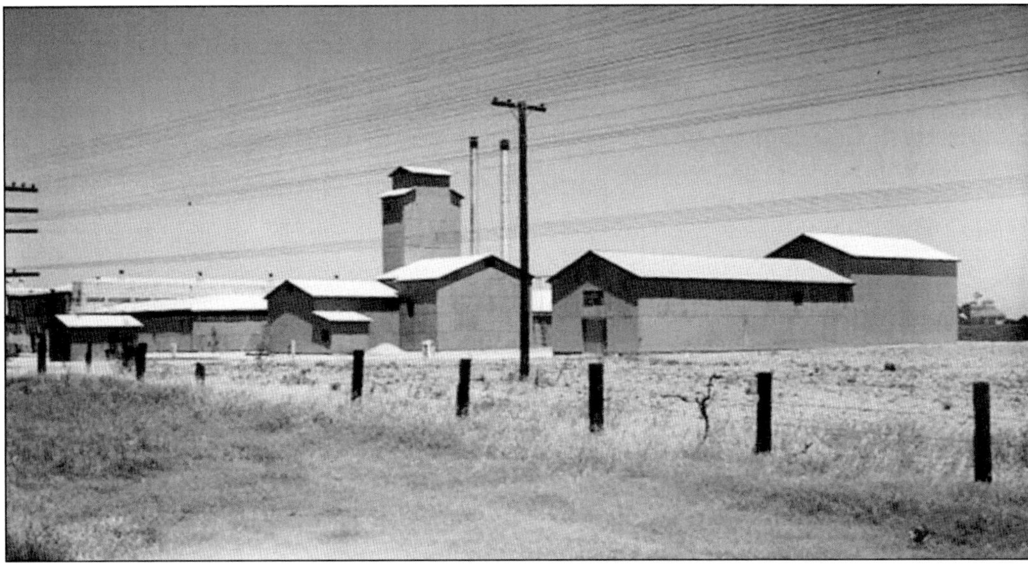

These well-kept agricultural buildings are protected by a barbed wire fence. In 1919, California established a single department that was responsible for agriculture. The California Department of Food and Agriculture is now split into six divisions and operates at about 100 locations throughout the state. (Courtesy of the Library of Congress.)

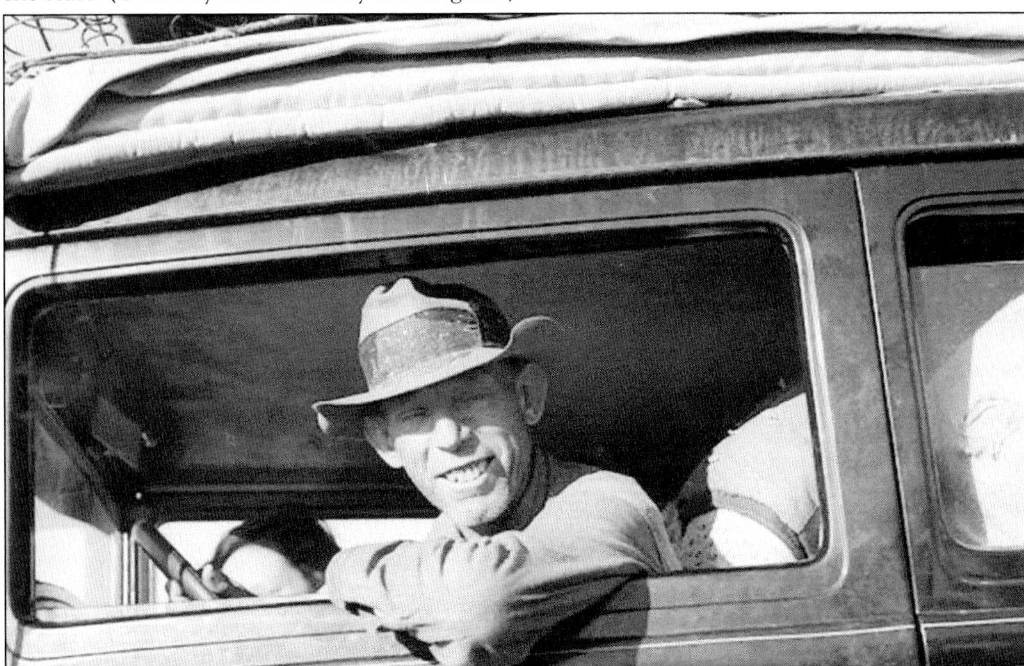

A Depression-era migrant farmer is seen here moving his goods in and on top of his truck. The Great Depression had devastating effects in many countries. Unemployment in the United States exceeded 25 percent, and some countries reached 33 percent unemployment. Cities in several countries suffered greatly, particularly those dependent on industry. Construction was virtually halted in many countries. Rural areas were affected as well, and crop prices fell by approximately 60 percent. (Courtesy of the Library of Congress.)

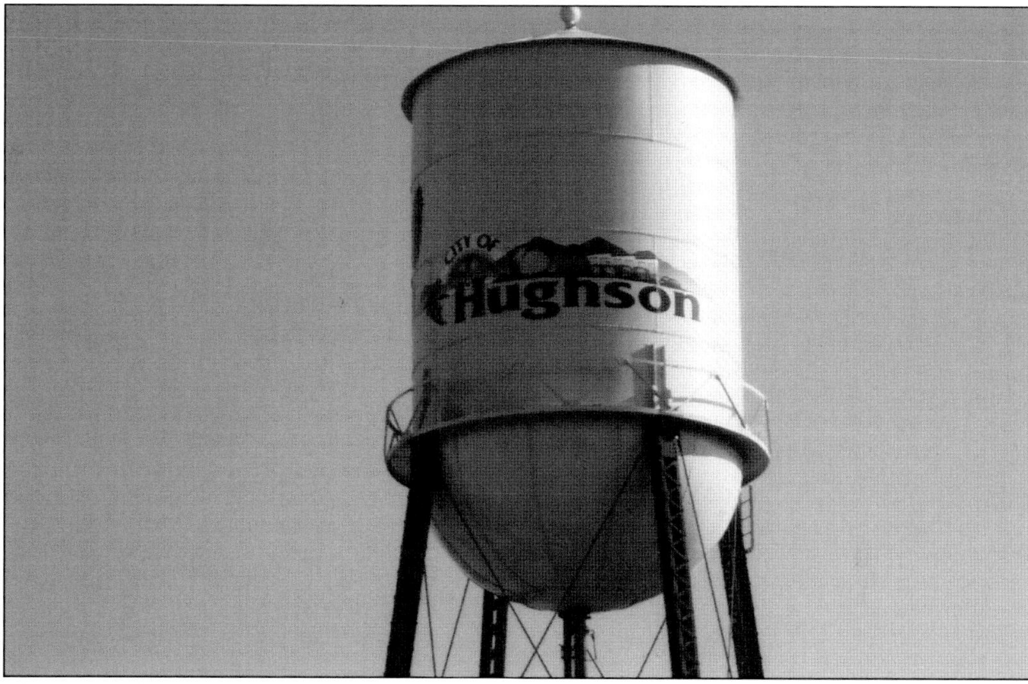

The town of Hughson, which is located south of Modesto, is surrounded by orchards and was initially known for its production of peaches, which earned it the title "The Peach Capital of the World." Peaches are no longer the primary crop, having been largely replaced by almonds. Hughson was founded as a township in 1907. Prior to 1907, it primarily consisted of a grain ranch that was owned by Hiram Hughson.

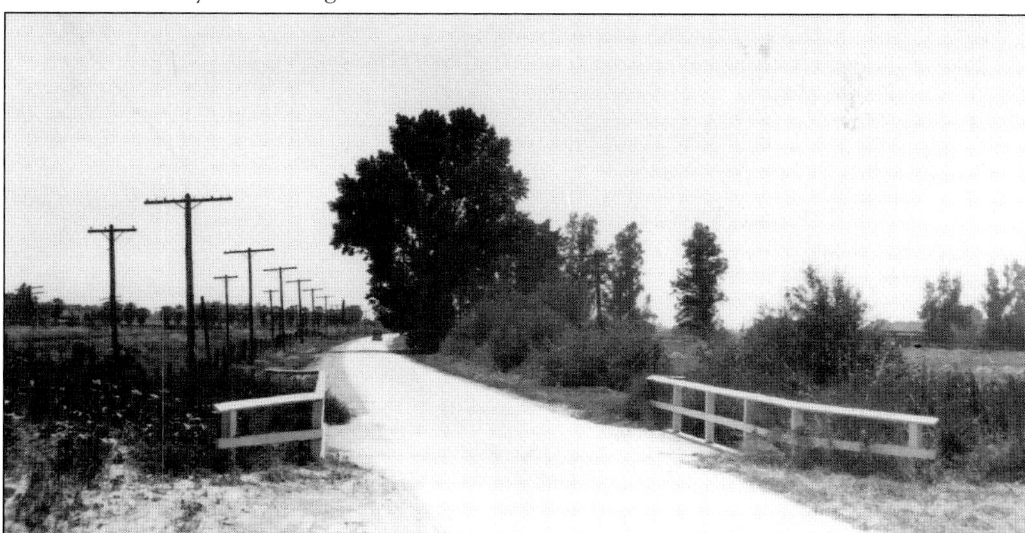

This photograph of a small bridge crossing south of Kingsburg in Tulare shows Highway 99 when it was only two lanes wide. The town of Tulare was established in 1872 by the Southern Pacific Railroad. The Tachi Yokuts people built and fished on Tulare Lake before the arrival of European settlers. The town was later named for the lake. (Copyright © California Department of Transportation.)

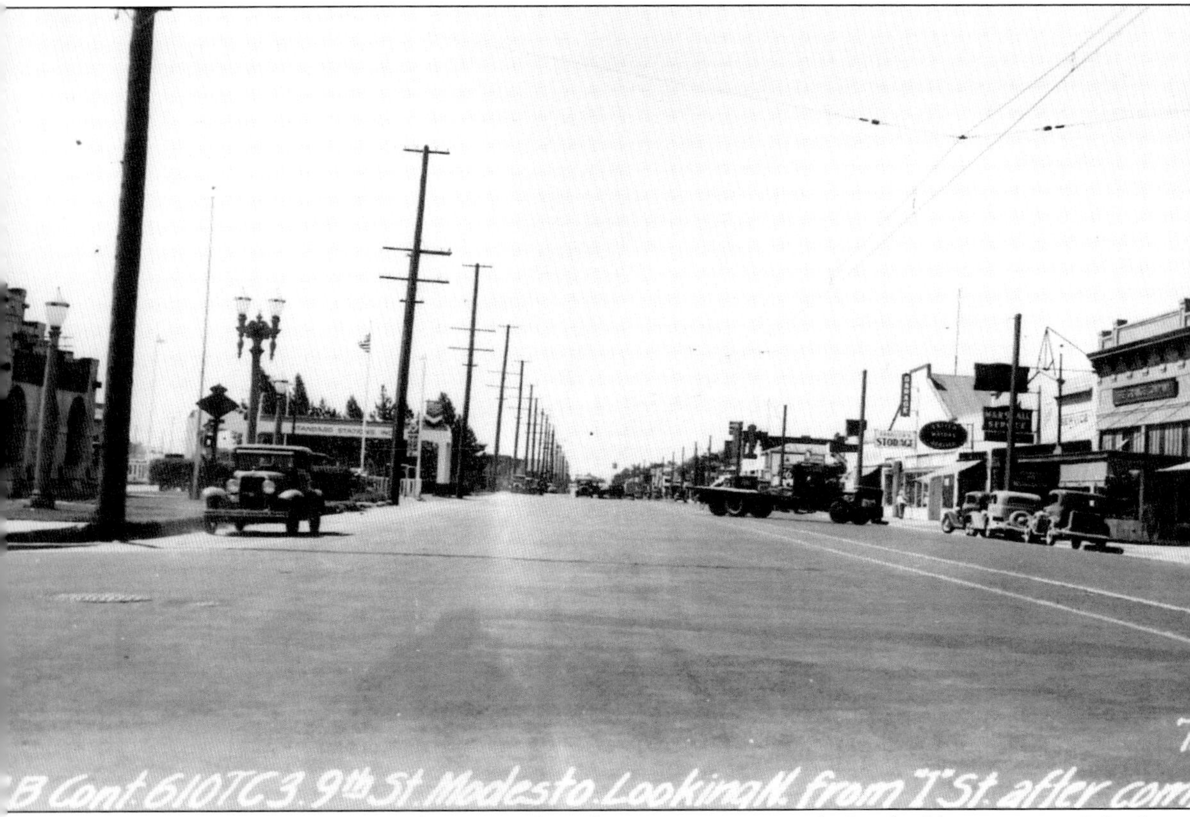

This engineer's photograph from 1934 describes construction work that had been accomplished on Ninth Street in Modesto—which was a portion of Highway 99 at the time. In the 1940s and 1950s, teenagers and young adults started congregating in this area to hang out. This activity was glamorized in the 1970s film *American Graffiti*, which was set in Modesto. (Copyright © California Department of Transportation.)

Six

An Egalitarian Route

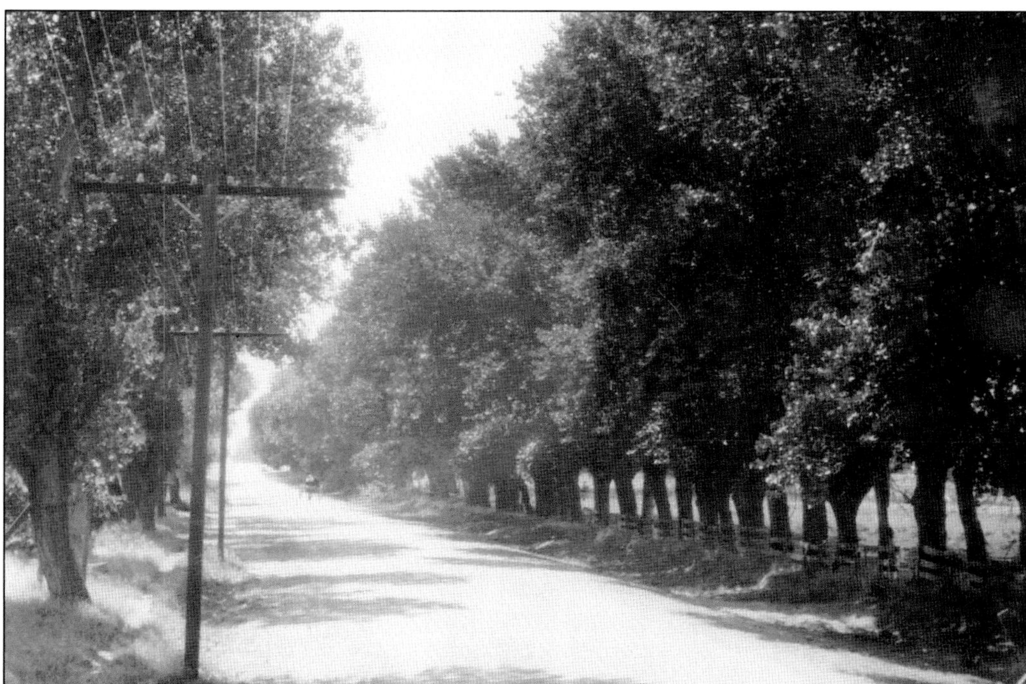

This photograph shows a section of a tree-lined roadway in Kern County north of Bakersfield. It was taken in about 1916. World War I was taking place at the time that this photograph was taken. The war began on July 28, 1914, and lasted until November 11, 1918. More than 9 million soldiers were killed in the fighting. (Copyright © California Department of Transportation.)

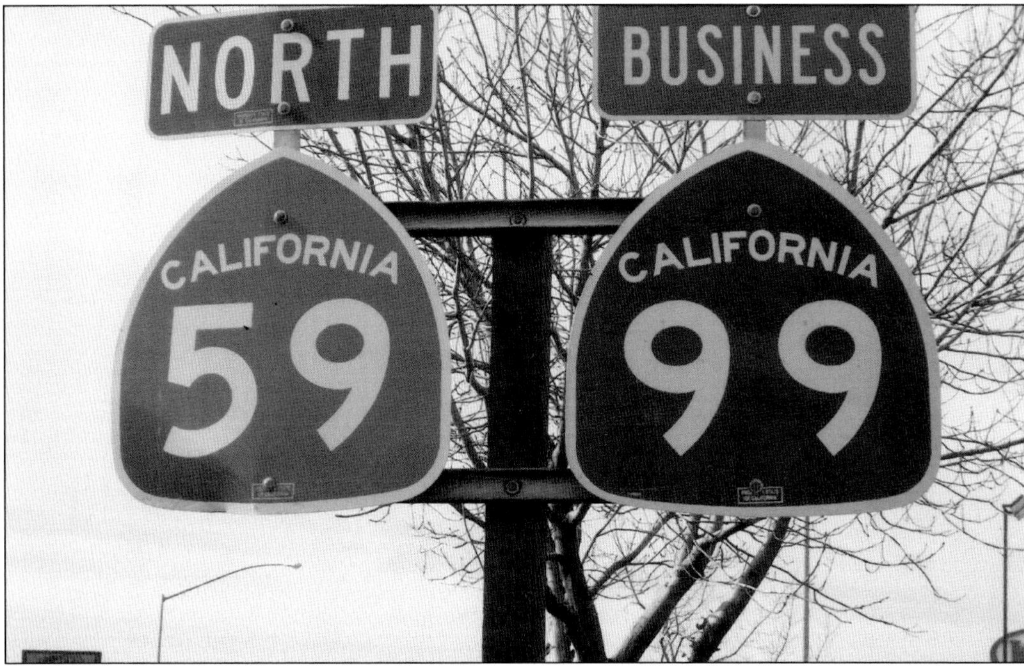

Business 99 in Merced is still an important roadway that runs through downtown Merced. The four-lane, urbanized road is lined with industrial, commercial, and retail establishments. Many businesses in Merced were subject to the restrictions imposed by the rationing of materials during World War II. Rationed items included tires, cars, bicycles, gasoline, fuel oil, kerosene, stoves, rubber, and shoes.

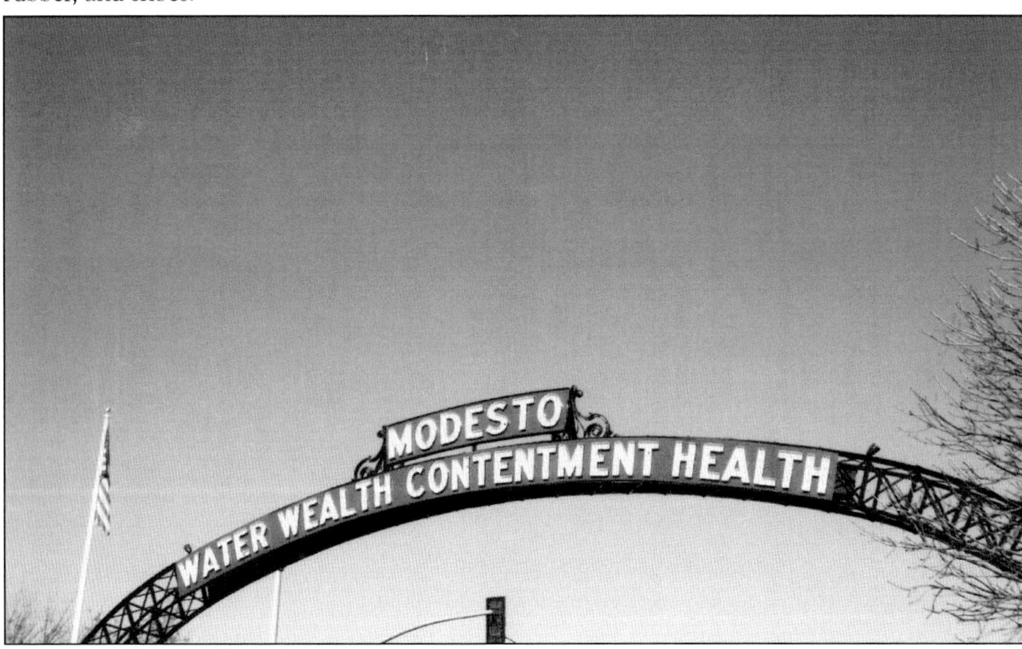

"Water Wealth Contentment Health" is the slogan on the Modesto Arch, which was installed on Ninth Street. These four elements express the life and goals of Modesto's early residents. The arch was established in 1912 and was both welcomed and detested by various groups.

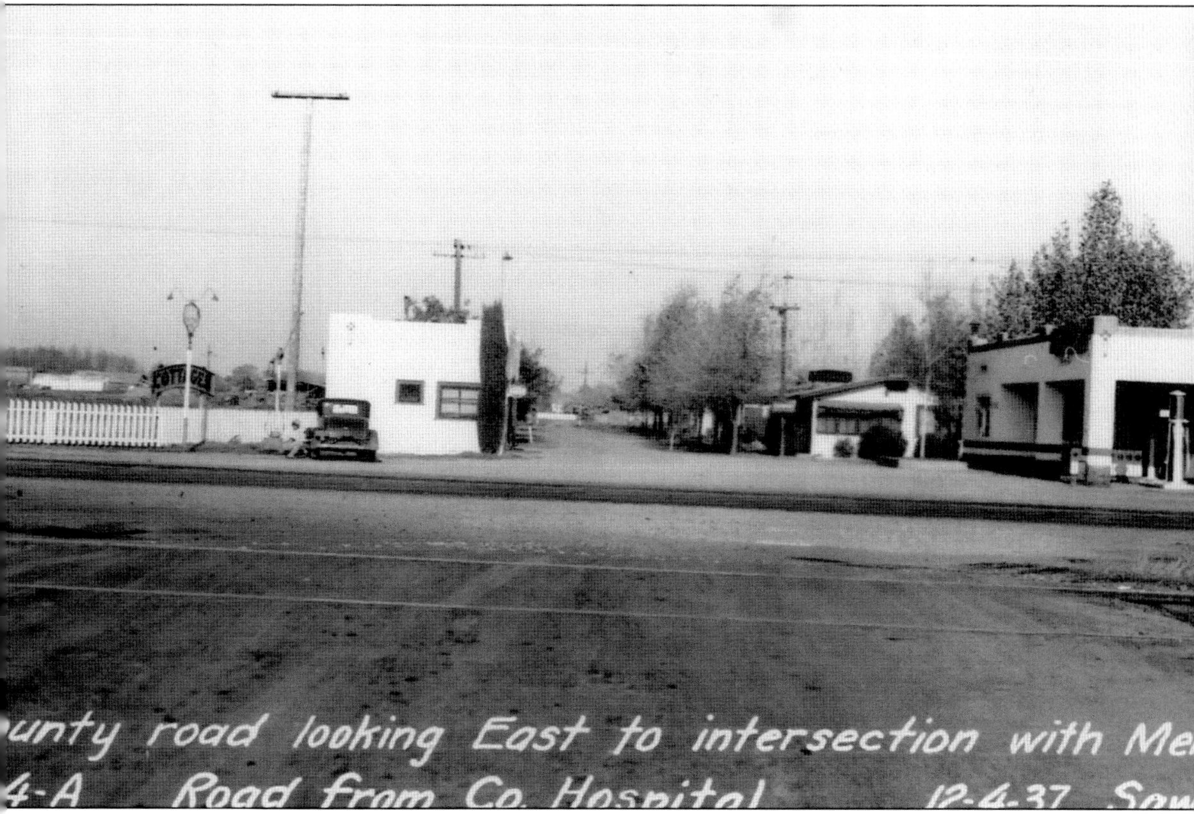

Cottages, residences, gas stations, and stores grew around the highway in 1930s Merced County, as shown in this 1937 photograph. Merced County was established in 1855. Improvements to Highway 99 made area hospitals more accessible, as a poorly made road could significantly increase the time required to travel to a hospital. (Copyright © California Department of Transportation.)

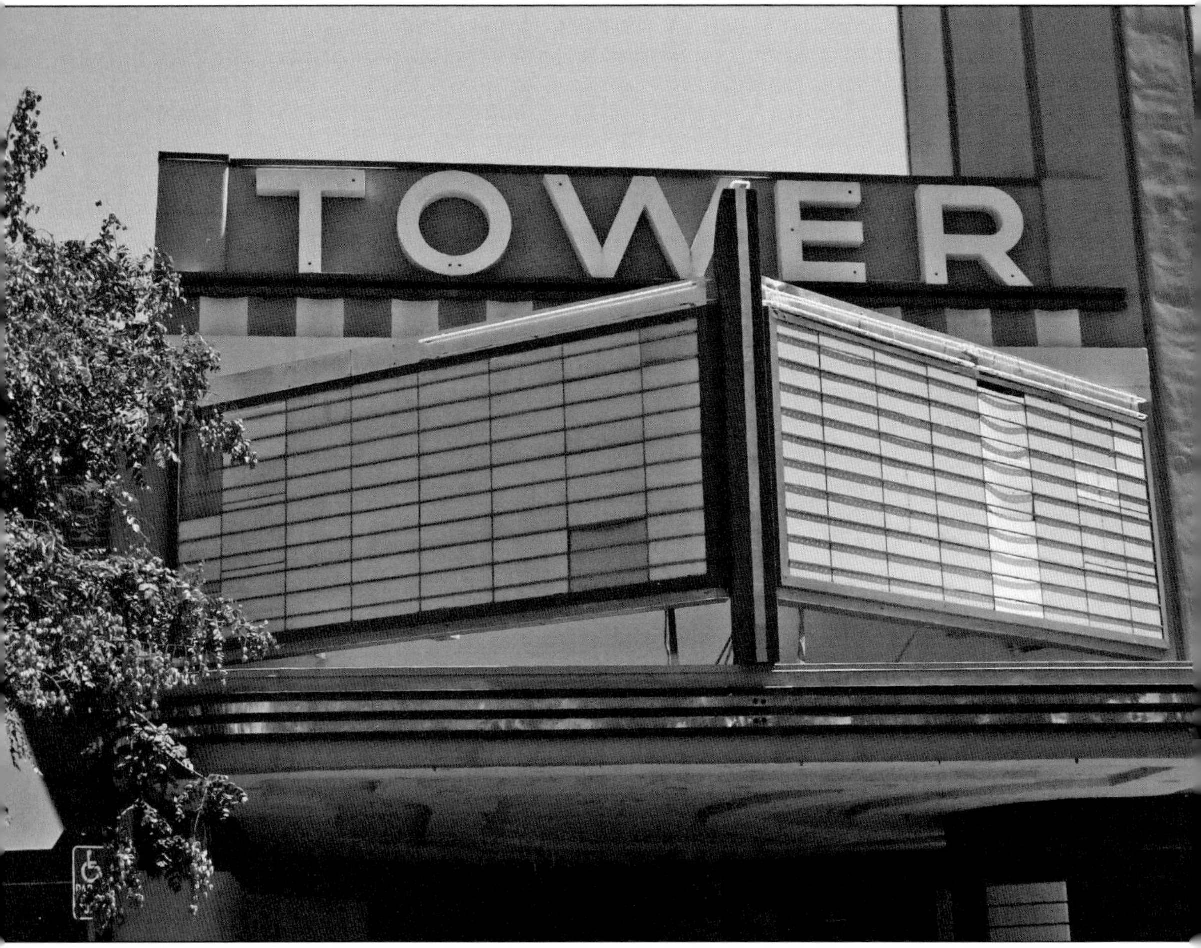

The Tower Theatre, a cinematic treasure, was designed, engineered, and built in 1939–1940 and opened in January 1941. It is located in downtown Marysville, a historic gold rush town, at 103 D Street. The theater, which is situated next to many historic buildings and antique shops, has been abandoned.

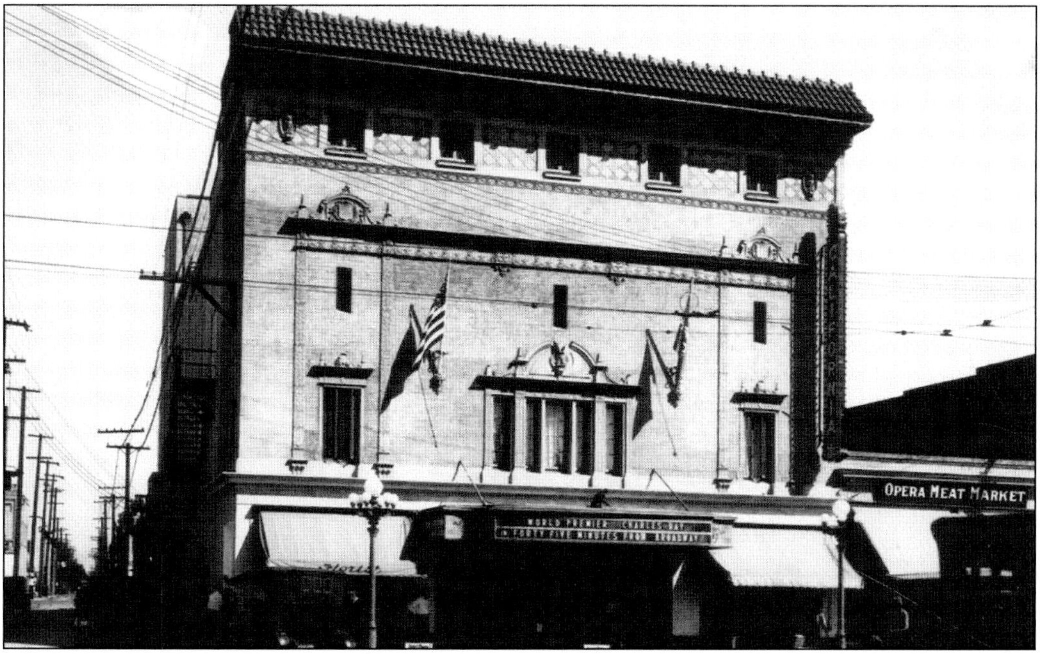

The opera and theater have been important parts of Bakersfield's culture from the early 1900s to the present day. California State University, Bakersfield—which was established in 1965—has a music department that contributes to this element of the city's culture. (Courtesy of the Kern County Library.)

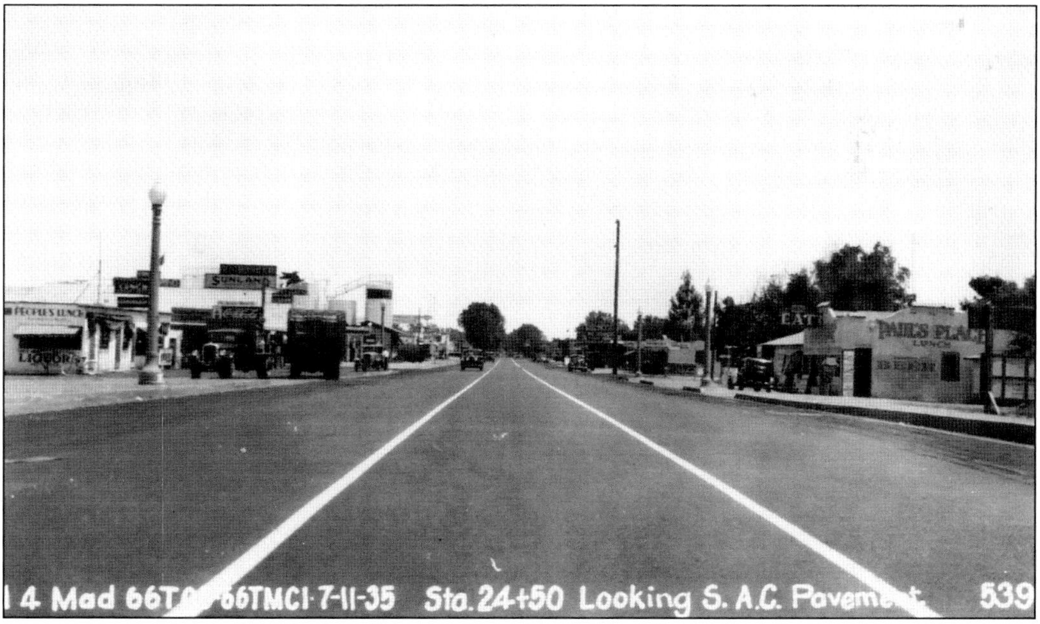

Station 24+50—as referred to in this photograph—means that something is 2,450 feet from an established point. This distance was measured by metal tapes, held under tension to obtain an accurate measurement. Construction photographs such as this one were used by contractors, civil engineers, and contracting officers. The asphalt on roads such as this one was typically three to six inches thick. (Copyright © California Department of Transportation.)

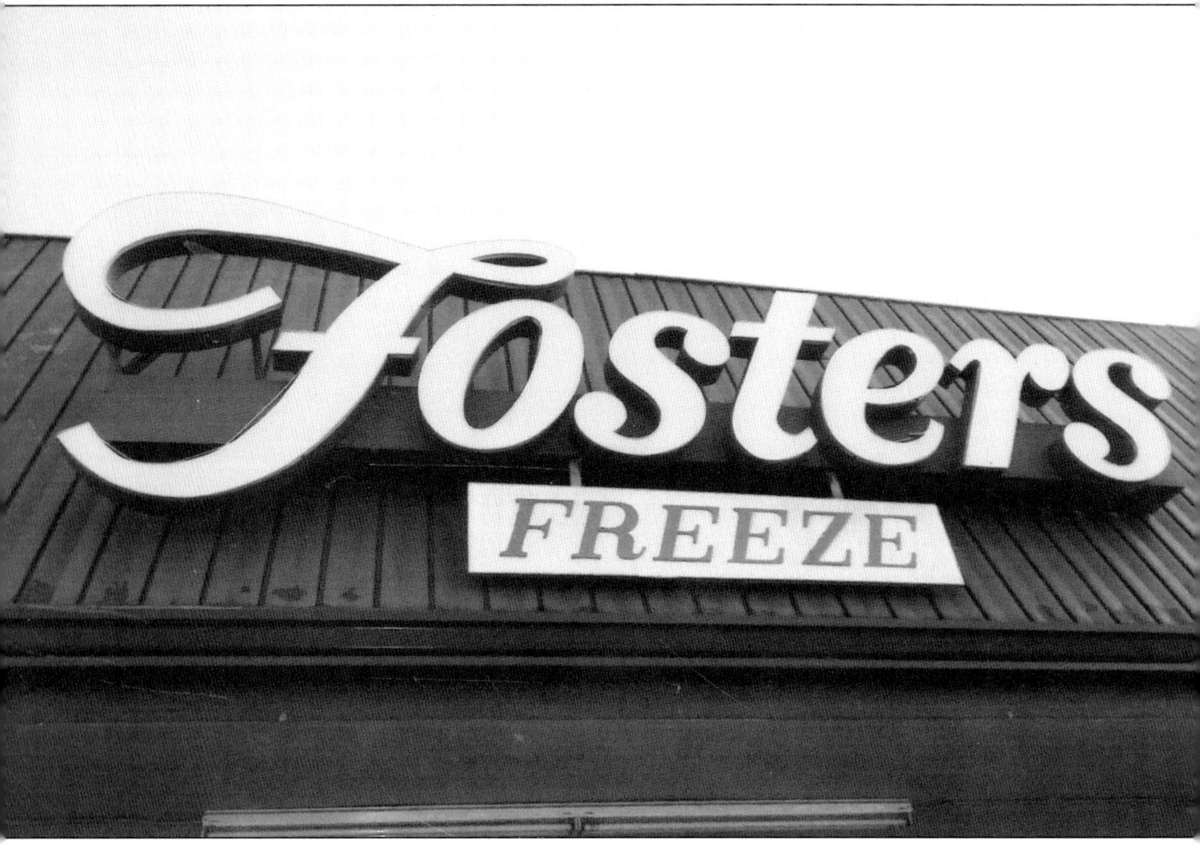

Fosters Freeze is a chain of old-fashioned hamburger stands that is found in many towns in the Highway 99 corridor. There are two locations in Bakersfield, one in Atwater, and five in Fresno. These restaurants are traditionally patronized by both travelers and residents of the cities and towns along Highway 99.

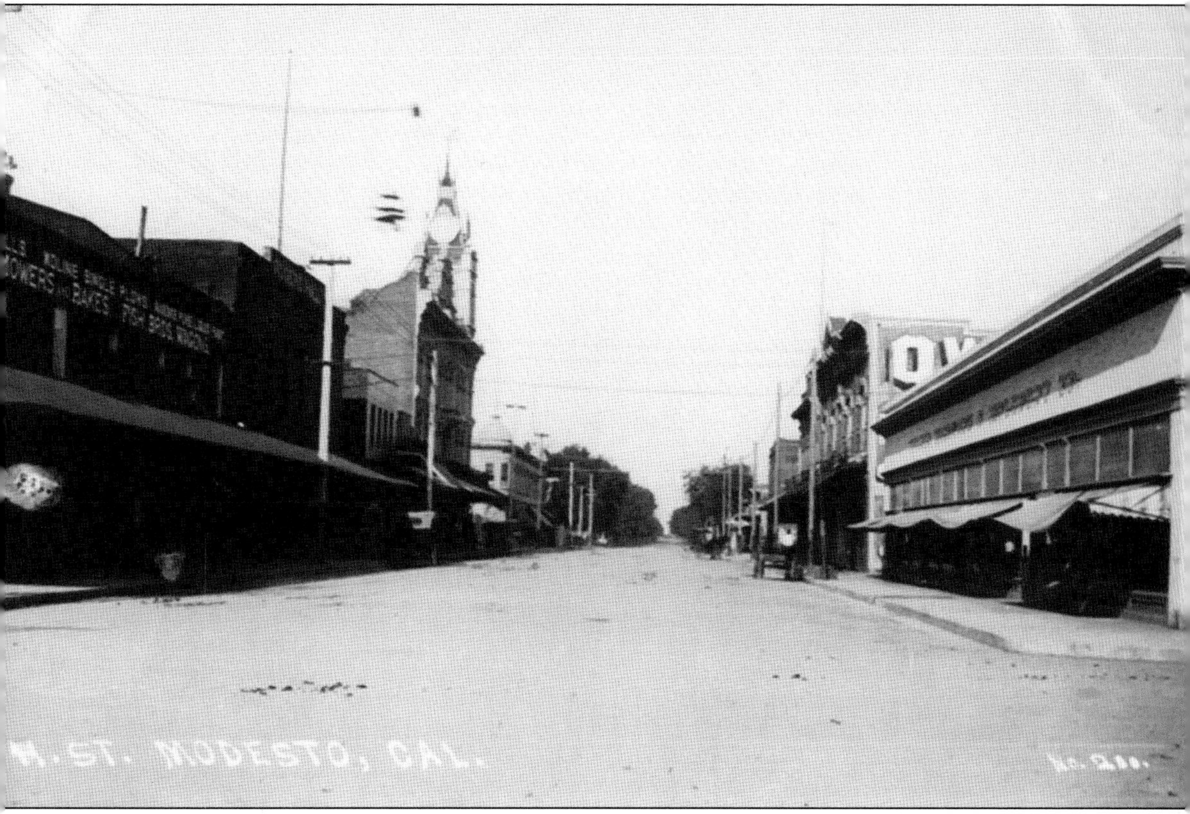

H Street, in downtown Modesto, is near the McHenry Mansion, the A&W hamburger stand, and the offices of the *Modesto Bee* newspaper. At the time that this image was taken, there were already large signs on buildings that advertised several manufacturers and retailers. (Courtesy of the California State Library, Sacramento.)

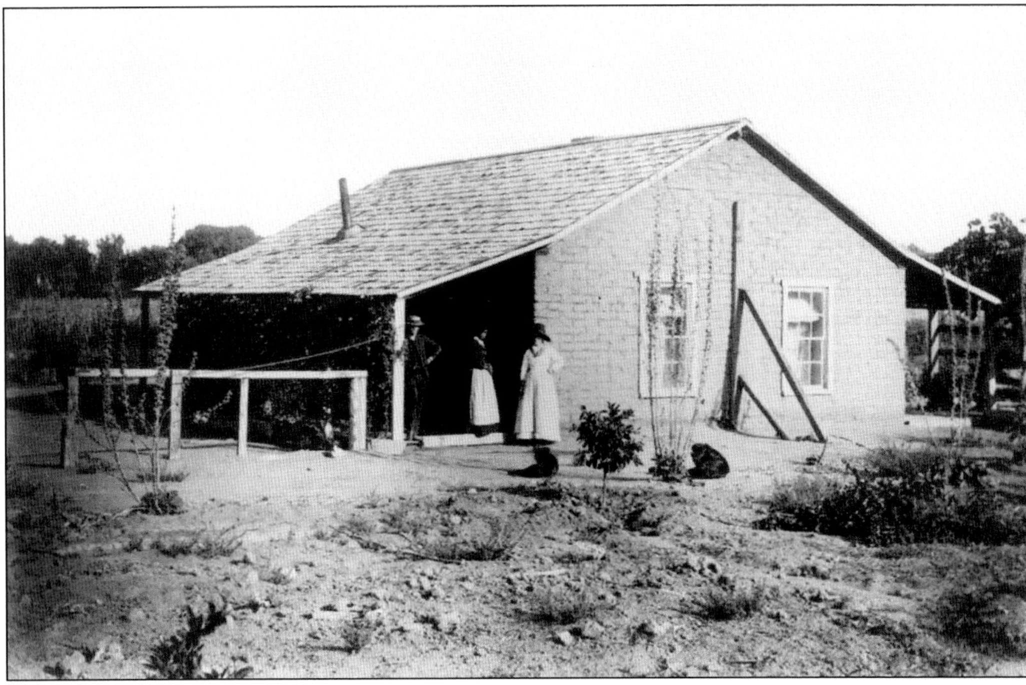

Photographed in the early 1900s, this cabin was typical of those found on ranches and farms in Kern County. While much of Kern County is flat agricultural land, there are mountains within its boundaries. The county's economy is linked to agriculture and the petroleum industry. (Courtesy of the Kern County Library.)

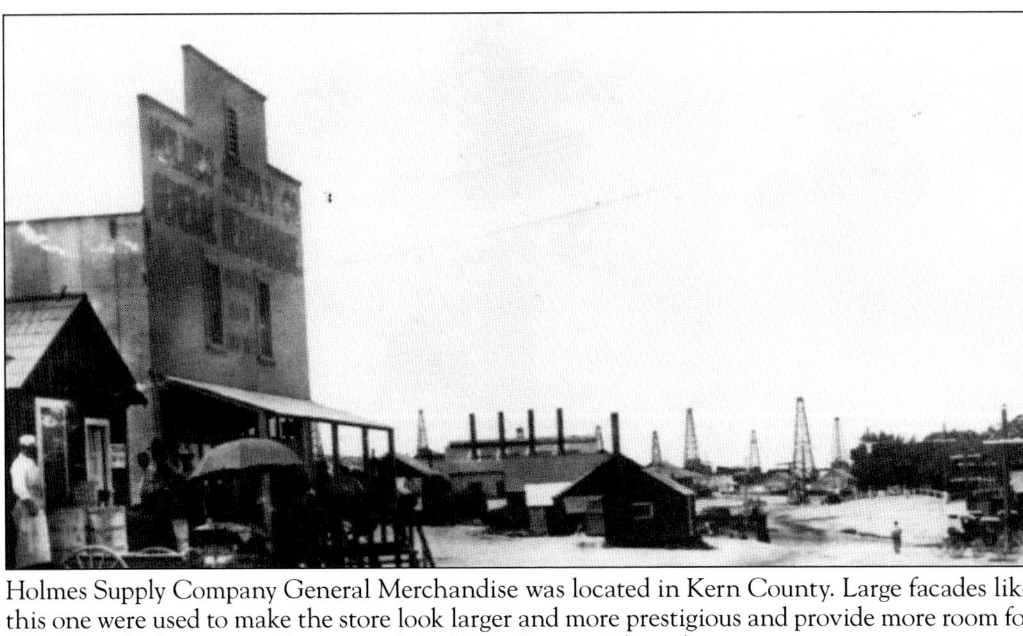

Holmes Supply Company General Merchandise was located in Kern County. Large facades like this one were used to make the store look larger and more prestigious and provide more room for signage and advertising. (Courtesy of the Kern County Library.)

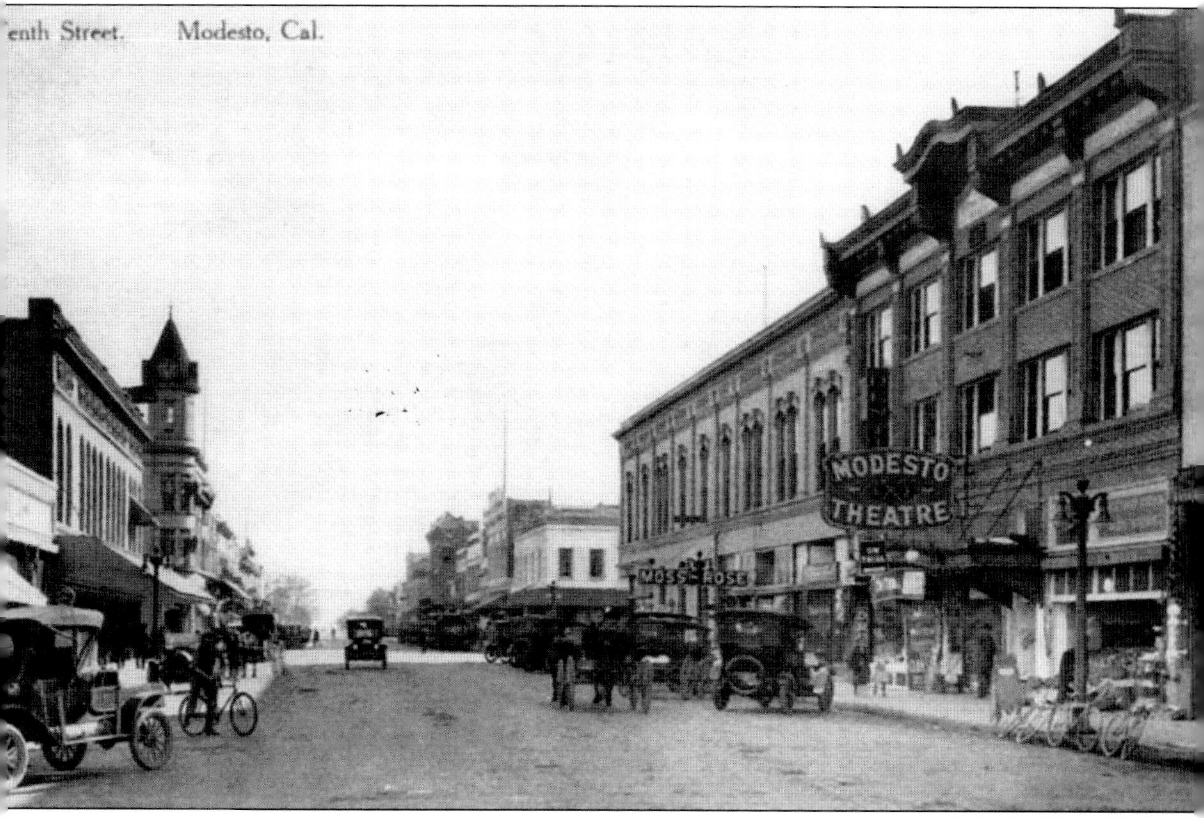

Tenth Street in Modesto was home to the Modesto Theatre, as well as many retail and office structures. Teenagers cruised "the strip" of Tenth Street in the 1950s, 1960s, and beyond. This activity was romanticized by the film *American Graffiti*. (Courtesy of the California State Library, Sacramento.)

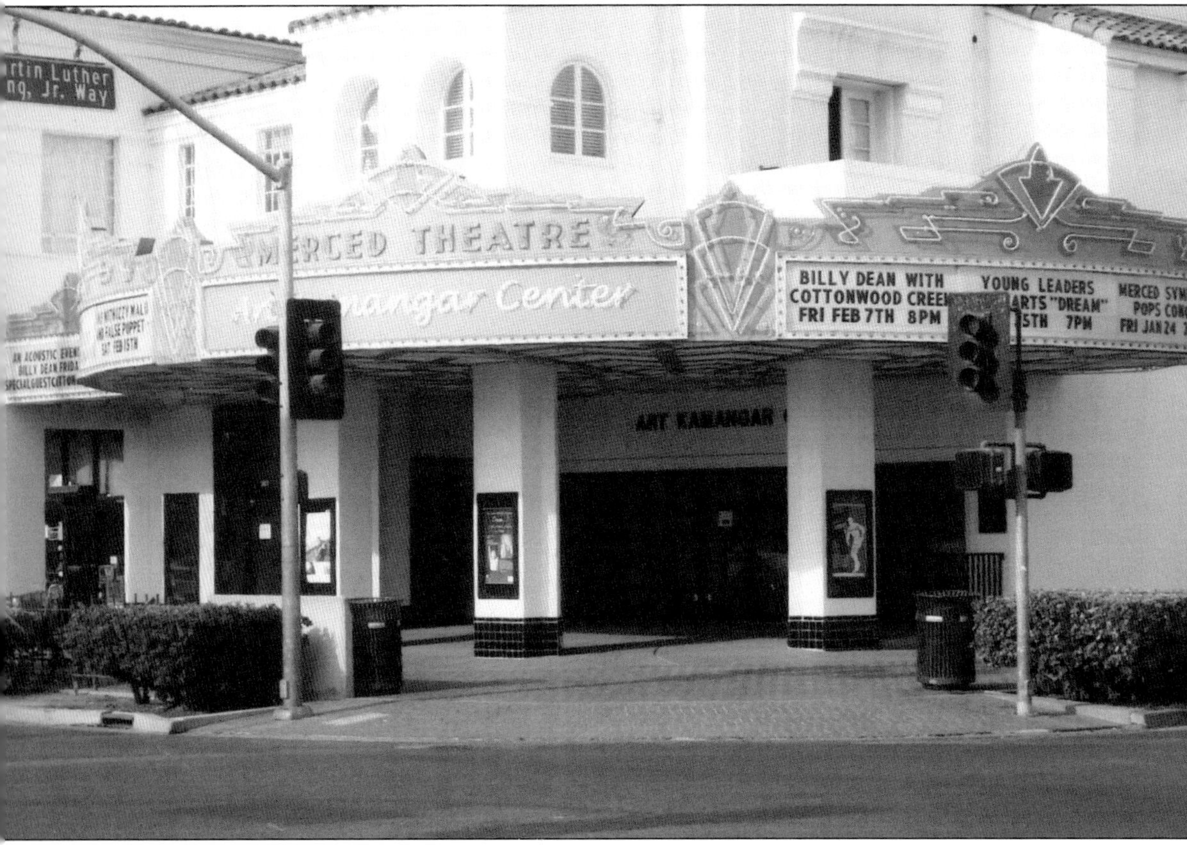

The Merced Theatre is designed in the Art Deco architectural style, which was popular from the 1920s to the 1940s. This theater, which is popular among both residents of and visitors to Merced, is located in the center of Merced's historic downtown—on the corner of West Main Street and Martin Luther King Jr. Way.

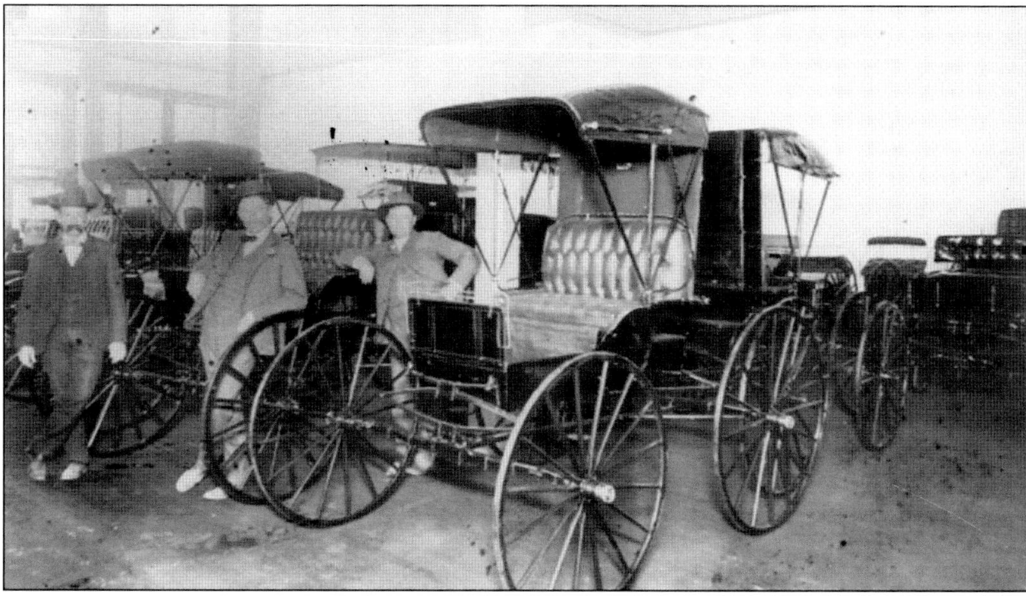

In this photograph, a group of Kern County gentlemen admires several handmade horse-drawn carriages. The carriages' thin wheels made it difficult to travel safely in inclement weather. Kern County was established in the 1860s and consists of about 8,000 square miles of land. (Courtesy of the Kern County Library.)

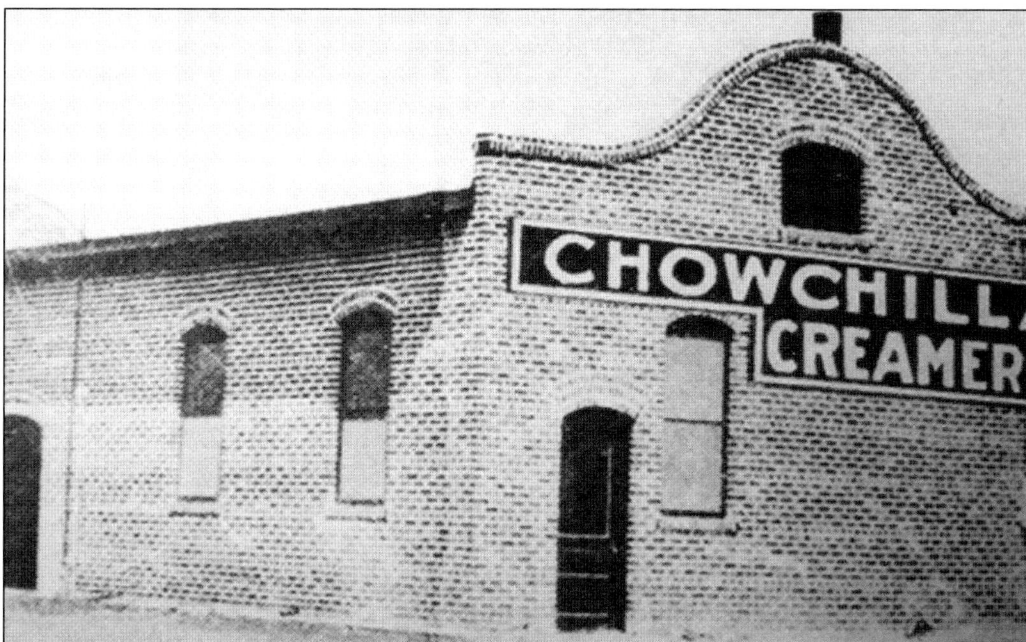

The Chowchilla Creamery in Chowchilla—in Madera County—was opened before Highway 99 was designated as US 99. This was an era of specialty food shops as opposed to supermarkets. The creamery was located close to several farms and ranches in the vicinity of Chowchilla. Chowchilla—which boasts the palm tree–lined Robertson Boulevard—was established in 1844. (Courtesy of the California State Library, Sacramento.)

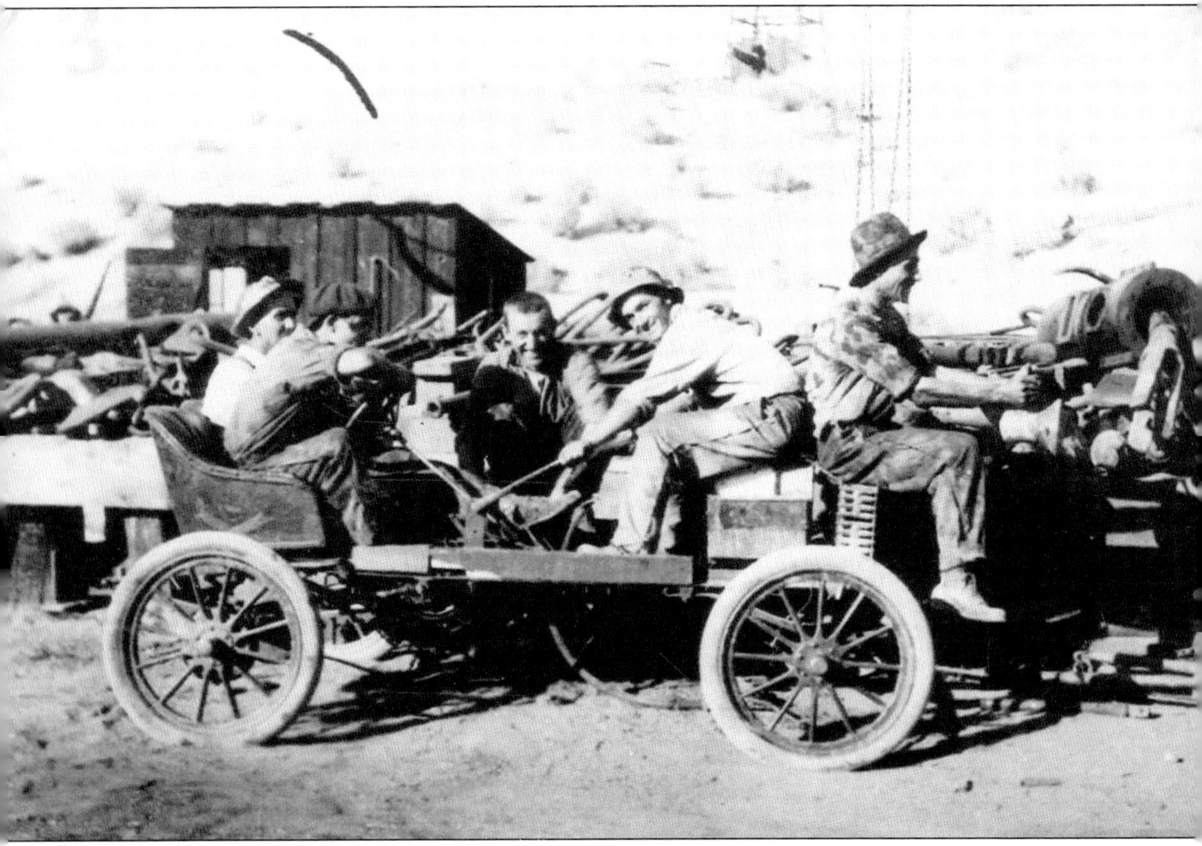

This early Reo automobile was photographed on the Mascot Lease at 25 Hill Road in Taft. Vehicles such as this one were used for transportation, recreation, and to perform work on agricultural lands. The areas surrounding Taft are recreational and agricultural centers. (Courtesy of the Kern County Library.)

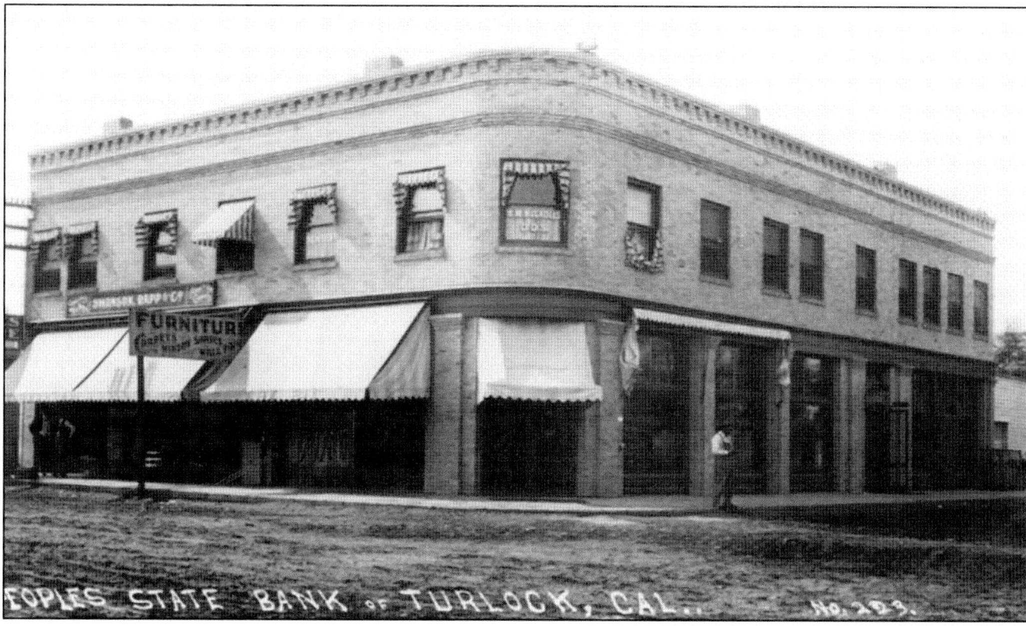

In this photograph of the People's State Bank of Turlock, multiple signs advertising dental services, furniture, shades, and window coverings are visible. The photograph was taken in what was, at the time, the downtown area of Turlock. Turlock is in Stanislaus County, which was formed in 1854. (Courtesy of the California State Library, Sacramento.)

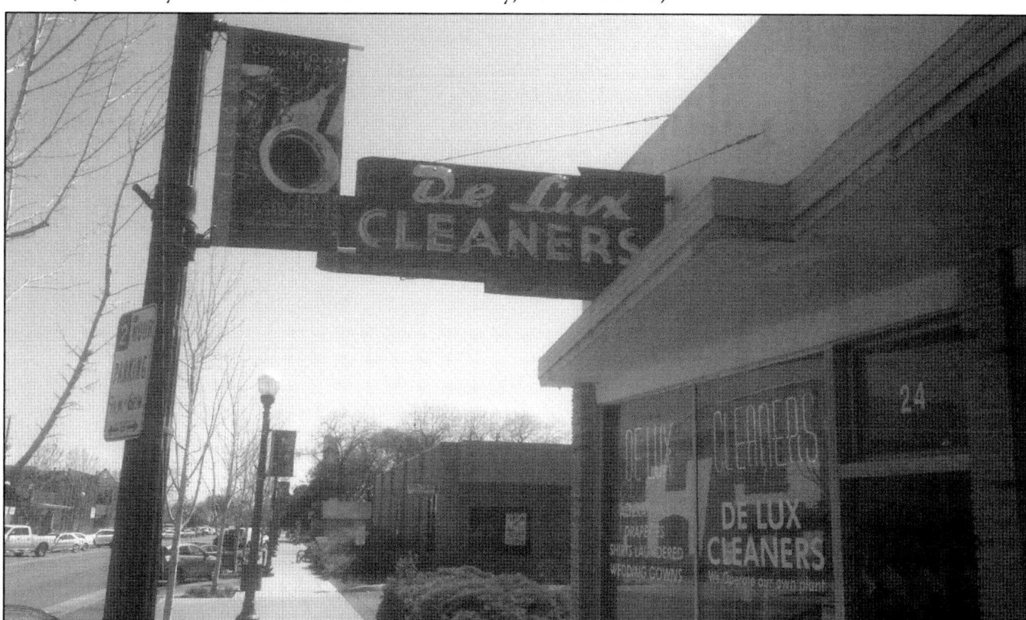

De Lux Cleaners has been operating in Tracy since the 1970s. It is situated along Tenth Street, which is in the center of Tracy's historic downtown. The other prominent street in downtown Tracy is Central Avenue, which runs perpendicular to Tenth Street. Tracy's downtown has been undergoing a steady redevelopment over the past 20 years. When De Lux Cleaners was established, the population of Tracy was about 5,000, as opposed to 80,000 today.

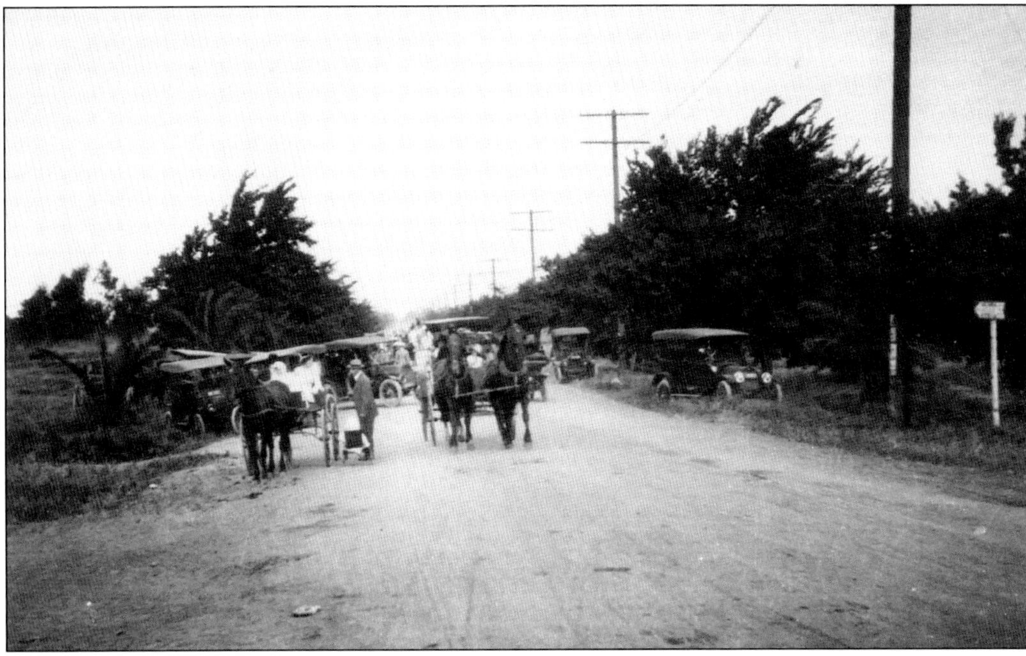

The life of a farmworker was a rough one, particularly during the Depression. Landowners often took advantage of the workers' plight. One individual, Cesar Chavez—born March 31, 1927—took action and worked to help farmworkers in the Central Valley and the Highway 99 corridor. Chavez went on to found the National Farm Workers Association. (Courtesy of the Library of Congress.)

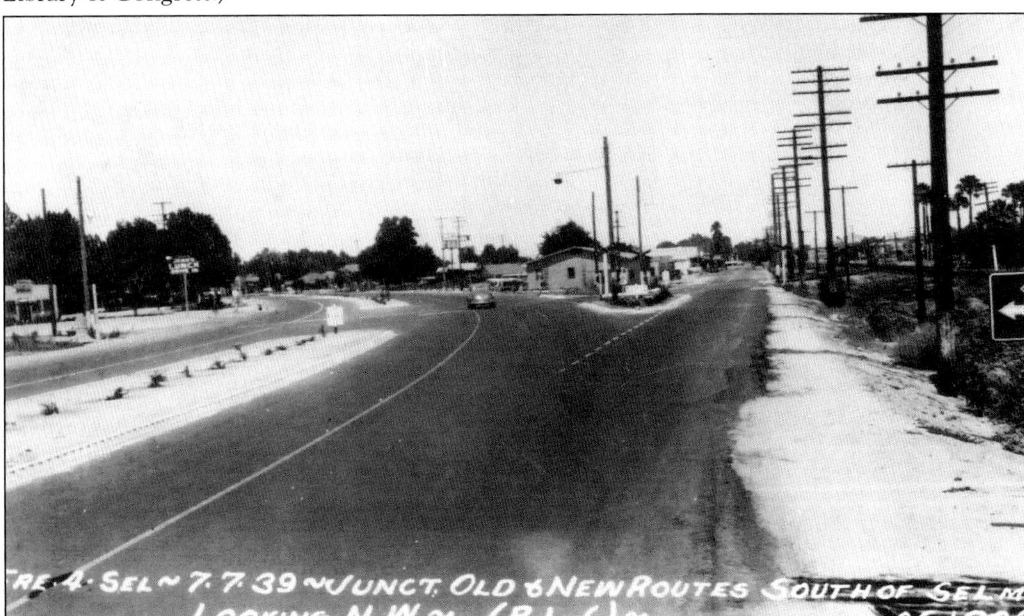

The Federal Emergency Relief Administration (FERA) was formed due to the rampant poverty during the Great Depression. FERA was the name given by the Roosevelt administration to President Hoover's 1932 Emergency Relief Administration (ERA). FERA was replaced by the Works Progress Administration (WPA) in 1935. (Courtesy of the Library of Congress.)

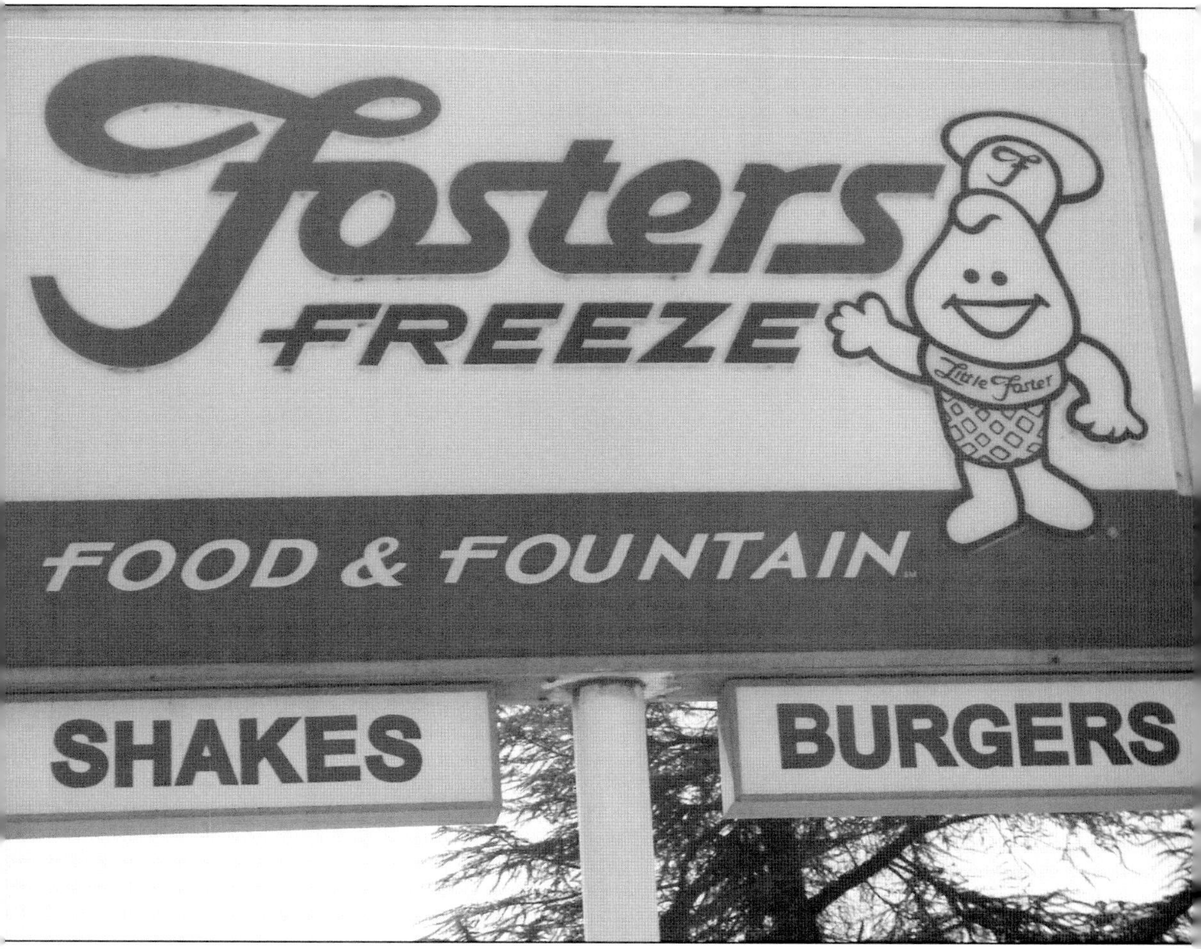

The Atwater Fosters Freeze is similar to many other fast food restaurants along the Highway 99 corridor. Atwater is a city on Highway 99 in Merced County. It is located north of Merced at an elevation of 151 feet. The population when it was incorporated in 1922 is estimated to have been less than 5,000.

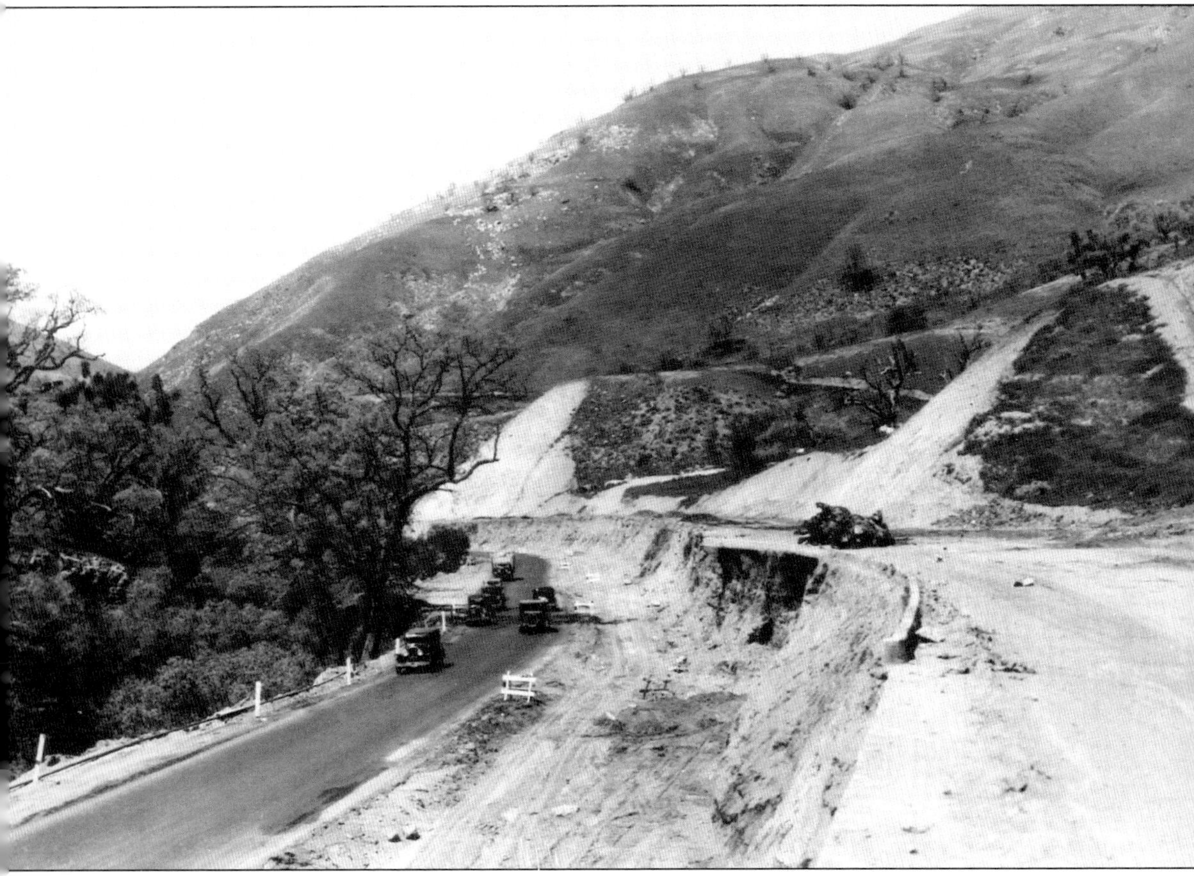

Heavy construction equipment was necessary to perform the excavation and grading that widened and reconfigured this stretch of highway, located south of Bakersfield. The terrain was mountainous, as opposed to the generally flat terrain of the Central Valley. Simple mechanical transits, surveyor's rods, and metal measuring tapes were used to perform the land surveying for this project. (Copyright © California Department of Transportation.)

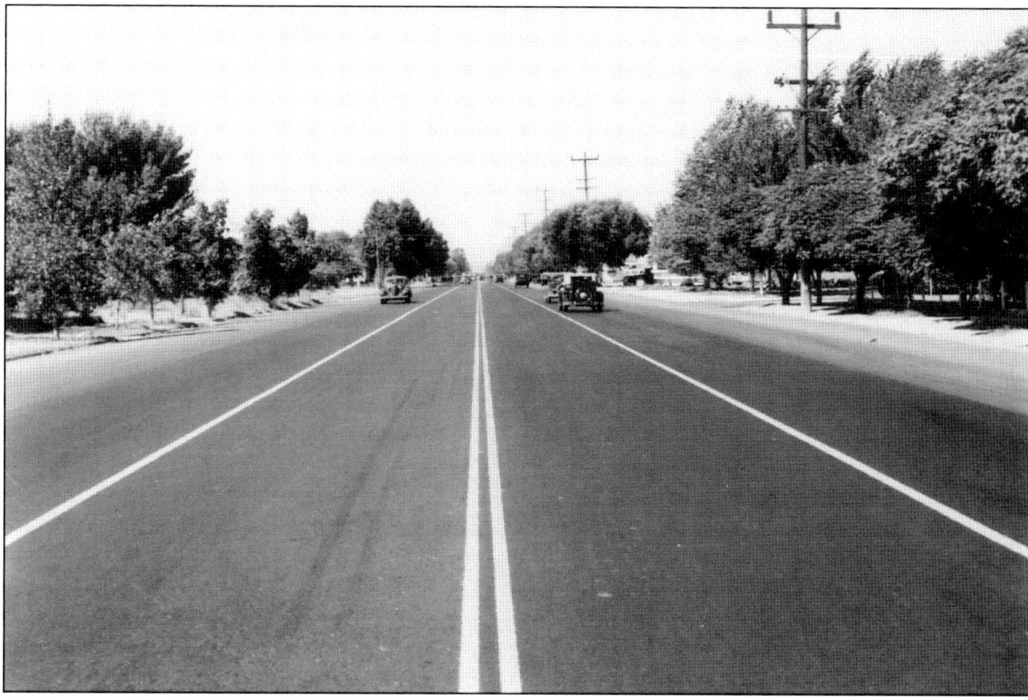

At the time that this photograph—depicting a four-lane section of Highway 99—was taken, the United States was still in the midst of the Great Depression. In addition to a 25 percent or greater rate of unemployment, small businesses and farms suffered financial reversals as well. (Copyright © California Department of Transportation.)

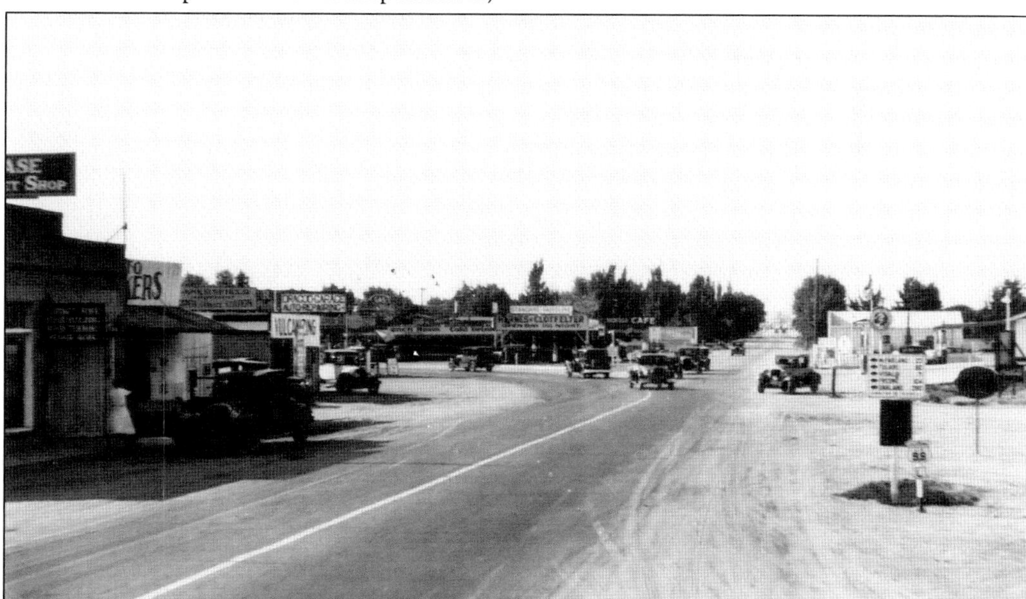

Dragoo Garage and Auto Repairing, Standard Gasoline, and other small businesses are visible in this photograph. Oildale is a suburb of Bakersfield, which was home to many emigrants from Oklahoma. Oildale, which is in Kern County, was founded in 1909. (Copyright © California Department of Transportation.)

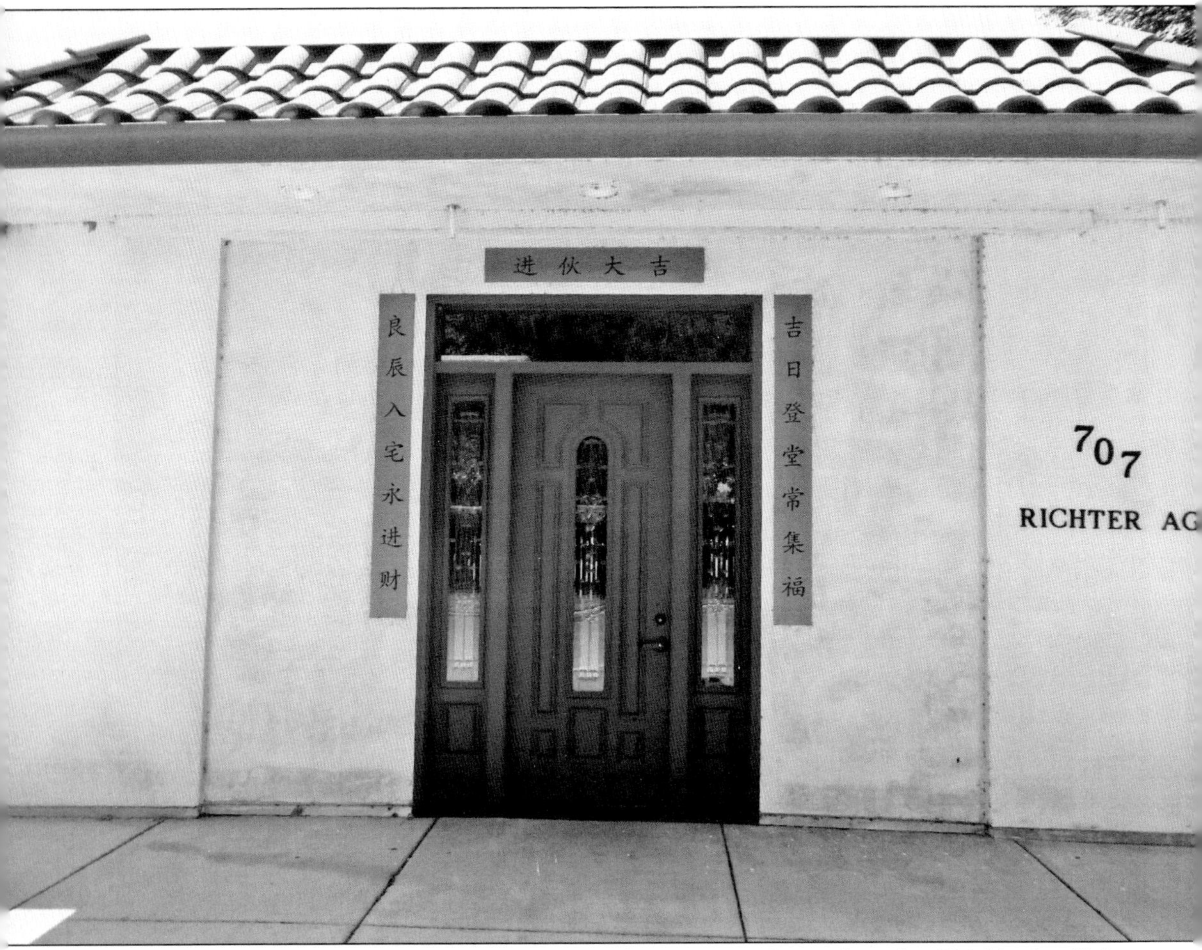

One of the remaining buildings in Colusa's Chinatown is located in the 700 block of Main Street. It was built in the traditional Chinese style of architecture, which includes a protruding sloped roof and Chinese symbols surrounding the doorway. There were three tunnels underneath Main Street that the Chinese residents used for gambling, opium smoking, and to hide from the authorities whether they were guilty of a crime or not. While the author mentions these vices, he still maintains the highest level of respect for the past and current Chinese American populations in California.

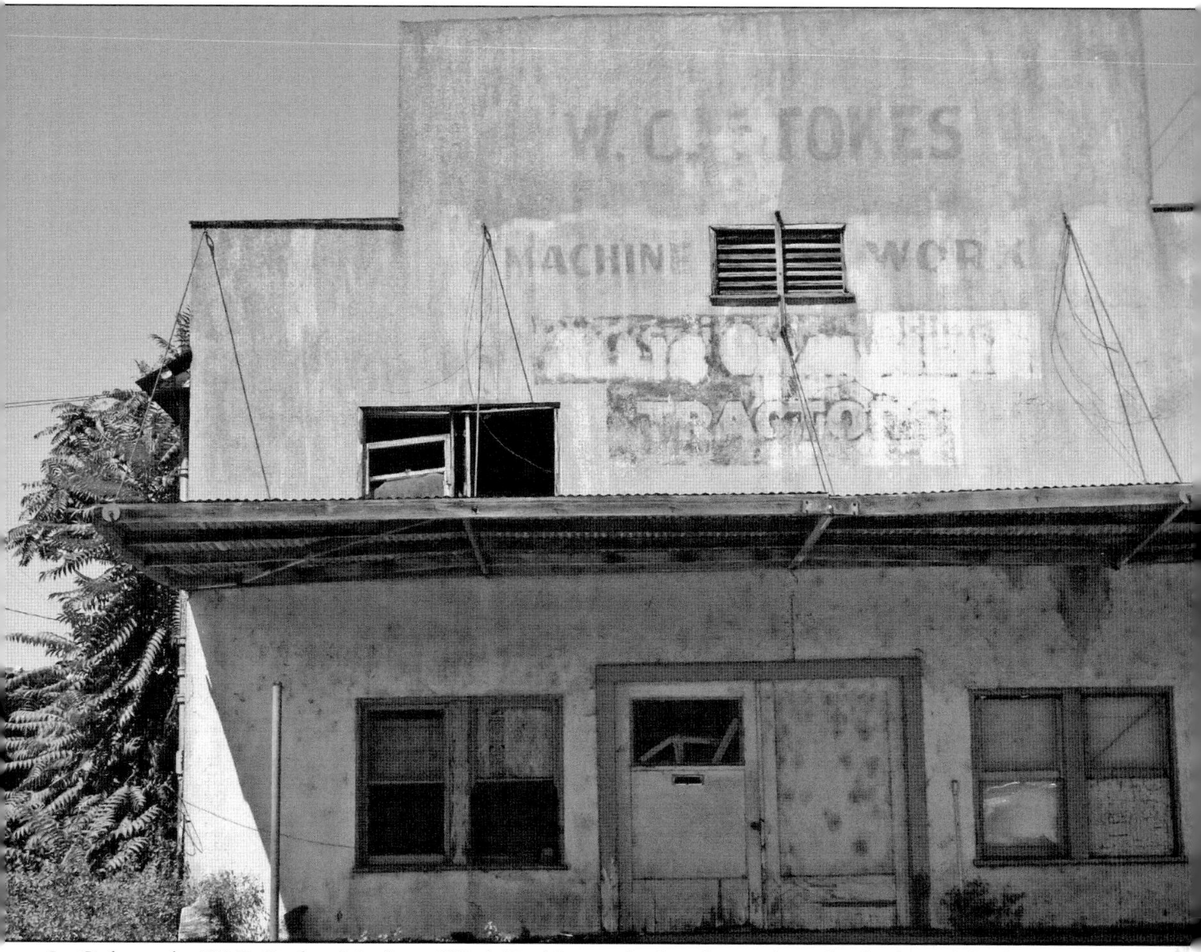

In Colusa, the W.C. Stokes Machine Work Building, which is located on the fringes of the historic downtown area, was built in the traditional Western frontier style of architecture. The building was designed with a large storefront on which a prominent sign was painted. As noted on the sign, this business performed work on tractors and other agricultural implements.

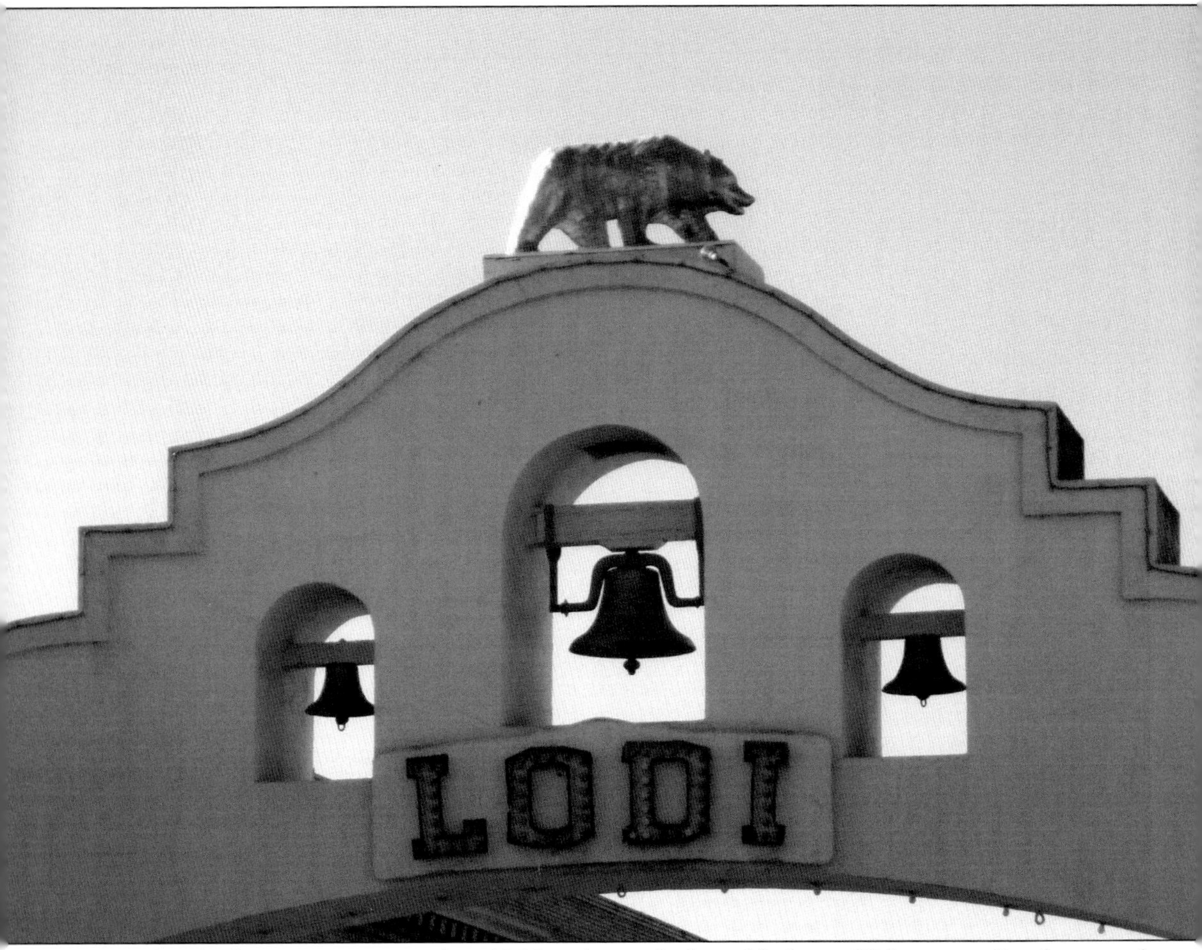

Lodi, which was incorporated in 1906, is located along Highway 99 between Stockton and Sacramento. A group of families decided to establish a school around 1860, which they built on a site near Cherokee Lane and Turner Road. Around 1870, the Central Pacific Railroad created a new route through Lodi. In 1906, the population of Lodi is estimated to have been less than 5,000.

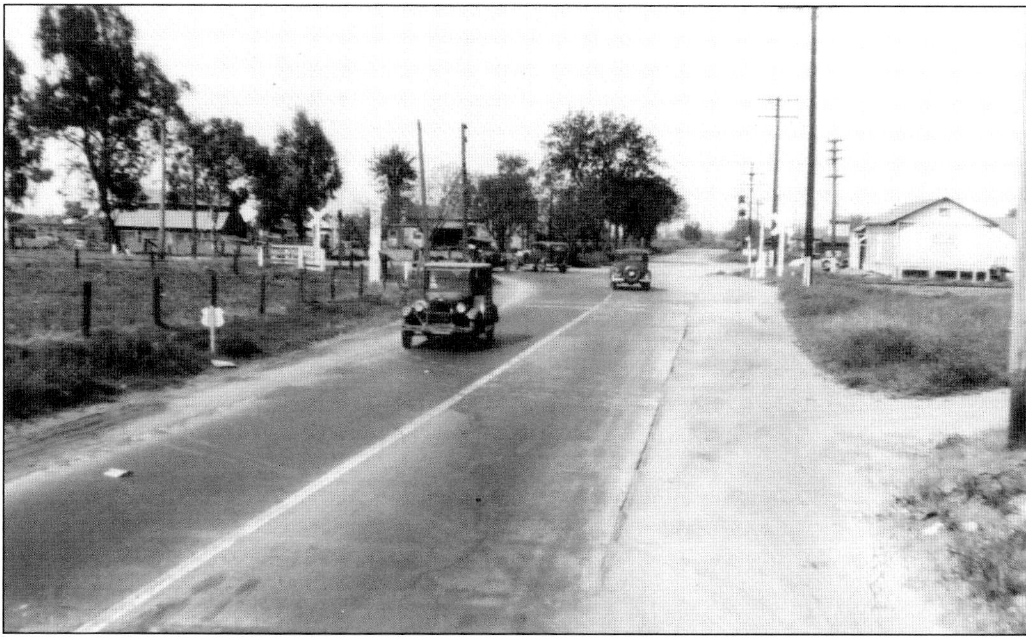

This photograph shows US 99 as a two-lane paved road with an unpaved shoulder, which provided a safe means for cars to exit the roadway and access roadside businesses or agricultural facilities. A railroad crossing is visible in the background. The photograph was taken in the 1930s. (Copyright © California Department of Transportation.)

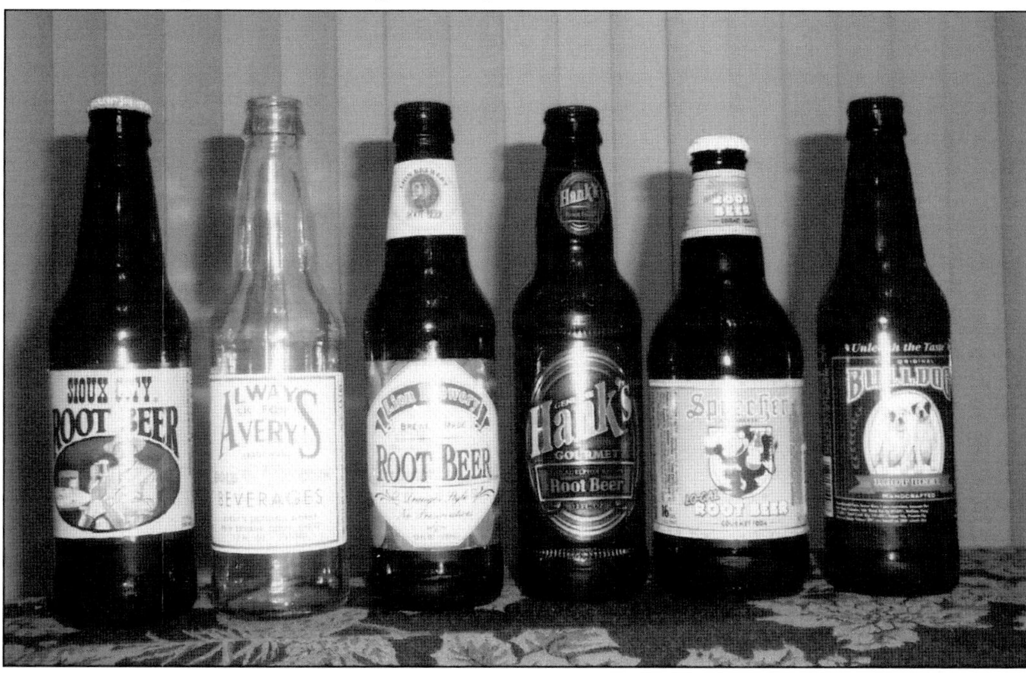

Soft drinks—including root beers—have been advertised and sold along Highway 99 from the time of the highway's origins. A favorite old-fashioned beverage was sarsaparilla. Sarsaparilla often contained extracts from the *Smilax regelii* plant. It was popular from the mid-1800s through the mid-1900s.

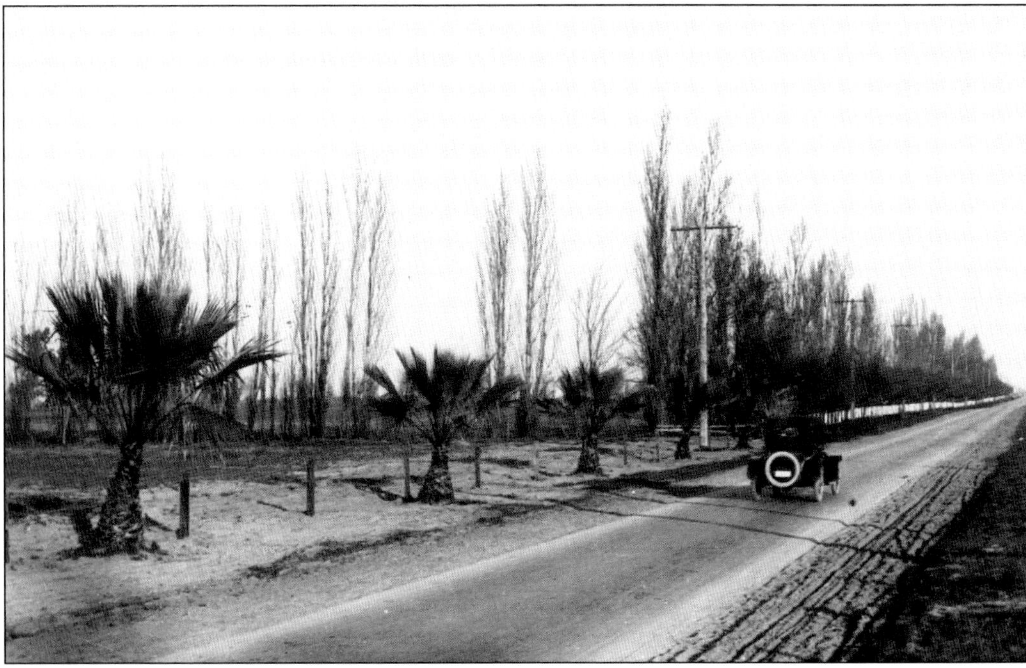

There were several makes of automobile in production by the time that Highway 99 had been paved. One of these was the Packard, which was an American luxury car manufactured by the Packard Motor Car Company of Detroit, Michigan. Another was the Buick. The Ford Model T was one of the most common vehicles in production at that time. (Copyright © California Department of Transportation.)

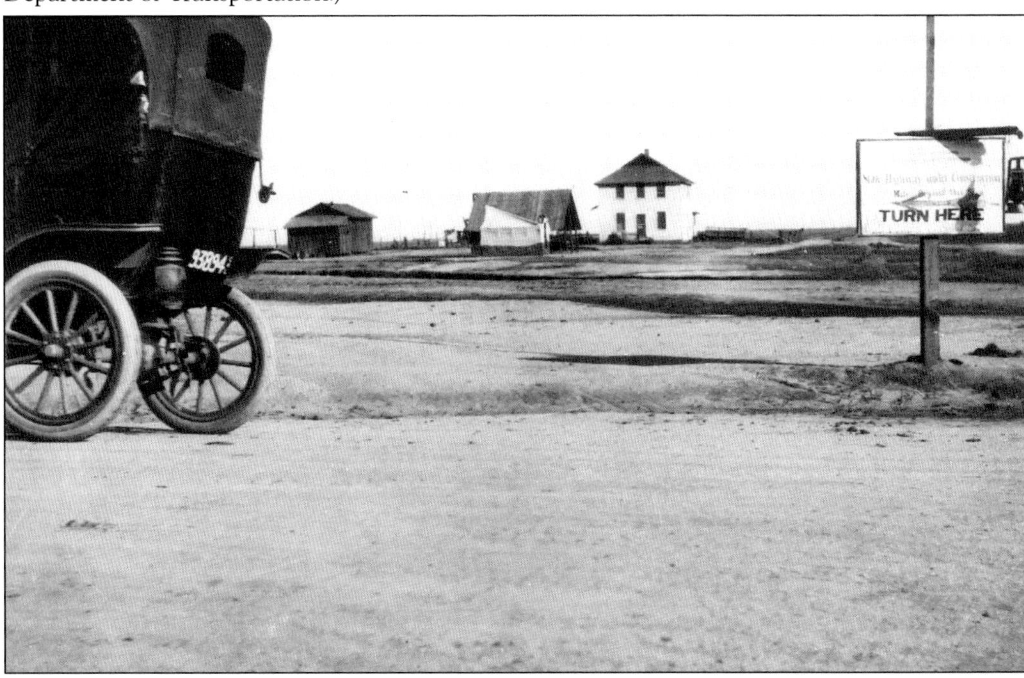

Initially, there were numerous automobile manufacturers, but by the end of 1930s, most American cars were made by General Motors, Ford, and Chrysler. (Courtesy of the Library of Congress.)

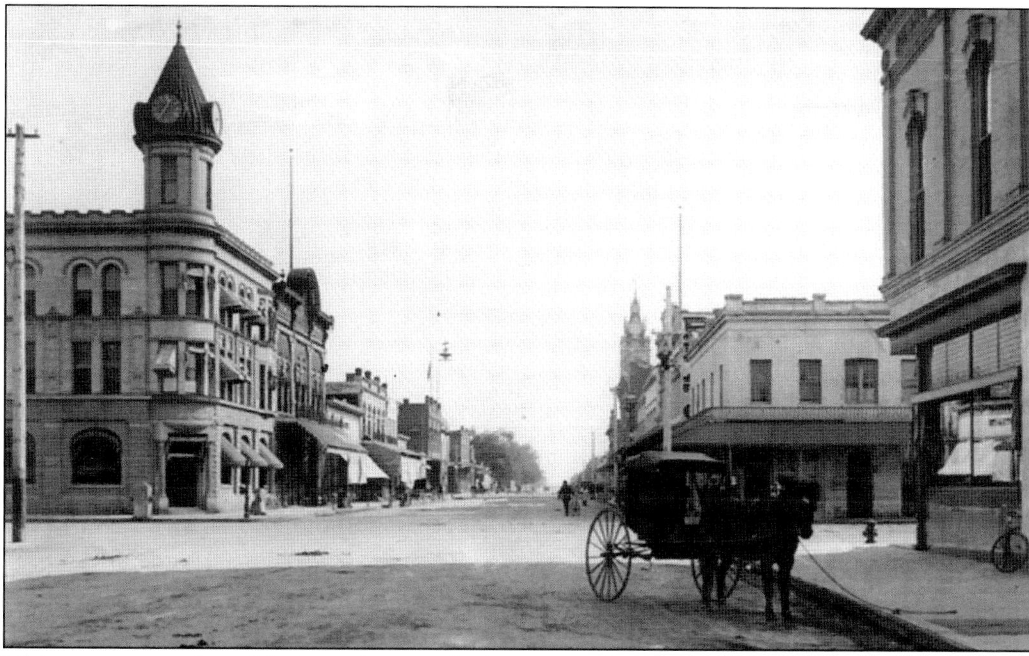

This street scene from Modesto shows a clock tower and several modern amenities. At the time this photograph was taken, horses were still a common mode of transportation—as illustrated by the carriages parked along the side of the road. Currently, the Modesto Regional Fire Authority provides fire protection services for Modesto and Salida, which borders Modesto on the north side. (Courtesy of the California State Library, Sacramento.)

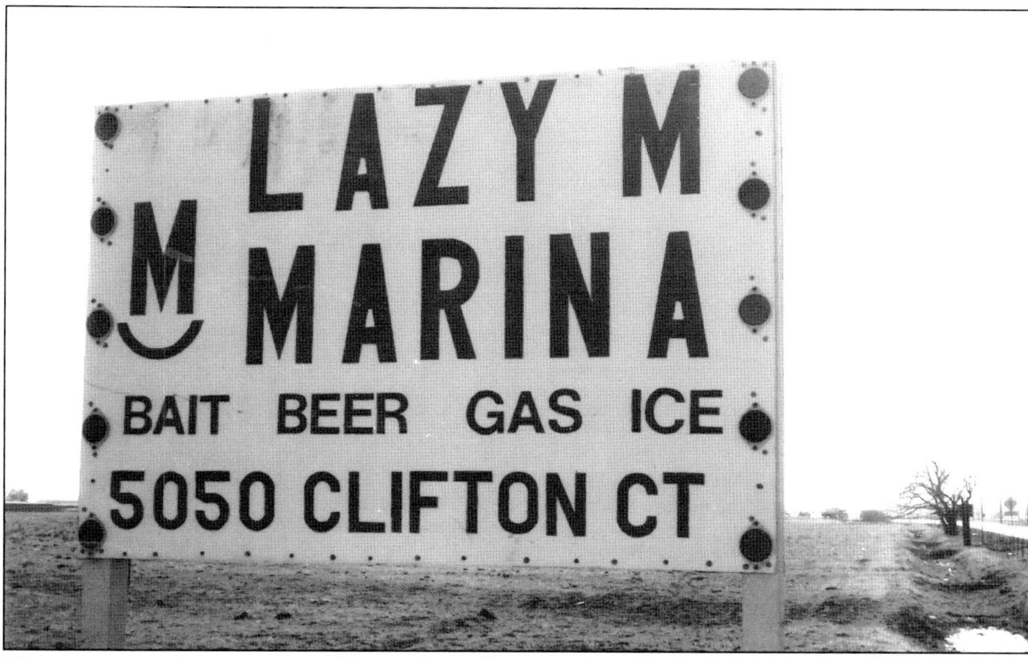

The tourism and recreation industry along the US 99 corridor provided many cities and towns with their identities and livelihoods. This is reflected in festivals that still occur today, such as the Melon Festival in Turlock and the Dry Bean Festival in Tracy.

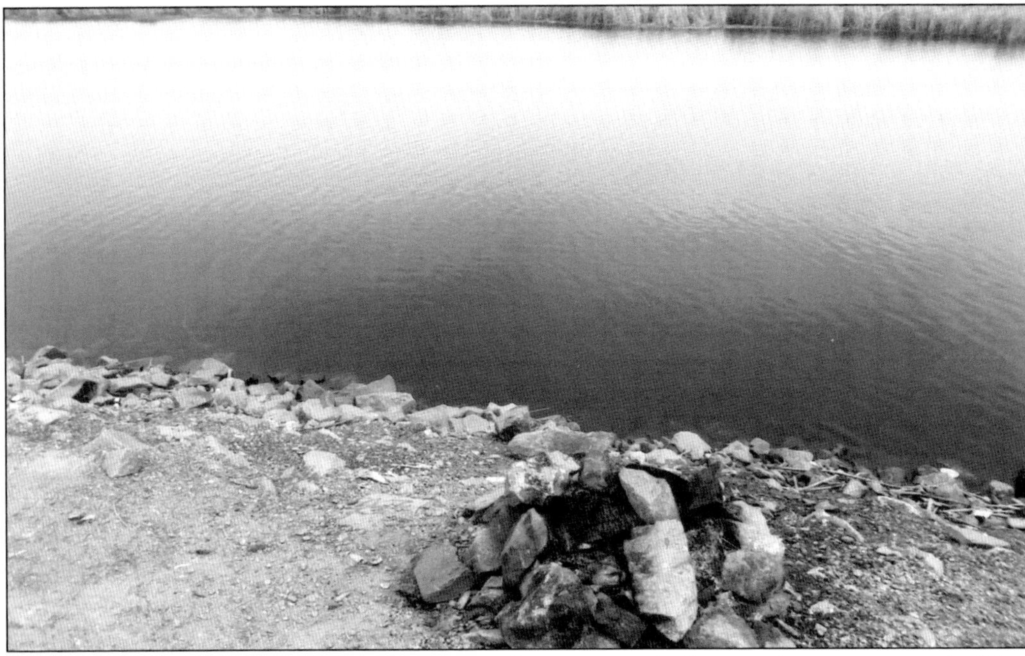

The early residents of Holt, including those of Japanese and Chinese descent, routinely fished in Whiskey Slough. To smoke the fish and to keep warm, fire pits were built on the top of the levee. These practices can still be observed today, as fishermen still regularly fish for bass and bluegill. There is also a Jewish population along Highway 99 in the larger cities of Stockton, Fresno, and Bakersfield.

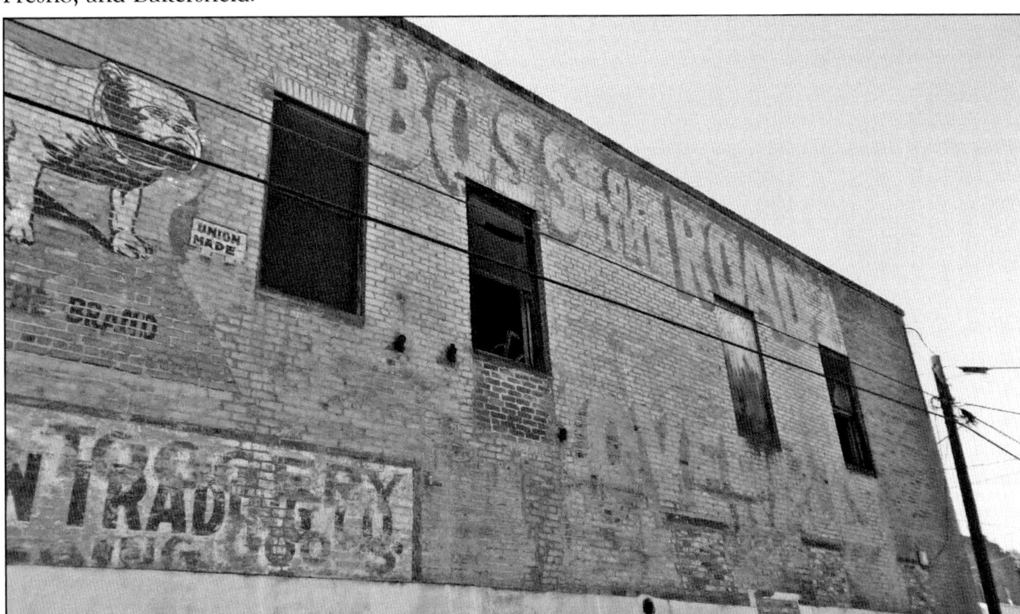

On the side of a picturesque brick building in one of Colusa's industrial sectors is a prominent sign advertising Boss of the Road overalls. The company that made this clothing, C.B. Cones and Son, was based in Indianapolis. These rugged American-made overalls that were manufactured from the 1860s to the early 1900s were sold to railroad workers as well as other hard-working individuals.

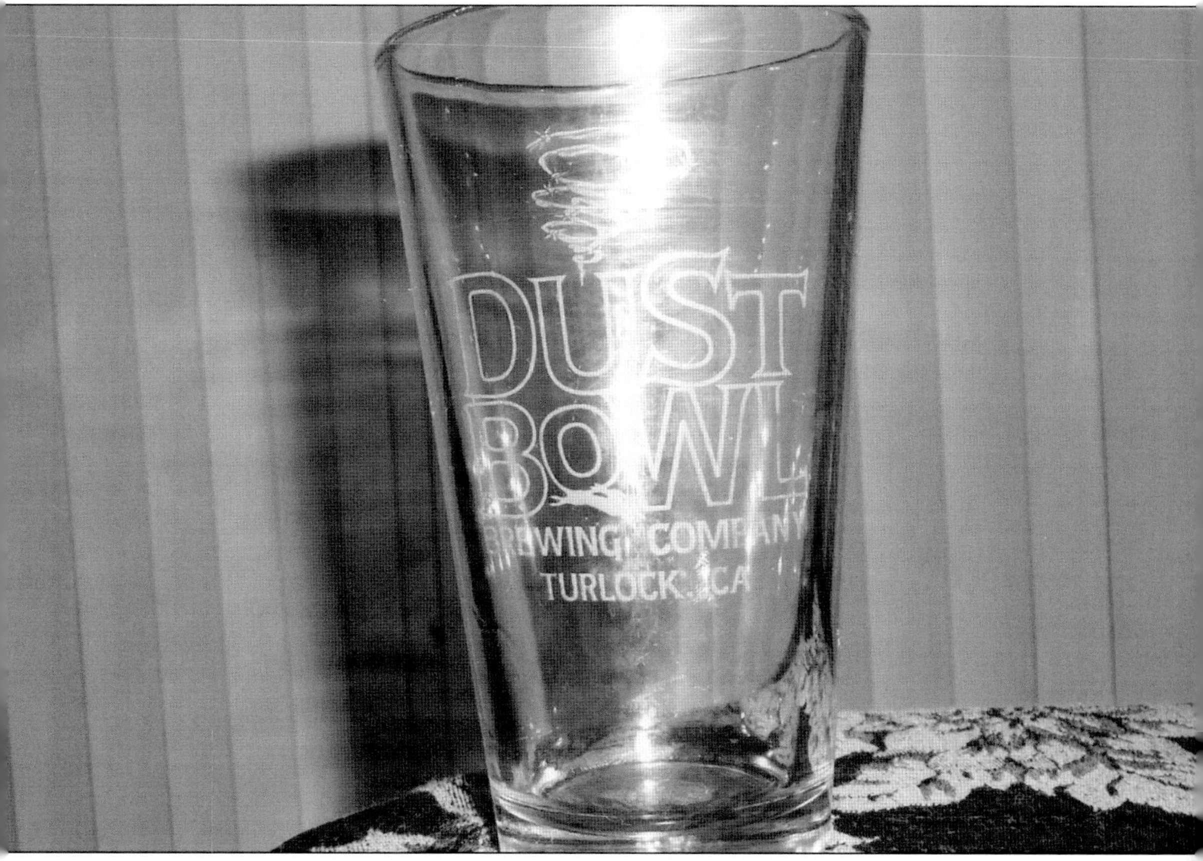

The Dust Bowl Brewing Company is a popular bar and restaurant. It is themed as a reminder of the obstacles that drought refuges faced when they attempted to reestablish their lives in California. It is located at 200 West Main Street in Turlock, at the center of the historic downtown area.

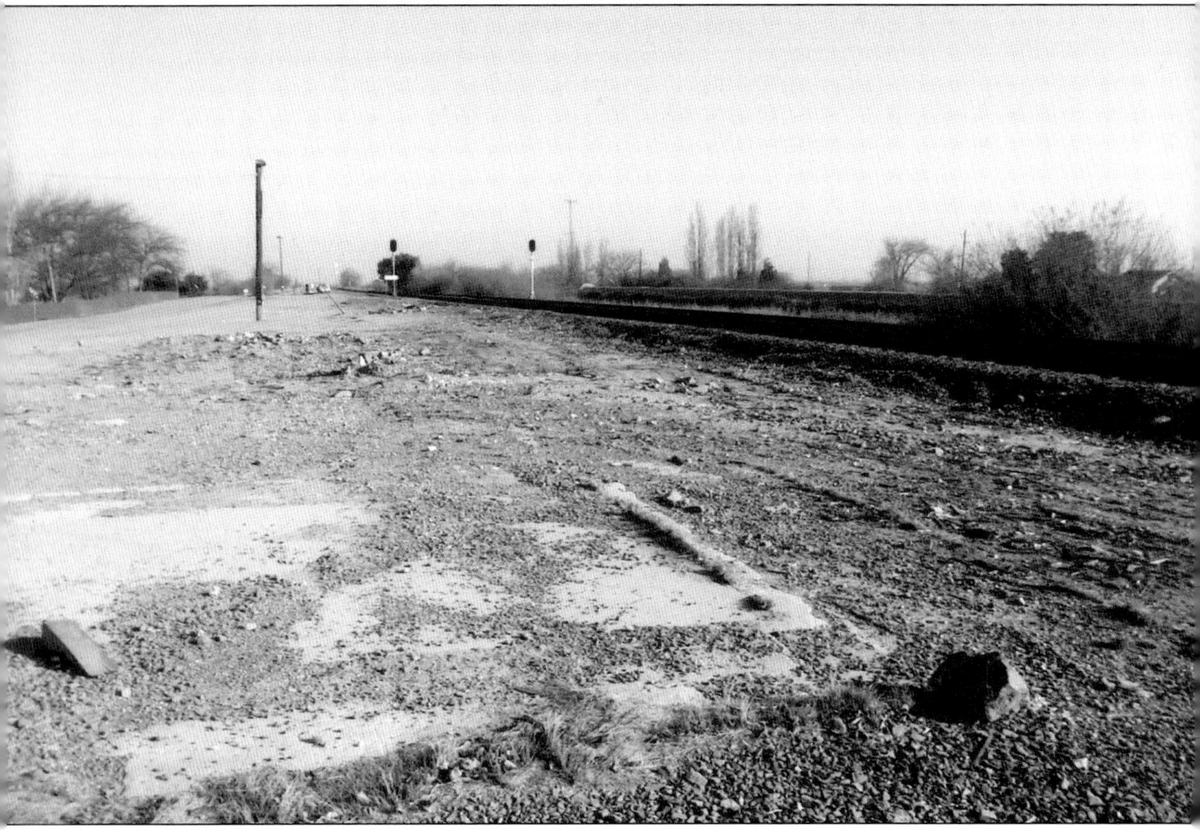

The railroad station in Holt was built in the 1900s and removed in 1970. This foundation is the only visible remnant of old station. Holt once served as an entertainment center for local communities. It was continuously populated by Chinese Americans and Japanese Americans from the 1880s through the 1930s, with a peak population of about 100.

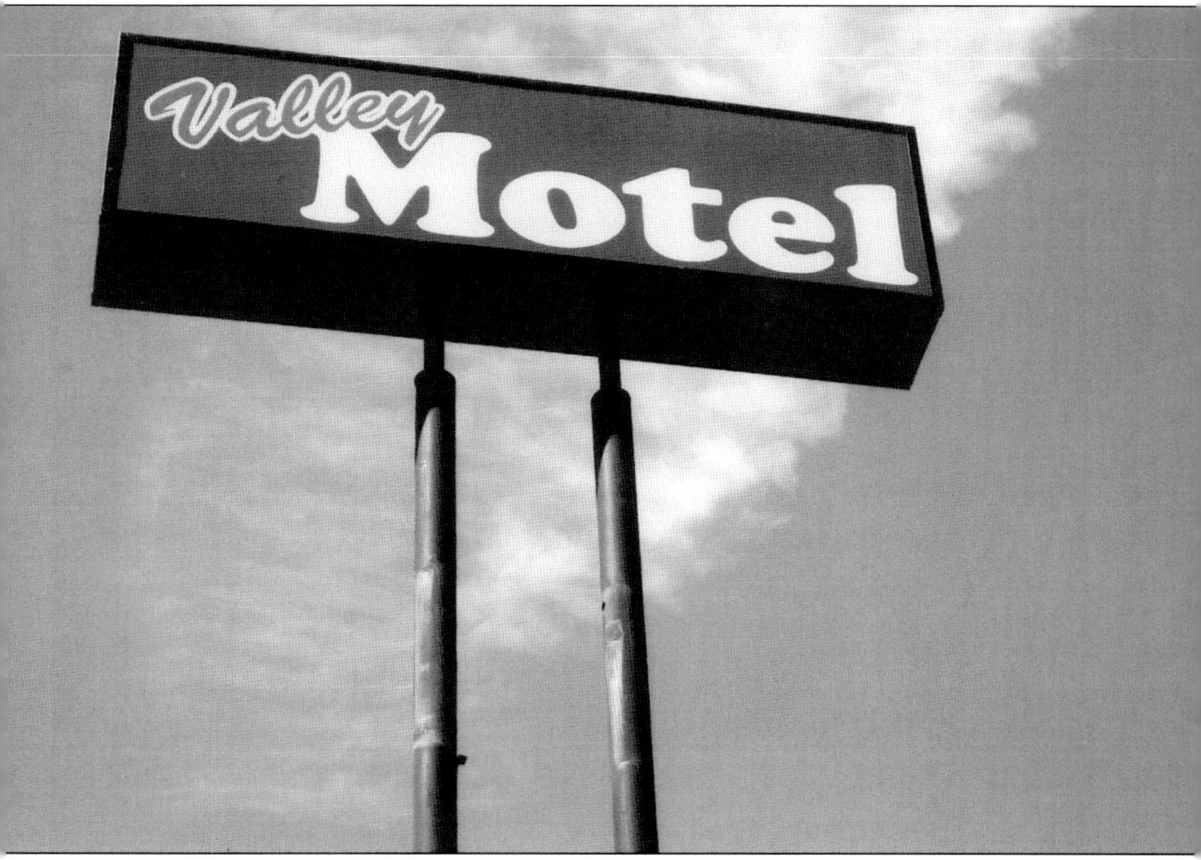

From the late-1800s until the mid-1900s, a wide variety of building materials were used to construct signs, columns, buildings, houses, and other structures. The types of material used inside and outside of homes varied greatly due to the cost, resilience, and appearance of the material. Wood framing was a common method of constructing buildings, while steel was used for towers and columns. Concrete block and brick were also popular. Brick buildings, which were attractive and popular, were typically unreinforced and did not offer much resistance to seismic forces.

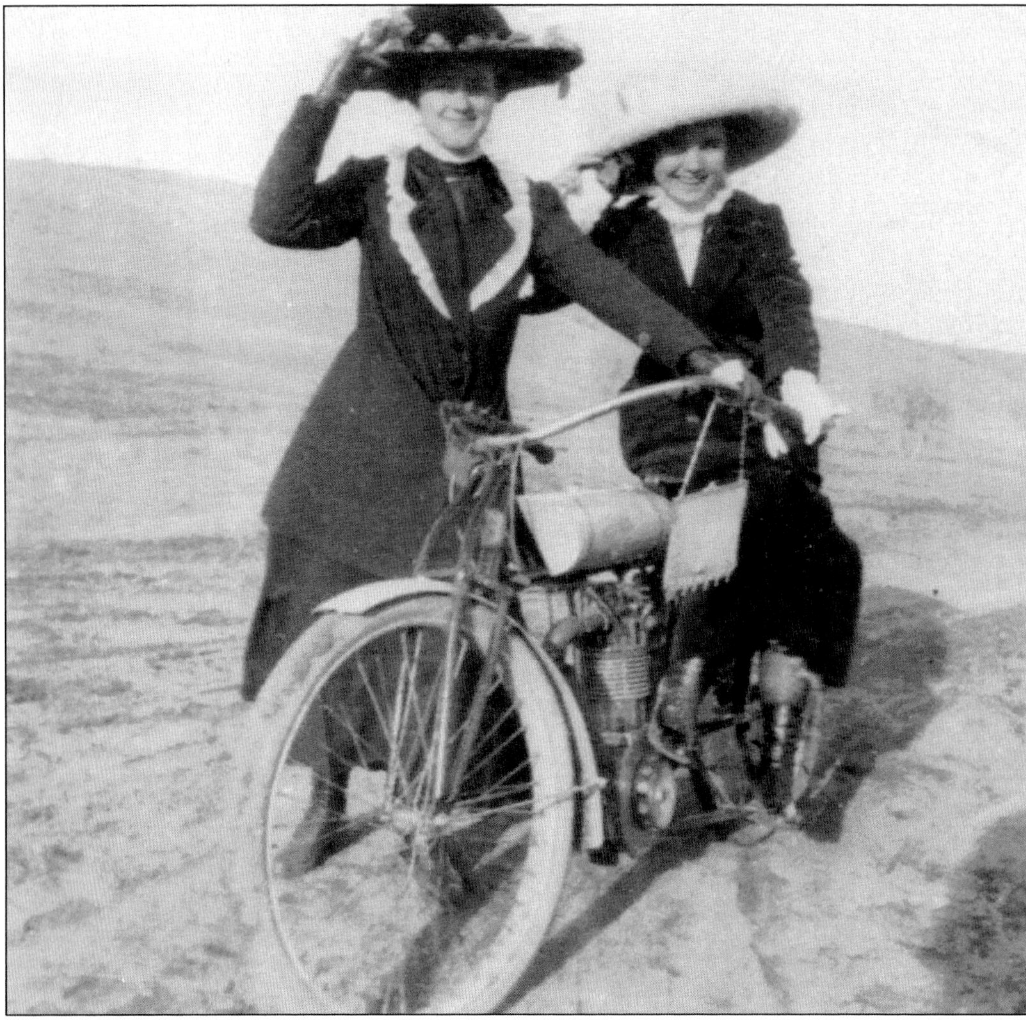

Two young ladies are seen here standing next to an early-vintage motorcycle. It is likely a Harley-Davidson, Indian, or one of the other American-made motorcycles that were in production at that time. The State of California began registering motor vehicles in 1905. (Courtesy of the Kern County Library.)

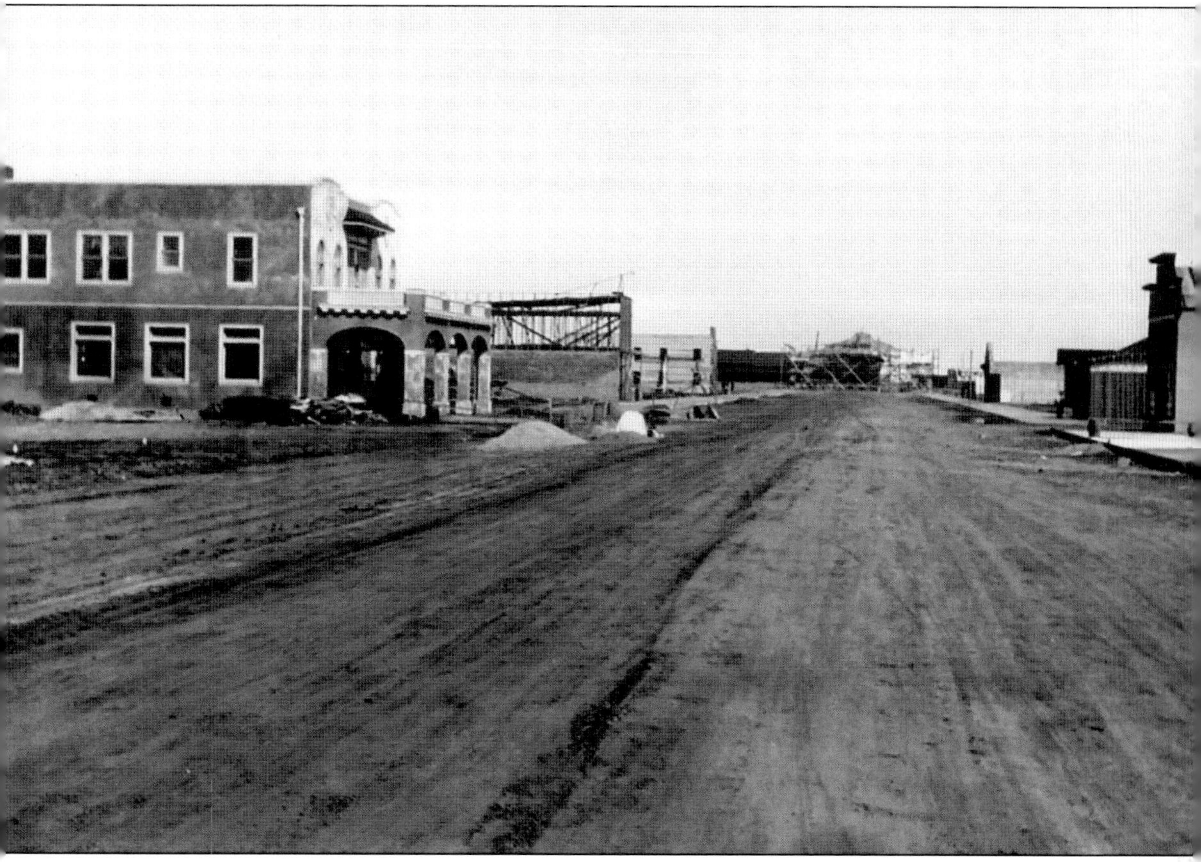

The palm lined Robertson Boulevard—along with other nearby roadways—serve as the main streets of Chowchilla. Chowchilla is located along Highway 99 between Merced and Fresno. Many buildings, including the famous arch, had been built by the time that the highway was being designated US 99 in the 1920s. (Courtesy of the California State Library, Sacramento.)

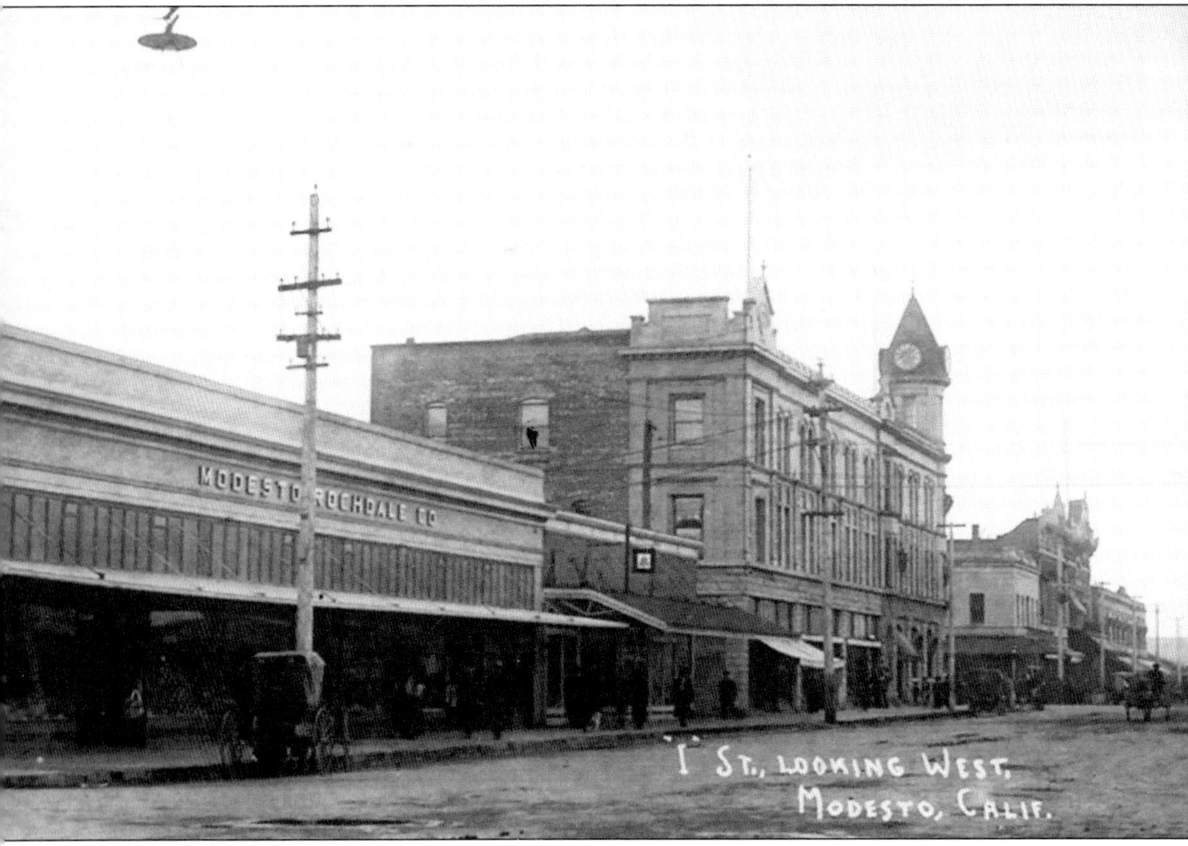

This photograph is of I Street in downtown Modesto. I Street travels through what is now a busy commercial and retail district. In the 1880s, homes were built east of the existing downtown. Today, only one of those prominent homes remains: the McHenry Mansion, built in 1882–1883. (Courtesy of the California State Library, Sacramento.)

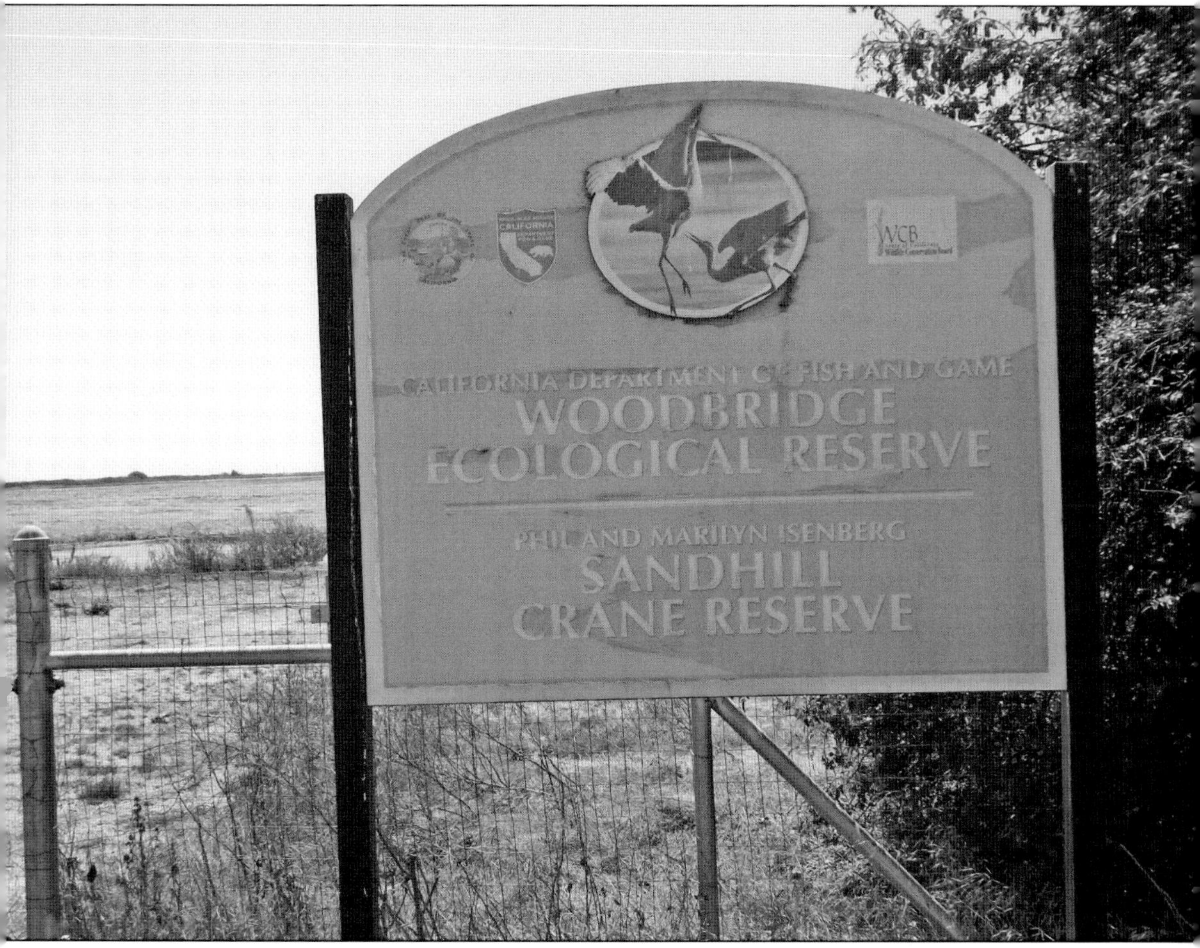

The Woodbridge Ecological Reserve, which is also known as the Sandhill Crane Reserve, is located to the north of Stockton. The cranes are a natural treasure that have been in this location much longer than people have, so they deserve sensitivity and consideration. Approximately 20,000 visitors per year visit the reserve primarily to observe the ritualistic dance of the sandhill cranes.

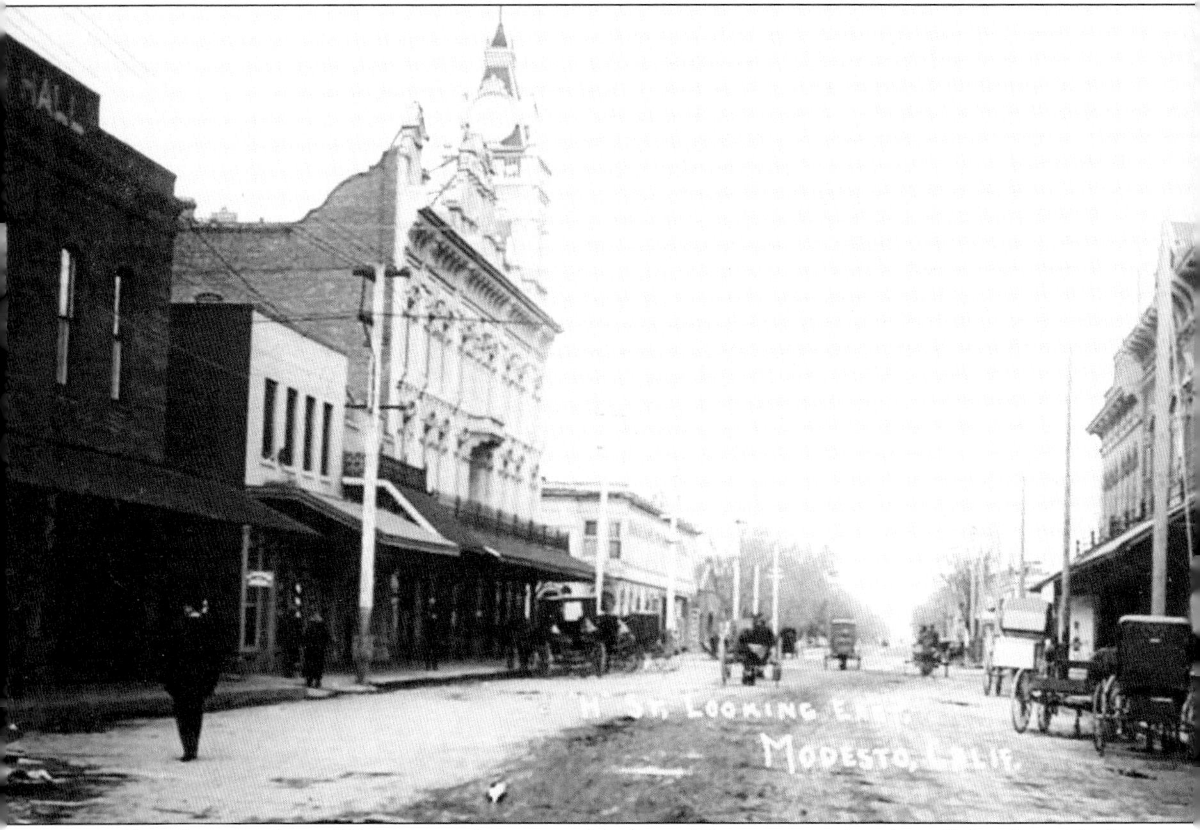

This photograph is of H Street in downtown Modesto. The city was already well developed before State Route 4 and Highway 99 were constructed. In a few decades, downtown Modesto would be well used by local teenagers who had embraced automobiles and the newly developed cruising culture. (Courtesy of the California State Library, Sacramento.)

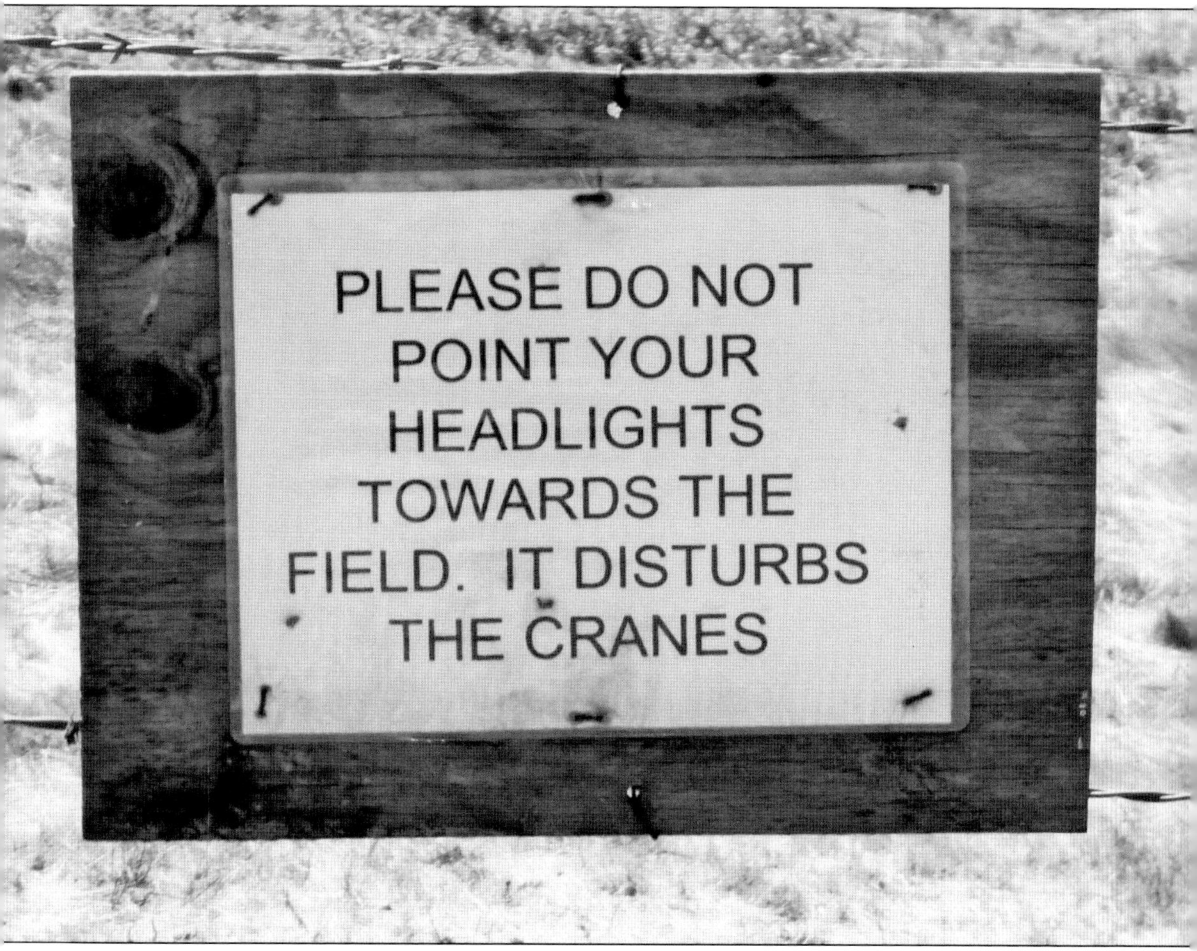

This crudely made but highly effective sign posted at the Woodbridge Ecological Reserve warns visitors about the cranes' vulnerabilities. The cranes are active at night, so they deserve the visitors' contribution to the quality of their lives in the reserve. The sign is posted between the parking lot and the reserve itself.

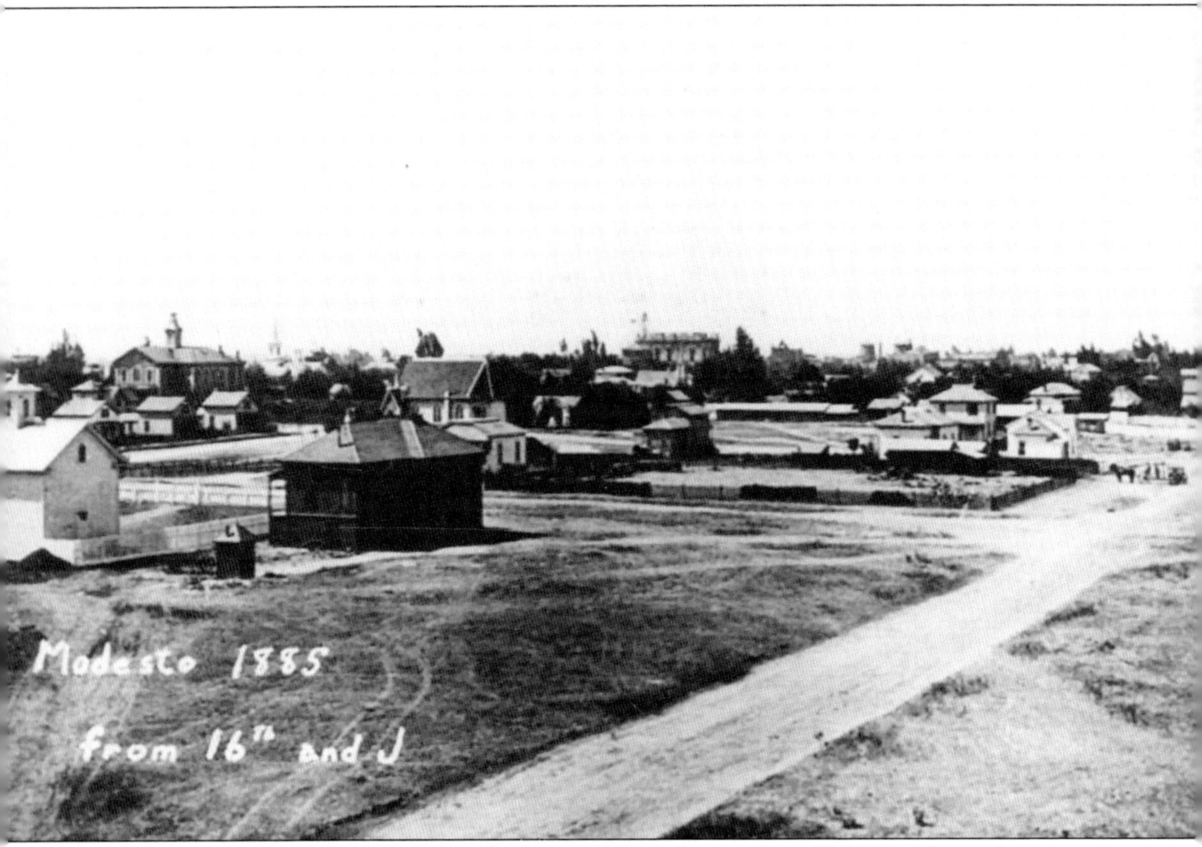

This 1885 photograph of Modesto, which was taken at Sixteenth and J Streets, shows the beginnings of the town. It was taken a few blocks from what would become State Route 4, and then US 99. The roads of the time were simply cleared spots in the soil, which became impassible following a strong rain. (Courtesy of the California State Library, Sacramento.)

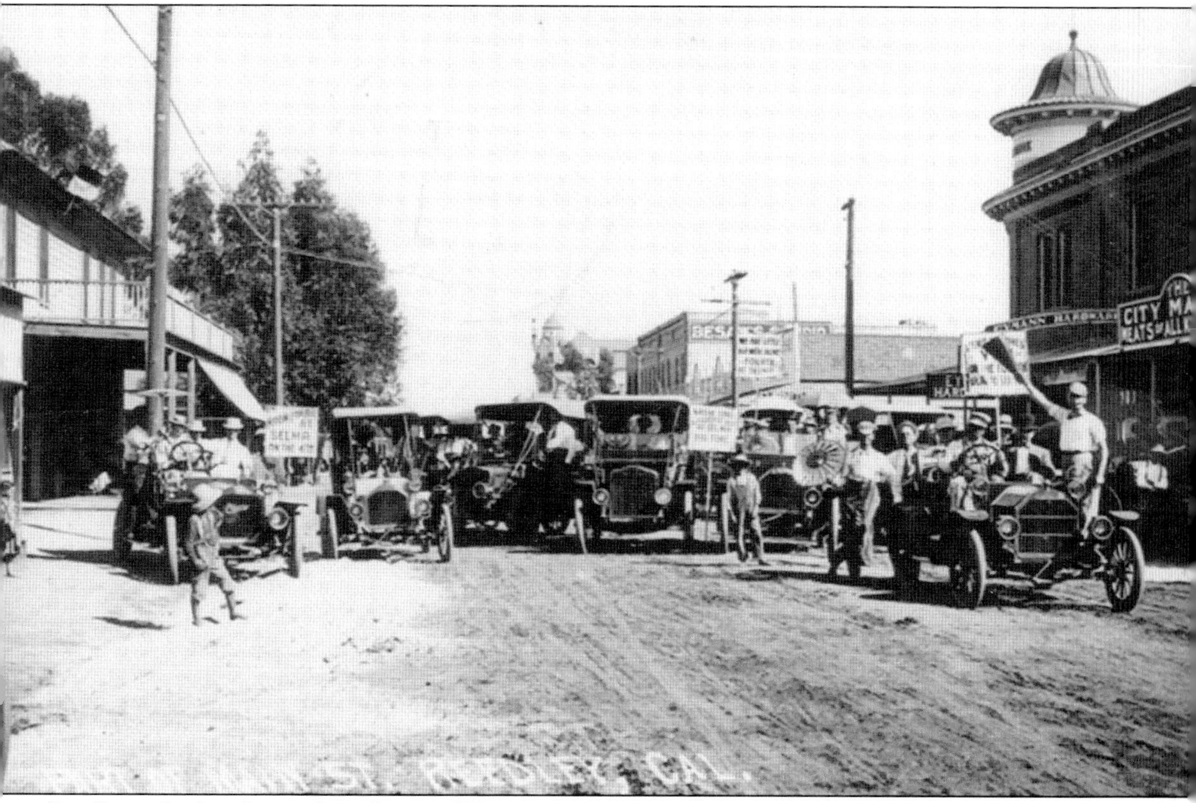

Reedley, which is located southeast of Fresno in Fresno County, is an agricultural center that is near to a number of recreational areas. Reedley was incorporated in 1913. An important element of Reedley's culture is the colony of German Mennonites whose strong traditions were, and still are, a great benefit to the city. (Courtesy of the California State Library, Sacramento.)

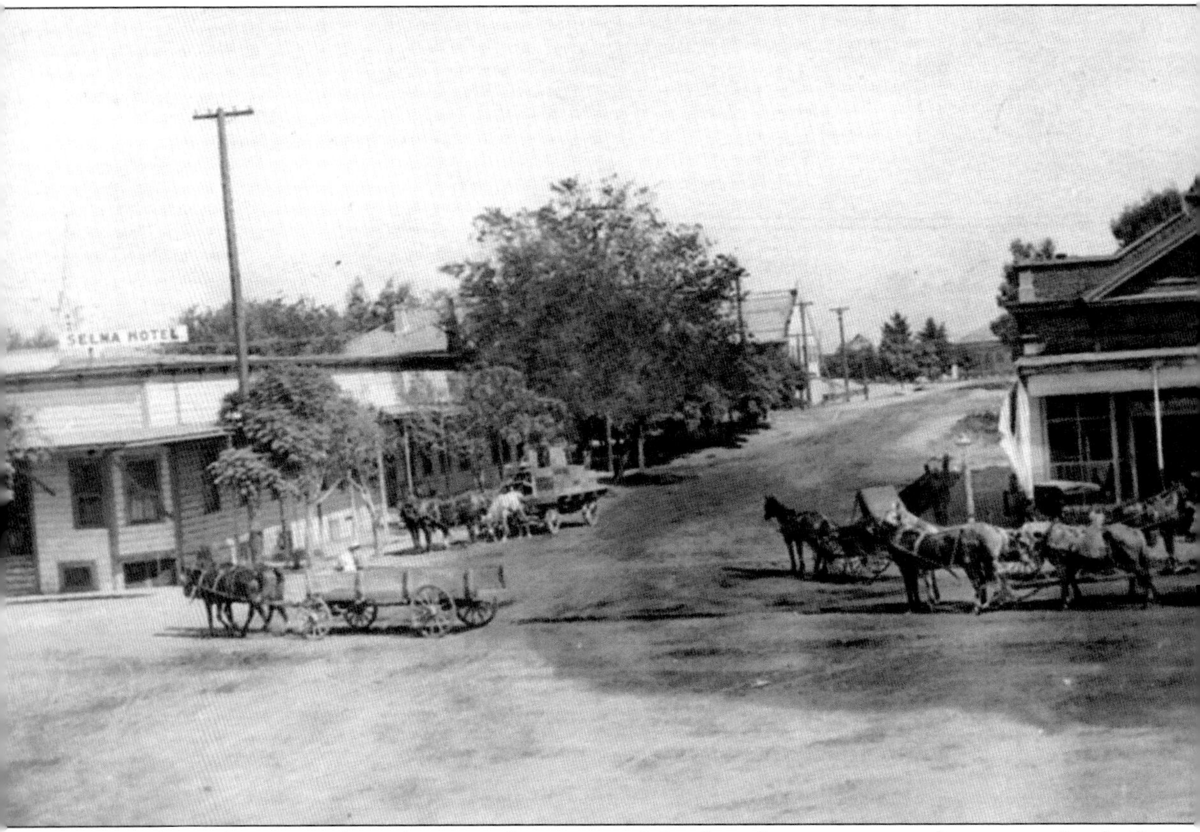

In the early 1900s, the Selma Hotel was one of the few places in town where an individual could find lodging. Selma was formed in the 1870s and was associated with the Southern Pacific Railroad. Selma is located Fresno County, to the south of Fresno. (Courtesy of the California State Library, Sacramento.)

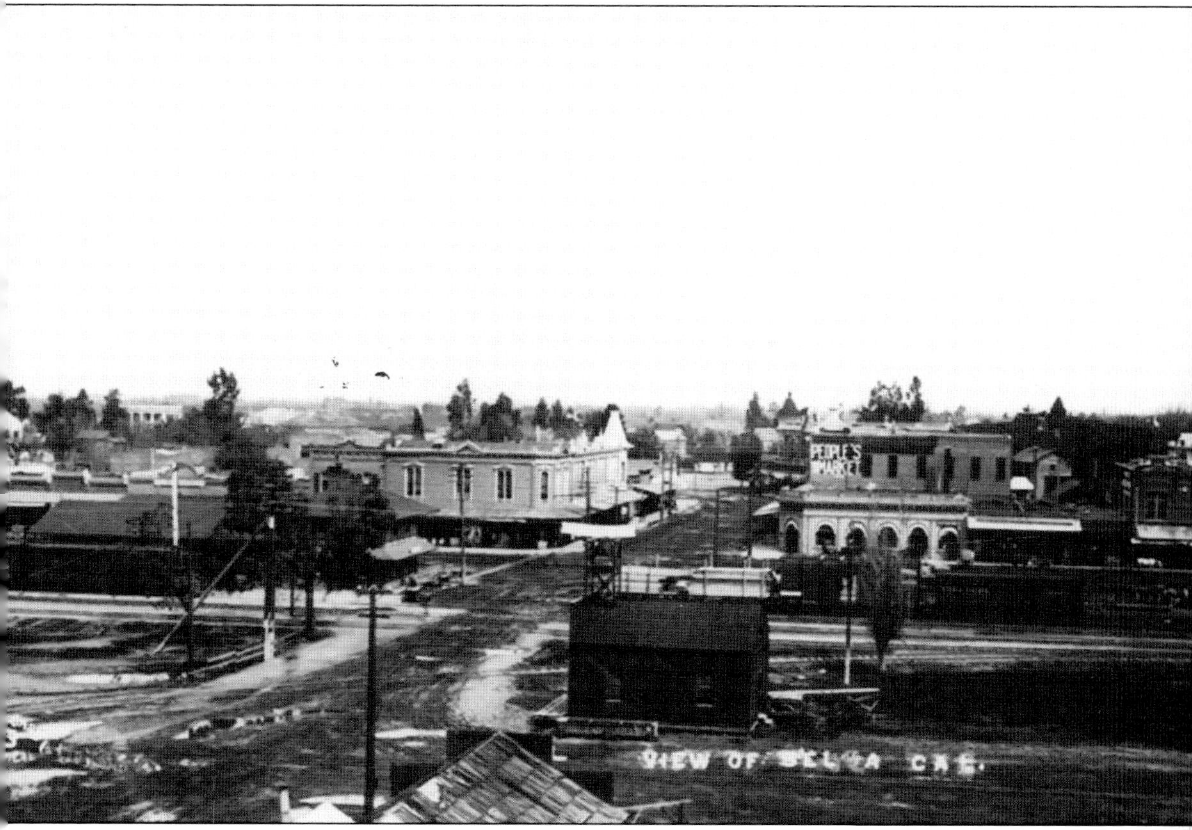

The Selma Hotel was opened in downtown Selma around 1900. In the 1950s, the Selma Motel—situated along Highway 99—opened, and it remains in operation until this day. In this photograph, Selma's roads do not appear to be paved, which indicates that horses are still the primary mode of transportation. A store, the People's Market, can be seen on the right side of the photograph. Highway 99 was eventually routed through this general area. (Courtesy of the California State Library, Sacramento.)

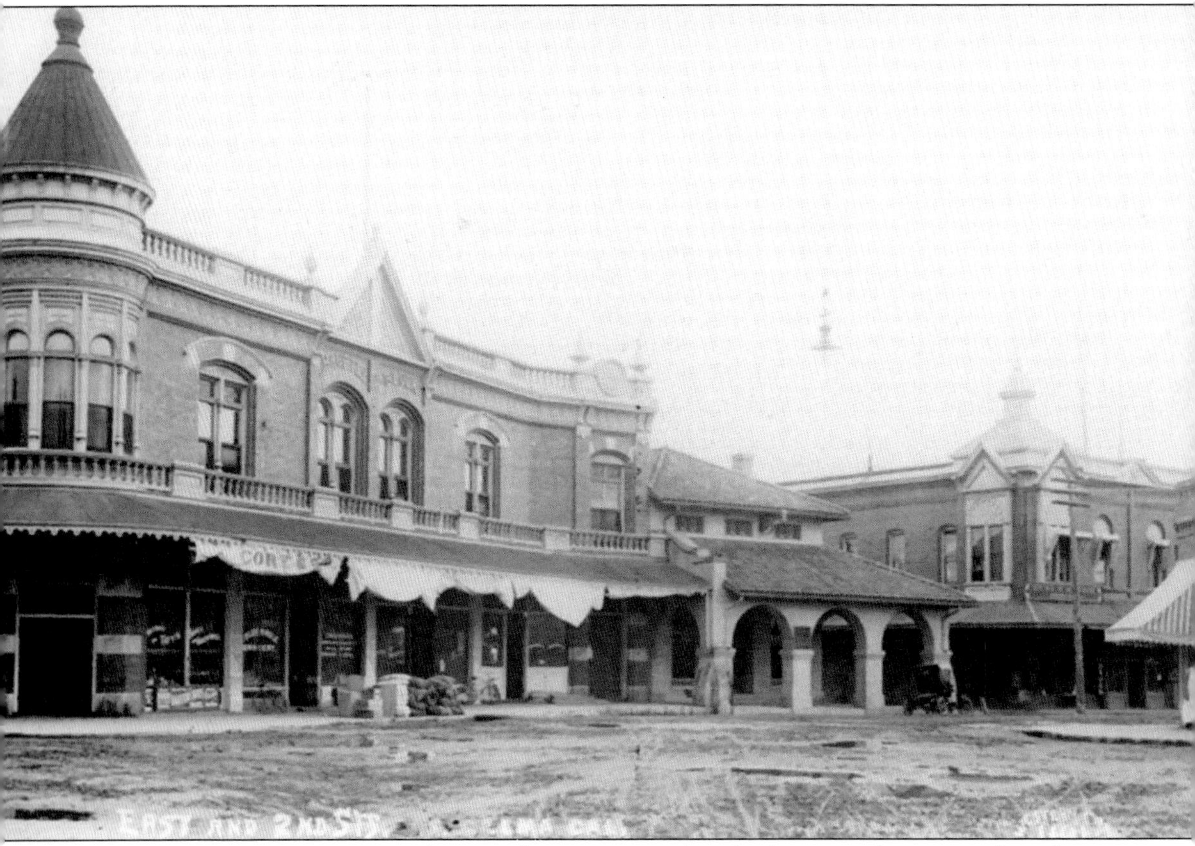

The intersection of East and Second Streets in Selma had not yet been paved at the time this photograph was taken, which lends the area a frontier appearance. A businessman can be seen standing in front of his store on the right side of the photograph. Selma grew along with the Southern Pacific Railroad, which began in the 1870s. (Courtesy of the California State Library, Sacramento.)

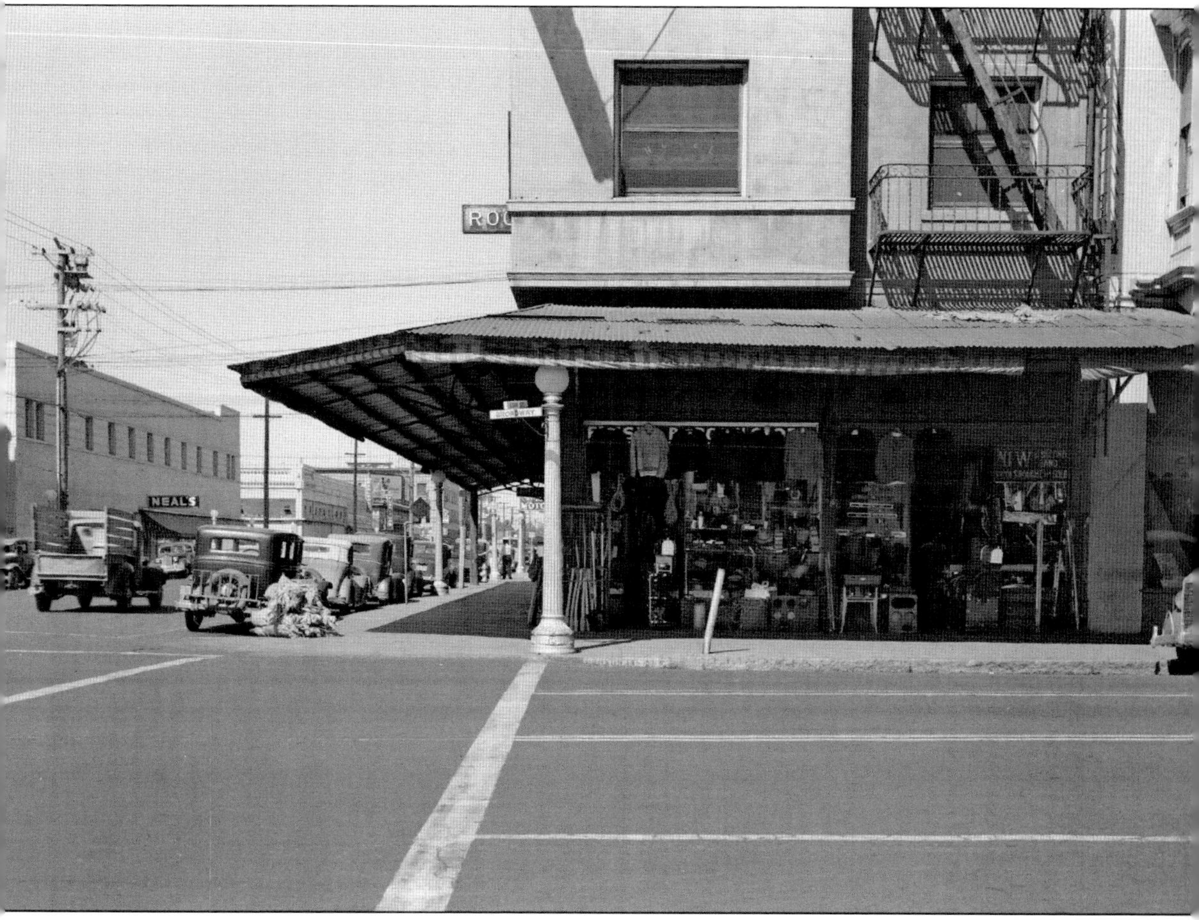

In this busy street scene, an external fire escape is visible from the second floor. In the 1930s and 1940s, automatic fire suppression systems were not commonly installed in buildings like this one, and residents were forced to rely on fire escapes. (Courtesy of the Library of Congress.)

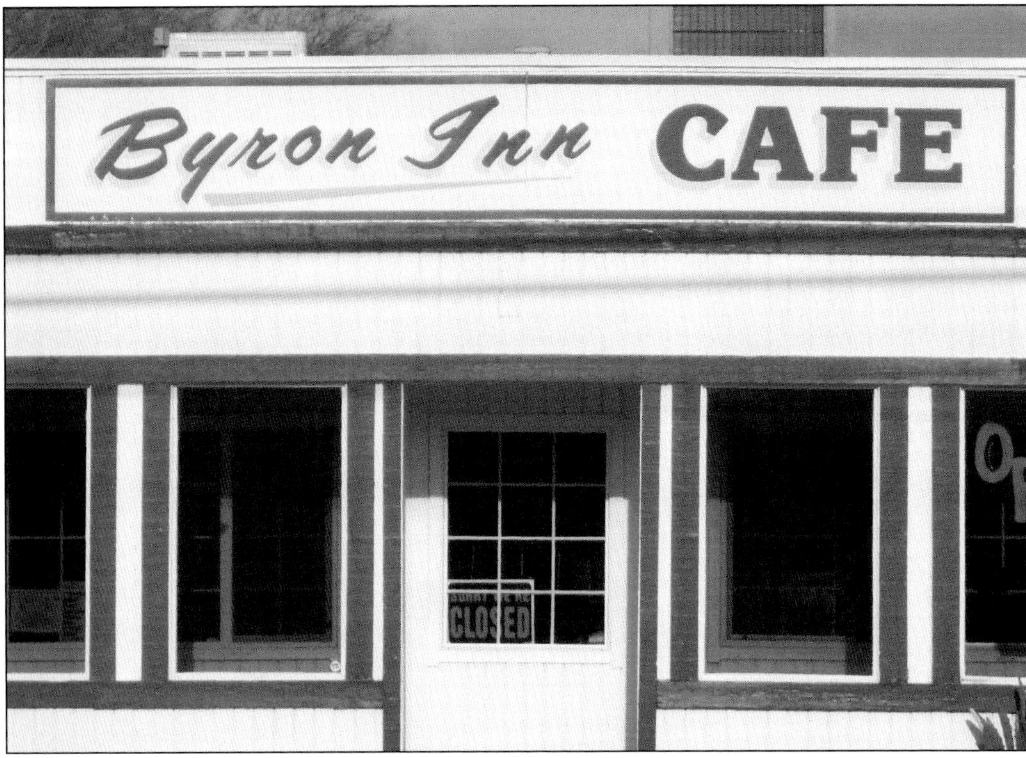

In the early 2010s, the Byron Inn Café closed after a fire caused significant damage. It was refurbished and reopened for business in 2014. Located in Contra Costa County, Byron is a census-designated place with a population of over 1,000.

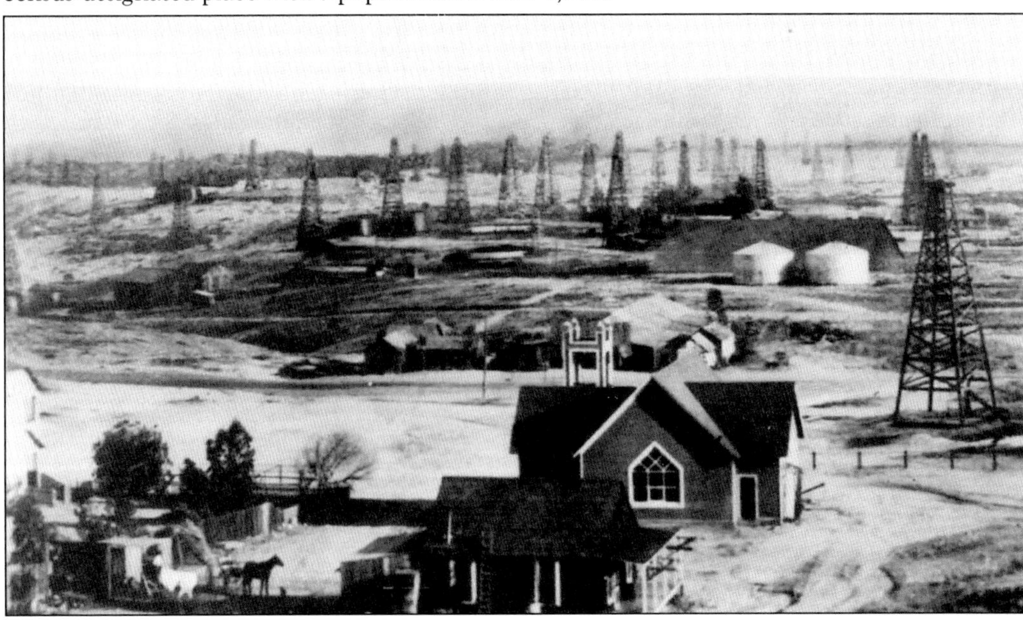

The Oil Center Congregational Church, located in Bakersfield, was formed prior to 1900. Congregational churches are Protestant churches that are built on the belief that each congregation should independently run its church. (Courtesy of the Kern County Library.)

Seven

A Simpler Life

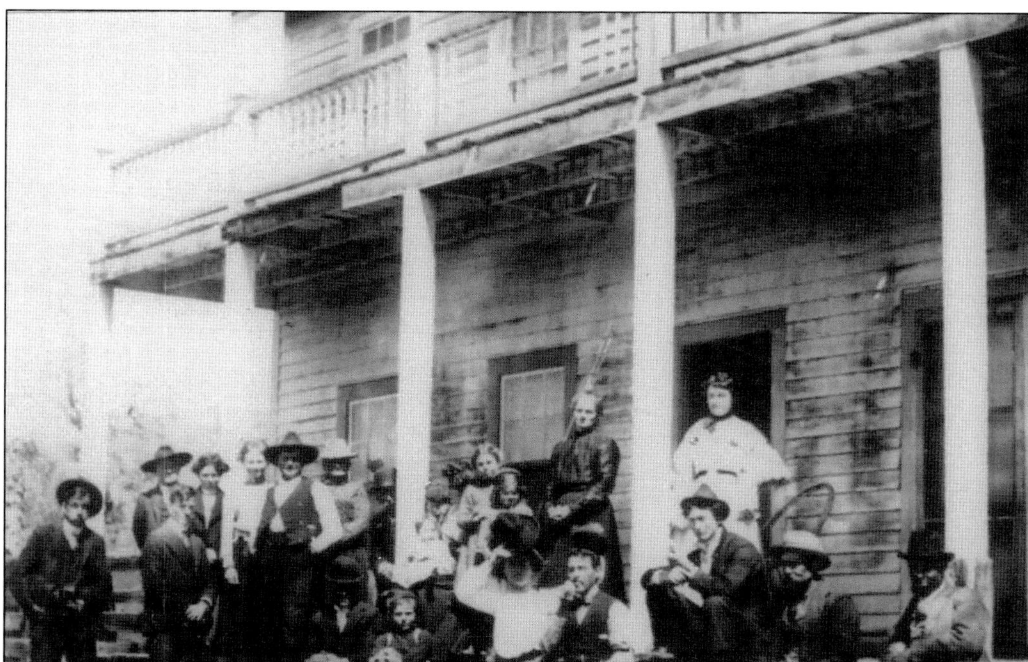

People congregated at the Glennville Hotel, which was centrally located in the town—as shown in this c. 1880 photograph. A community in Kern County, Glennville is located north of Bakersfield. (Courtesy of the Kern County Library.)

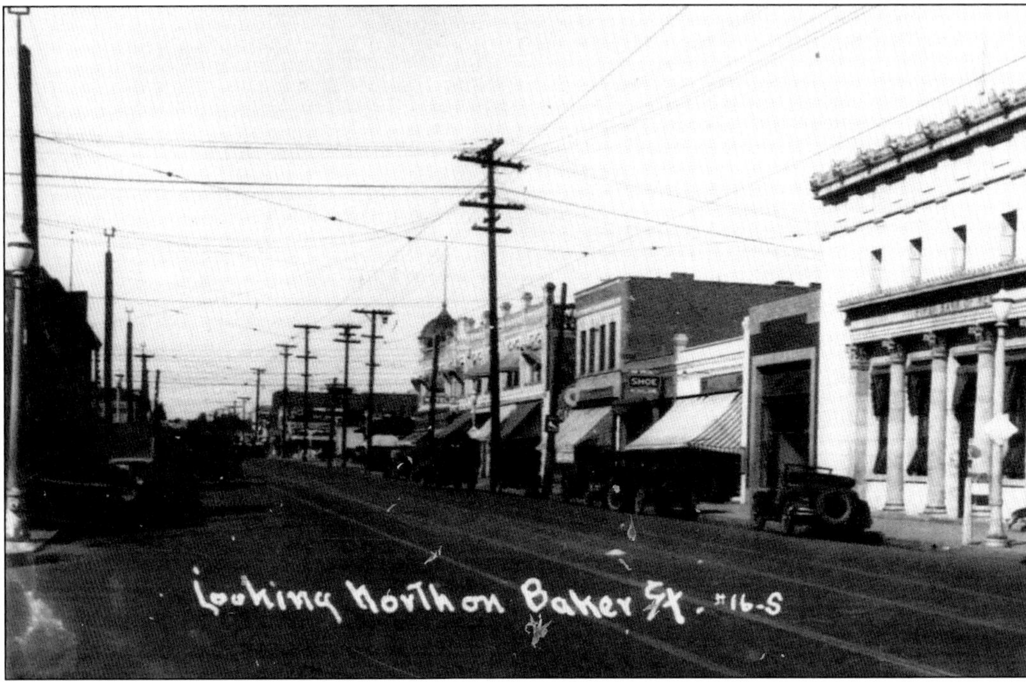

This photograph, which was taken on Baker Street in Bakersfield, shows the First Bank of Kern (located at 801 Baker Street) and the Western Hotel (located at 819 Baker Street). The president of the bank was A.S. Crites. (Courtesy of the Kern County Library.)

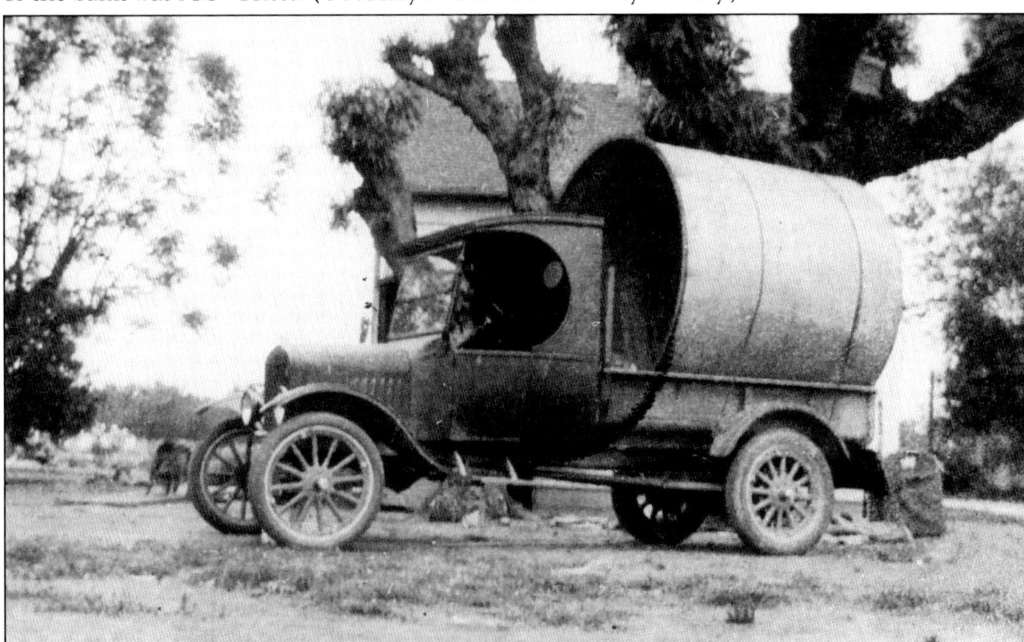

This Ford Model T, photographed in Kern County, was customized so that it could function as a water truck. When Bakersfield was incorporated in 1873, there were very few roads outside of the city limits—almost none of which were passable for the automobiles that would be invented 25 to 30 years later. (Courtesy of the Kern County Library.)

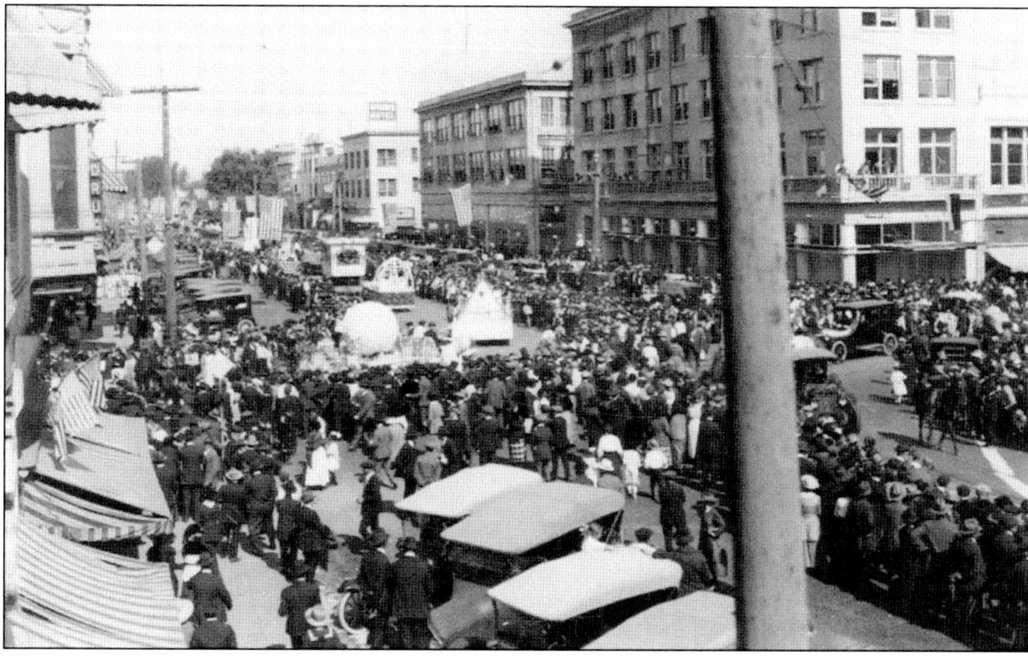

The Cotton is King Festival's parade along Chester Avenue in Bakersfield was a popular event. The town of Wasco's float can be seen on a square white vehicle at the left center of the image. A drugstore is visible on left side of street, while the Grand and Manchester Hotels can be seen on the right side. A fur and millinery shop can be seen on the side street at the far right. (Courtesy of the Kern County Library.)

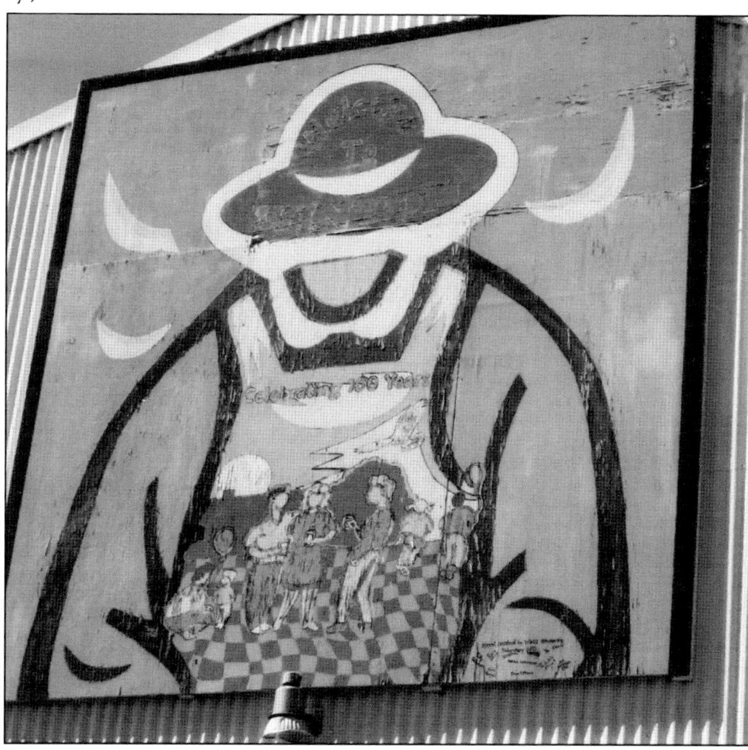

Visitors are welcome in the town of Winton, a census-designated area of Merced County located three miles from Atwater. Winton has a population of about 10,000 and an appreciation for the old-fashioned and nostalgic that is common in many towns along the Highway 99 corridor.

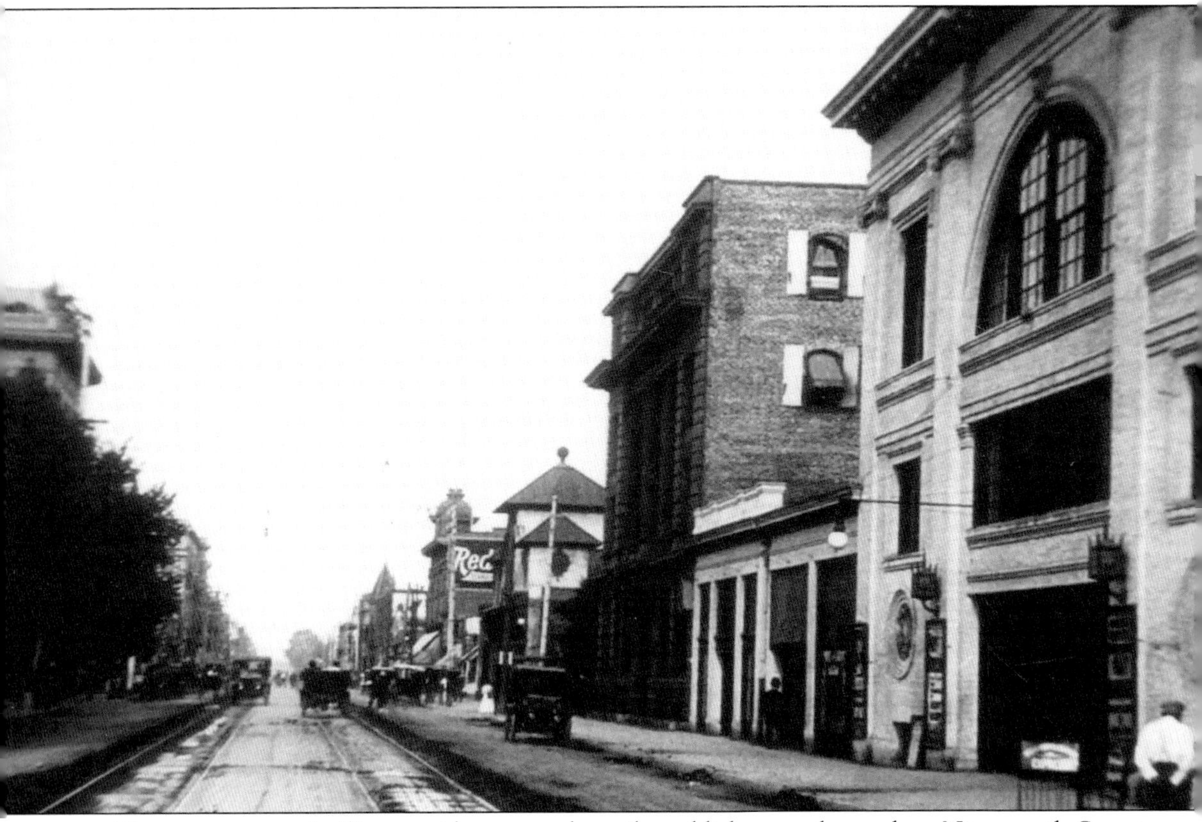

There were several offices, residences, and retail establishments located on Nineteenth Street in Bakersfield at the time that this photograph was taken. The Bakersfield Opera House was located along this thoroughfare. Bakersfield was incorporated in 1873. (Courtesy of the Kern County Library.)

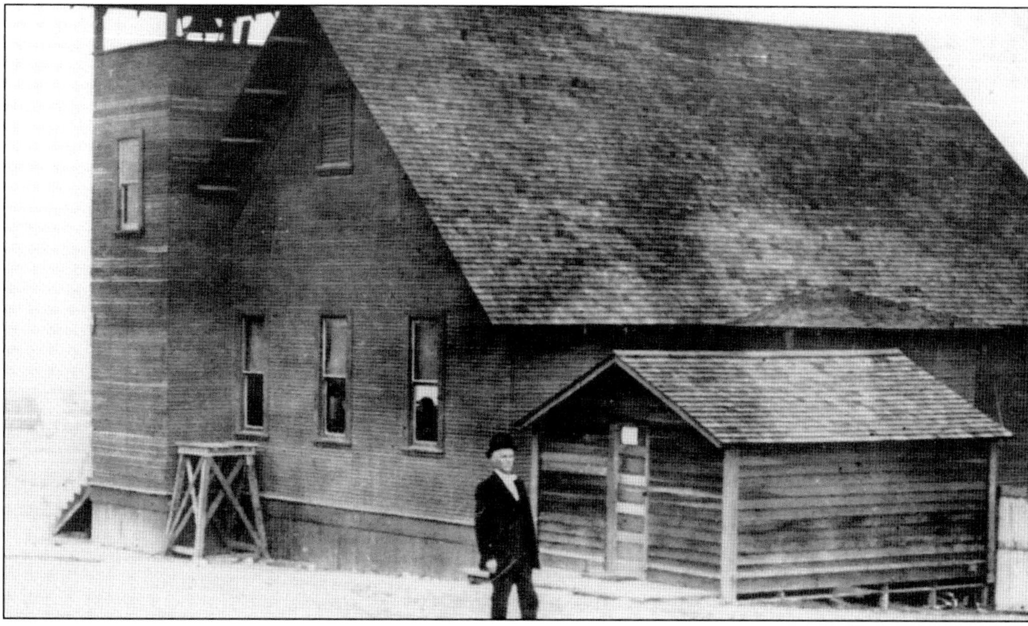

Built in 1910, Bakersfield's First Methodist Church was located at Pico and Asher Streets. A man named A.P. Peel once served as its pastor. The Methodist tradition continues in the cities and towns located along Highway 99, with several churches hosting active congregations and generally adhering to the same doctrines and theology as those who gathered in this structure. (Courtesy of the Kern County Library.)

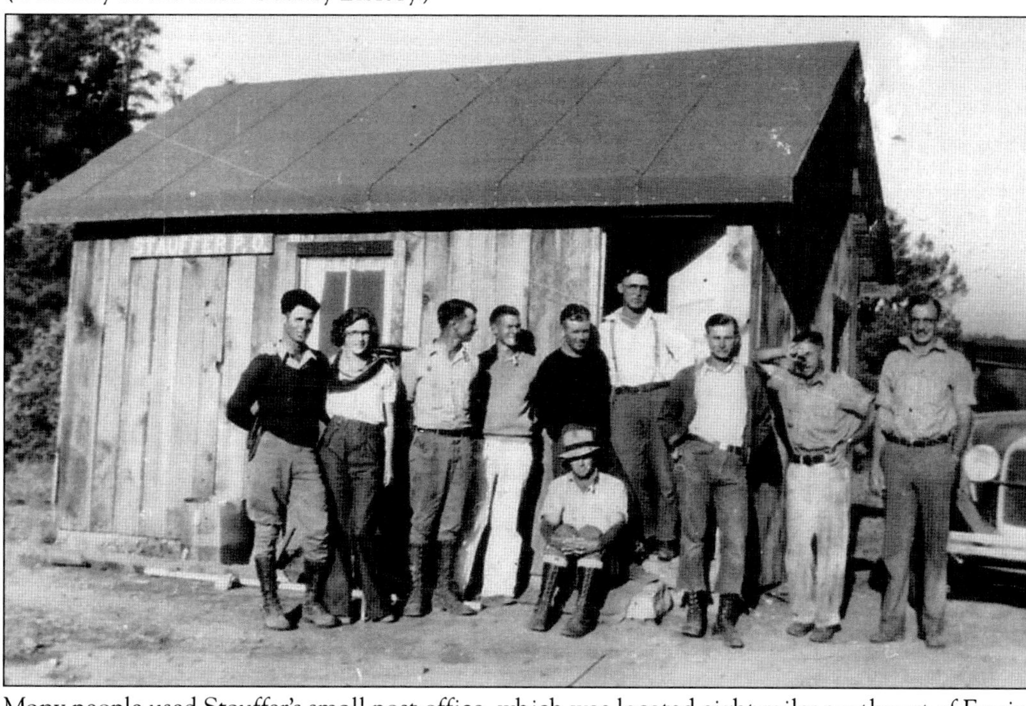

Many people used Stauffer's small post office, which was located eight miles southwest of Frazier Park in Kern County. Stauffer was a mining town that was located along Seymour Creek, south of the convergence of Highway 99 and Highway 5. (Courtesy of the Kern County Library.)

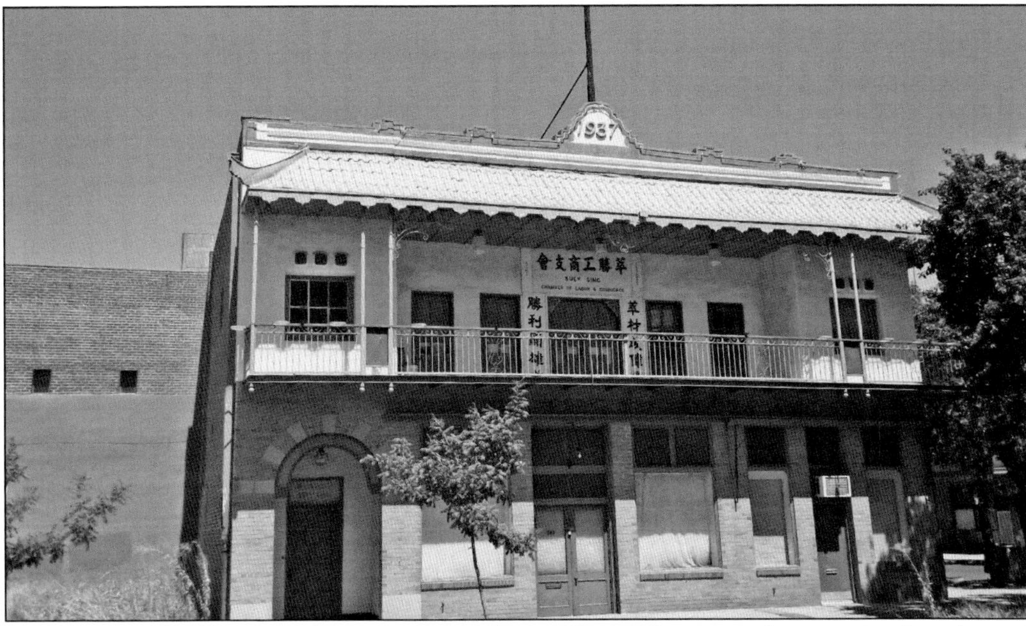

This two-story building, which was constructed in 1937 in a Chinese architectural style, is located in the heart of Marysville's Chinatown. At the time that this was constructed, there were over 50 businesses in this Chinese American sector and a sizable number of residents living there. In general at that time the Chinese population had not fully integrated into the American economy, so neighborhoods such as this served an economic purpose as well as a cultural one.

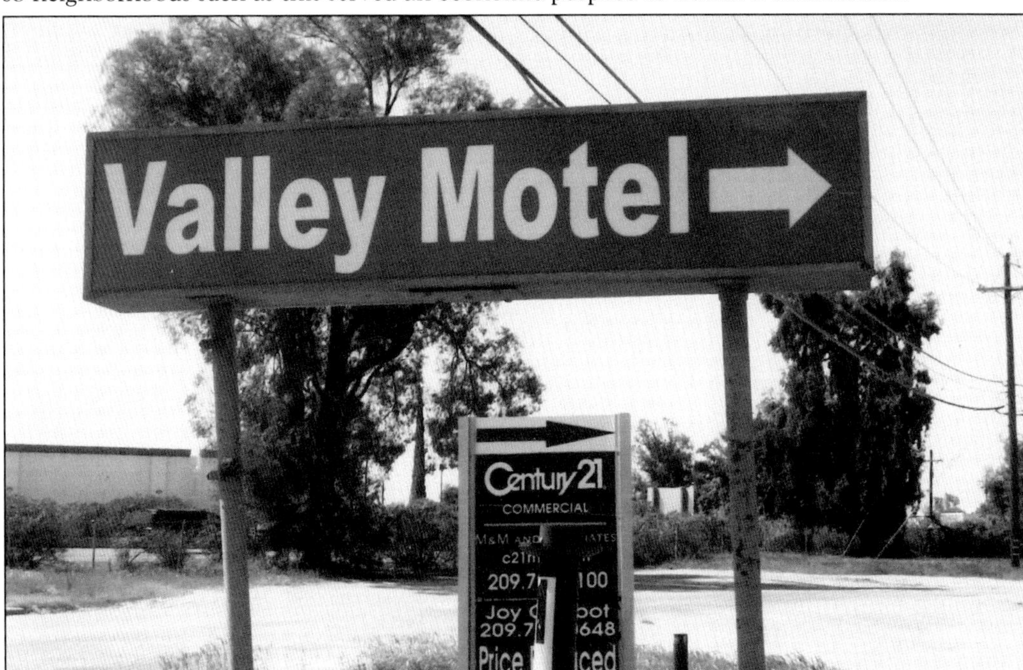

In the 1940s and 1950s, Highway 99 travelled through at least 15 town and cities. Traffic caused by ongoing construction work was common as well. This greatly increased the travel time between Northern and Southern California. Because of this, motels were abundant along the highway.

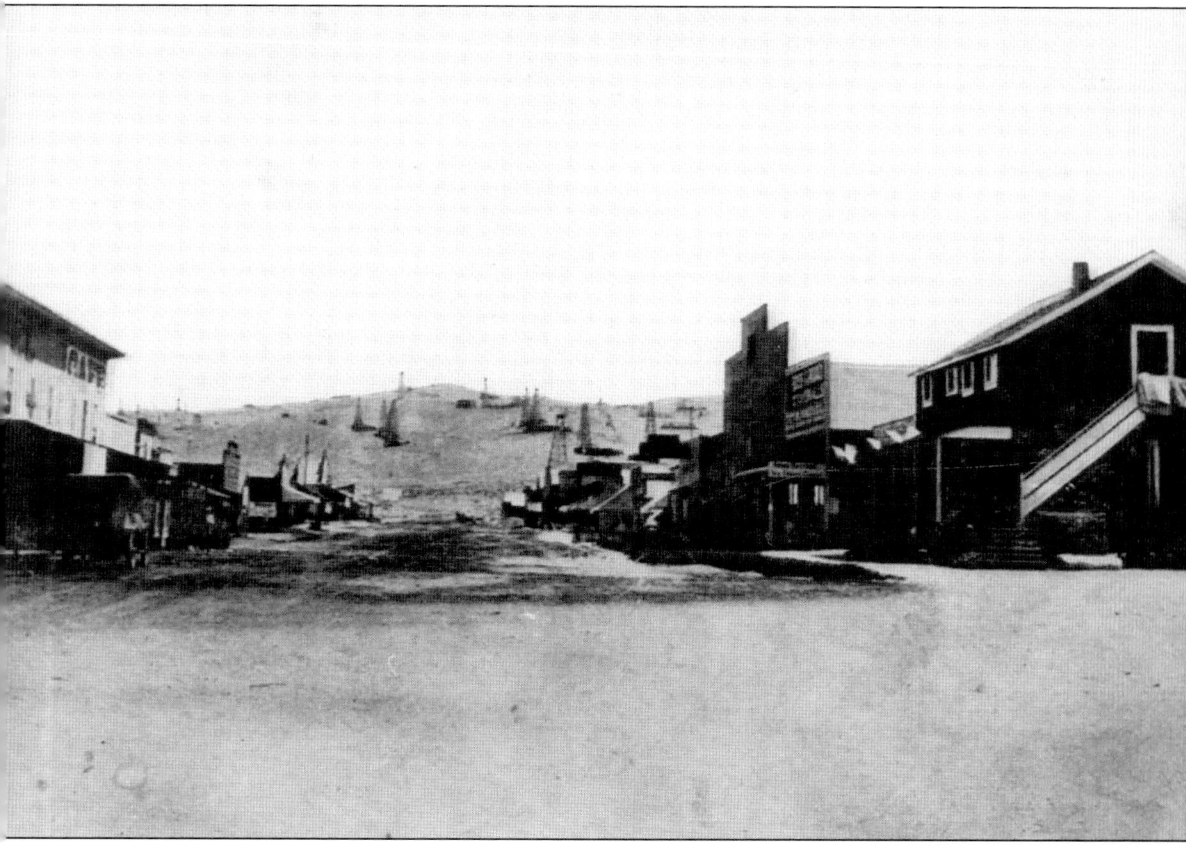

Prior to the construction of Highway 5, residents of Taft used Highway 99 as their primary north-to-south route. Taft is a small town located southwest of Bakersfield in Kern County. There was once a significant amount of oil production in the area surrounding Taft. (Courtesy of the Kern County Library.)

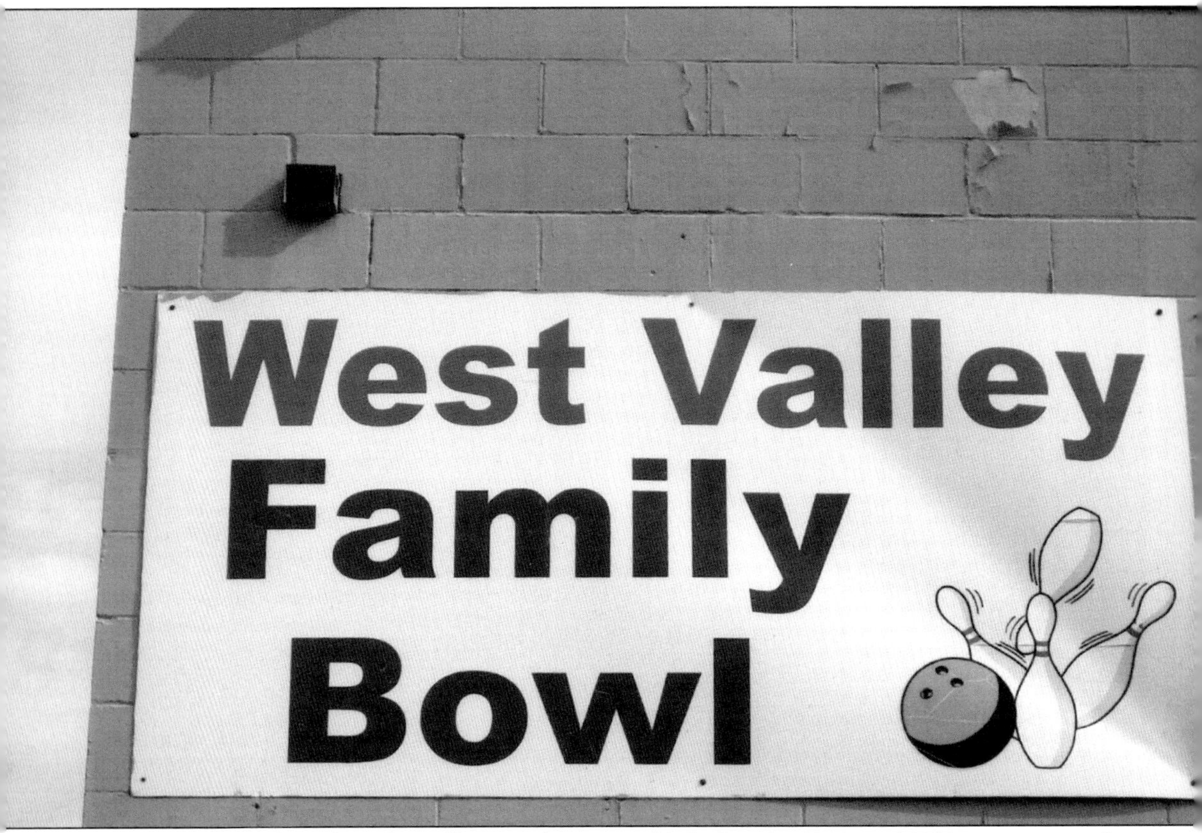

Numerous motels, such as the Valley Motel, were established in the 1940s and 1950s to accommodate the increasing number of travelers on the highway. They were usually moderately priced and easily accessible. Typically, there was a large sign near the hotel, installed about 30 to 40 feet above grade, to attract customers on Highway 99. Recreation centers such as bowling alleys—like West Valley Family Bowl in Tracy—were also common along the route. Bowling has been played for centuries and remains a popular pastime today.

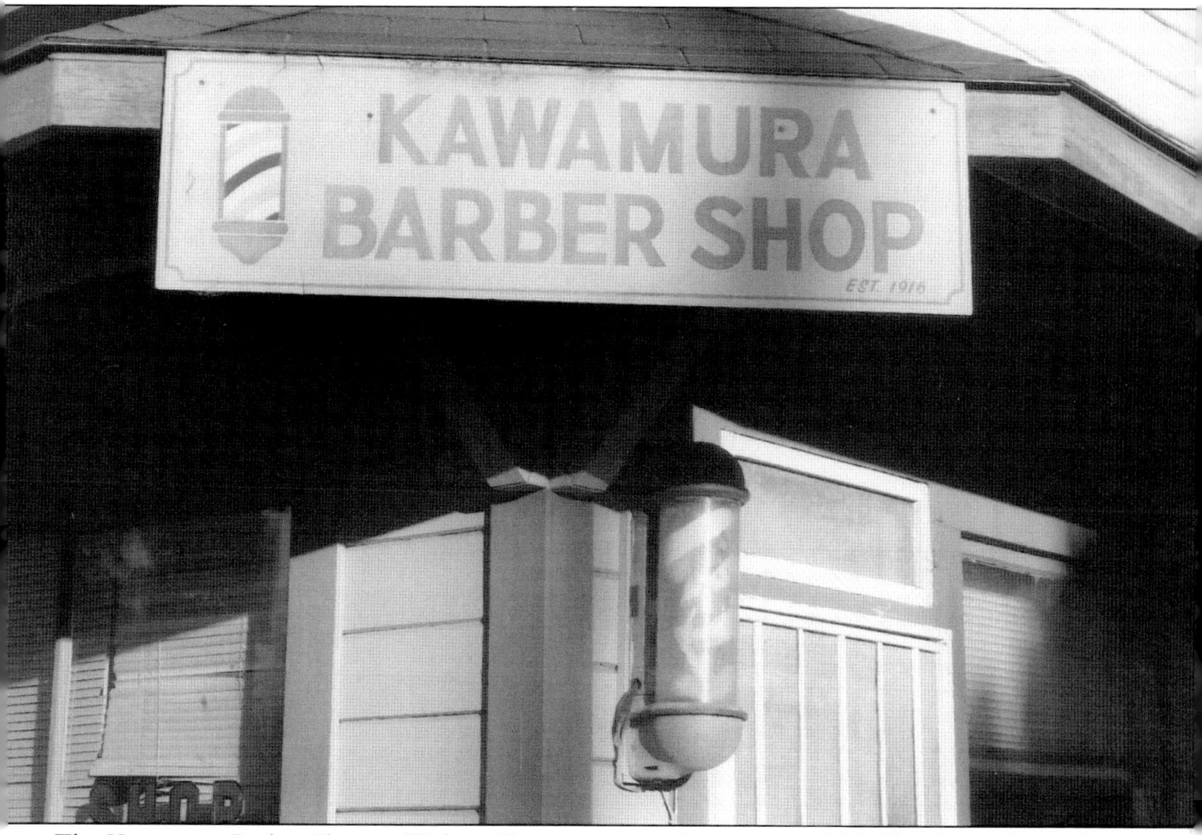

The Kawamura Barber Shop in Walnut Grove went into business in 1916. The shop is located on Market Street, which is the primary business street in the town. Much of the equipment in the barbershop was purchased in the 1960s or earlier. The shop has since closed, but members of the Kawamura family were giving haircuts there as late as 2012.